HENRI BÉCHARD S.J.

Kaia'tanó:ron Kateri Tekakwitha

Translated by Miss Antoinette Kinlough
Illustrated by Madame Andrée S. de Groot

KATERI CENTER
KAHNAWAKE
QUEBEC
1994

Béchard, Henri
    Kaiatanoron Kateri Tekakwitha
    includes bibliogr. ref.
    ISBN 2-9803283-1-6

    1. Tekakwitha, Kateri, 1656-1680. 2. Indians-
North America - Canada - Biographies. 3. Indians -
North America - Canada morals and customs.
4. Christian biographies - Canada. I.Kateri Center.
II. Title.

E90.T2B42 1992 971' .00497   C92-097349-3

Legal deposit - 2nd Semester, 1994
National Library of Quebec
National Library of Canada

BOOKS BY FR. HENRI BÉCHARD, S.J.

J'ai cent ans, l'Église Saint-François-Xavier de Caughnawaga, Éd. du Messager, Montréal, 1946. (Out of print).

The Visions of Bernard de Hoyos, S.J., Vantage Press, New York, Washington Hollywood, 1959. (Out of print).

L'Héroique Indienne Kateri Tekakwitha, Fides, Montréal, Paris, 1967, 2ᵉ édition.

The Original Caughnawaga Indians. International Publishers, Montreal, 1976.

Jérome Le Royer de la Dauversière, His friends and his enemies, The Apostolate, Bloomingdale, Ohio, 1991.

Les audacieuses entreprises de Monsieur de la Dauversière, Méridien, Montréal, 1992.

Founder and editor of the quarterlies:

KATERI, Lily of the Mohwaks (1948)

KATERI, Lys de Agniers (1951)

The portrait on the front page goes back to the Monday of Easter 1980, when Kateri's Beatification was announced. This painting inspired by the apparition of Kateri to Anastasia was displayed at the University of Montreal and at the Floralies. Mrs. de Groot has greatly helped in the reawakening of sacred art in Canada.

KAIA'TANÓ:RON KATERI TEKAKWI:THA

Kaiatanoron: precious, dear, blessed
Kateri: baptismal name
Tekakwitha: who walks groping for her way

Imprimi potest: Montreal, July 28, 1992
Jean Bellefeuille S.J.
Provincial

Nihil obstat: Saint-Jérôme, July 4, 1992
Lucien Campeau S.J.

Imprimatur: Saint-Jean-Longueuil, September 5, 1992
Bishop Bernard Hubert
Bishop of Saint-Jean-Longueuil

With gratitude
to Anne Scheuerman

Preface

It's with great joy that I present this posthumous work of our regretted Father Henri Béchard. It will crown and conclude the thousand of pages that this patient researcher and devout admirer of Kateri Tekakwitha has written on the Iroquois Virgin, on her nation and her time. It will also be the occasion of signalling the work of putting into form this text that the author was unable to achieve because of his primature death. It was done by Madame Madeleine Huet with an application, a disinterestedness and an intelligence that cannot be surpassed. The work will fill a need which was felt in Quebec, that of better knowing to better appreciate it, the work of evangelization accomplished by the French missionaries of the 17th century. At the same time it will illustrate the quality of Iroquois converts who chose to take refuge in New France, so that they could practice freely their new Christian faith. Even their names have fallen in an immerited oblivion. Fr. Béchard brings them to life to our astonishment and admiration.

Kateri is an exceptional example but not unique, of the intelligence and the heart with which the Iroquois accepted the Christian message. Left as an orphan and saved herself from the smallpox, she showed, even before her baptism, dispositions towards virtue that her own milieu could not give her any example. Baptized in her native village by Fr. Jacques de Lamberville, April 11, 1676, she strived from this day to reproduce in her life the examples of sainthood proposed to her. However, as the dissolution and insolence of the young warriors did not allow her a peaceful exercise of her faith, she took profit of the help of an Oneida neophyte to go and join her people already regrouped in the Mission of Laprairie, in 1677. She had at heart but to practice heroically charity and purity, associating herself with a few companions and competing with them. In 1679, she pronounced the vow of chastity. The next spring, having fallen sick, she died on the 17th of April, 1680. After five years only as a Christian, she was admired by all for her heroic virtues. It is not so much her own but the French who made her this reputation, not only those close to her but of the whole colony. Fathers Cholenec and Chauchetière, who had known her, narrated what we now know about her. Fr. Béchard puts in relief the companions of the heroine, who also deserve to be known for their faith and courage to confess it. He testifies passingly but efficaciously, of the spiritual climate of New France at that time, when Kateri became an object of admiration and of cult.

May this book help to make appreciate better than we do the humane quality not only of the natives of our country but also of the apostles ready to die so that Jesus Christ be better known.

Lucien Campeau, S.J.

Acknowledgments

Our gratitude first goes out to Father Henri Béchard, S.J. who spent 43 years of his life studying the history of the Indian Missions of New France and in particular the existence of this little Mohawk Indian girl who, thanks to his efforts, was to be beatified in 1980, the Blessed Kateri Tekakwitha. An immense joy for the Vice-Postulator that he was at that time.

This last book of Fr. Béchard on the Lily of the Mohawks is the fruit of all his research work in Kahnawake, Montreal and France. It's a compendium of all his knowledge about Kateri, the work culminating his life.

This book could not have been finished without the indispensable help of Madeleine Huet researcher, corrector, coordinator of all his writings. She deserves very special thanks. Miss Marie Baboyant has also been a very regular and professional collaborator as a librarian; she had reviewed all his non-published manuscripts.

A name which cannot be forgotten in the work of Fr. Béchard is that of Madame Andrée de Groot, painter and artist. Associated to his work since 1952, how many drawings she made for the Kateri magazine and for the illustrations of his books. The painting on the cover is her painting. This contribution culminates her devotion to the Cause and her personal devotion to her dear Kateri.

Finally Fr. Lucien Campeau, S.J. was kind enough to read the writings of Fr. Béchard and verify the corrections and additions of Madeleine Huet. A well-informed historian, he assures the authenticity of the historical facts related in this work which is one of full maturity.

The names of Lise Saint-Germain and Albert Lazare who contributed discreetly in many ways to the making of this book must also be mentioned.

May Kateri be honored by this work!

Jacques Bruyère, S.J.,
Vice-Postulator

Table of contents

First part
(1634 to 1677)

13

Second part
(1677 to 1680)

Third part
(After 1680)

Guide to reading and abbreviations

The works contained in the glossary are accompanied by an * when they appear for the first time in the course of the reading.

Most of all the old texts are translated in modern language for more facility.

Here is the list of abbreviations used:

DBC   Dictionnaire biographique du Canada, First Volume (1966)

EPC   CHOLENEC, P., Extract from a letter of Father Chonelec (Cholenec) which contains the narration of the Holy Life and extraordinary penances of a few Native women, written at Saint Francis Xavier Mission of the Sault, close to Montreal, February 1680.

EPE   SAINT-VALLIER, Mgr J.-B. de, Estat présent de l'Eglise et de la colonie française dans la Nouvelle-France (1856)

HI   BÉCHARD, H., L'Héroïque Indienne, Kateri Tekakwitha (1980)

HDNF   CHARLEVOIX, F.-X. de, Histoire et description générale de la Nouvelle-France   (1774)

HC   DEVINE, S.J., E.J., Historic Caughnawaga (1922)

JR   THWAITES, R.G. ed., The Jesuit Relations and Allied Documents (1959)

K   BÉCHARD, S.J., H., Revue trimestrielle Kateri, C.P. 70, Kahnawake, QC, J0L 1B0

LCC   CHAUCHETIERE, C., Lettre touchant la mission des Iroquois du Sault St. François-Xavier proche Montréal (1682)

LEC   Lettres édifiantes et curieuses, écrites des missions étrangères (1819)

MIC   OURY, G., Marie de l'Incarnation, Ursuline (1599-1672), Correspondance (1971)

MV   GRASSMAN, T., The Mohawk Indians and Their Valley (1969)

NA   CHAUCHETIERE, C., Notes autobiographiques (1695)

OCI   BÉCHARD, S.J., H., The Original Caughnawaga Indians (1976)

PO   SALOTTI, Card. Carolo, S.R.C., Positio super virtutibus (1940)

RDDC   CHAUCHETIERE, C., Recueil de ce qui s'est passé depuis le décès de Catherine.

REMY   RÉMY, P., Certificat de M. Remy, curé de la Chine, des miracles faits en sa paroisse par l'intercession de la B. Cath. Tegakwitha (1696)

VCT   CHOLENEC, P., La vie de Catherine Tégakoüta. Première Vierge Iroquoise (1696)

VBCT   CHAUCHETIERE, C., La Vie de la B. Catherine Tégakoüïta dite à présent La Sainte Sauvagesse (1695)

VI   MARTIN, F., S.J., Une Vierge iroquoise ou vie de Catherine Tégakoüita, texte dactylographié.

PART ONE

1

A Christian Mother

Little is known about Kateri's mother, only the fact that she was an Algonquin baptized in Trois-Rivières and brought up among French settlers, which gives us some idea of her country of origin.

Trois-Rivières, at that time, was a small outpost founded in 1634 by the Sieur de Laviolette by order of Samuel de Champlain. This natural stop-over visited by natives, traders, explorers and missionaries made it an ideal site for the first settlers from New France to establish a colony and for the fur traders from the north, sailing down the powerful Metabouritine* River, to set up a trading post.

Since 1641, the people known in Canadian history as Mohawks* and who lived in the eastern part of what is now the State of New York, had been getting their firearms from Dutch settlers further to the south. They used these weapons occasionnally for venison, but mostly to subject their long-time enemies , in this case and concerning our story, the Montagnais* and the Algonquins*. These two nations were sometimes visited by the Hurons on their way to trade in Trois-Rivières. Because of this, they too fell under the Mohawks' power.

From 1641 to 1653, the Algonquins, who were a nomadic nation, abandoned their native land east of Lake Ontario, and on Allumettes Island, to settle near the fortress of Trois-Rivières built by the French to protect themselves from Iroquois invasions. The Huron Federation*, which lived in settlements, "fell under Iroquois rule in 1649".[1]

It is possible that the young Algonquin maiden, later to become Kateri's mother and whom I shall call "Marie", migrated to the region of Trois-Rivières around that time with her nation. One thing is certain, according to modern biographers of Kateri Tekakwitha, Marie was a captive of war and was taken to the Iroquois canton as a slave.[2]

One day, young Marie was forced by her captors to travel the war path of the Mohawks in the opposite direction, as they headed home. They rowed up the Saint Lawrence River and then the Richelieu in a Mohawk-built elm canoe, less navigable and less intricate than the Algonquin model. They reached immense Lake Champlain and later came to the Andiatarocte*. Undoubtedly, they portaged their way through the forest until they finally reached the Mohawk River, which flowed through their homeland.

The Mohawk nation or "silex people" was the most warlike of the Five Nations*. They formed, with the neighbouring Oneidas, the group called the Lower Iroquois. Further west, as far as Niagara Falls, were the Onondaga, the Cajugas and, finally, the Senecas, otherwise known as the Upper Iroquois. All these together composed the Iroquois Confederation*.

On the south shore of the Mohawk River stood a lovely village named Ossernenon*. This small town perched on a green hill rolling down to the foamy waters, was encircled by a palisade made of tapered logs. The long-houses, in which three to seven families lived, contrasted with the single-family wigwams of the Algonquins. Stretching out around these dwellings were large fields of corn, beans and squash, to the amazement of young Marie, whose compatriots lived on fishing and hunting. This was the place where René Goupil* had shed his blood for the Lord on September 29th, 1642; not far from here, Isaac Joques and Jean de La Lande had also been murdered in 1646.

The young woman was soon married to one of the village chiefs.[3] Marie had to adjust to her husband and his customs, his country and his language. Though her social status must have provided amply for all her needs, one can imagine that this "fervent Christian" often missed her native village near the little chapel of Trois-Rivières. Here, there were no more Black Robes to provide the Eucharistic Presence. No missionary had passed through the land of the Mohawks since 1646.

Between 1655 and 1659, Fr. Simon Le Moyne went to Mohawk land four times, acting as a sort of ambassador for the Hurons, who had taken refuge in Quebec, awaiting orders from the Mohawks, whom they regarded as their masters. During his stays, Ondessonk* - the name of Saint Isaac Jogues which Fr. Simon had inherited - would visit the Christian Hurons, among whom were a few French captives. After each of his visits, this small Christian community impatiently awaited his return; Marie was probably among them. The missionary would comfort the afflicted, teach the unlearned, hear the confessions of the penitents who came to him, baptize the children, encourage all these people to pray, exhort them to persevere in the faith and to avoid sin. He would never let anyone go away without saying something about hell, heaven and the power of God who sees and knows all things and who punishes evil and rewards good.[4]

In 1656, Marie gave birth to a lovely baby girl, and later to a boy. Oftentimes, to calm them or help them to sleep, this attentive mother would sing them some of the hymns she had once learnt in the distant country of her youth; no doubt she must have whispered the morning and evening prayers to them. As for the little girl, said Fr. Chauchetière*, "the care her mother took of this little one, while she lived, which was only four or five years, had a great deal to do with her growing in age and wisdom."

As she grew up, the older child ventured farther and farther away from her longhouse. Sometimes she would go down to the river and play, throwing pebbles into the water. One after another, they would fall through the rushing ripples like gold in the sunlight. Thus did the months and years go by.

In 1660, a great calamity struck the village. Smallpox, probably caught from the neighbouring Dutch settlers, invaded the homes, killing both children and adults. The village medicine man was overworked. It can be assumed that he came to dance in the chief's longhouse to obtain healing for the members of the family. The ugly wooden mask, the turtle shell used as a rattle and shaken to the beat of a wild dance, and the demonic shouts of the dancer terrified the little ones more than they conjured away the smallpox epidemic.

The mother was the first one to die. We know that she prayed until her last breath for the grace of Baptism for her children. Her prayers remained unanswered in her lifetime, but, said Fr. Chauchetière, these prayers may "have obtained the grace of Baptism for her daughter and, for us, the grace of having a saint." Shortly afterwards, the dreadful disease swept the little boy away to the land of Bountiful Hunting.

The little girl, aged four, survived the virus, but her once beautiful face was completely disfigured by it. Moreover, she was left with a "very frail body and her eyesight remained especially weak". She could no longer sustain the brightness of daylight and was forced, from then on, to "cover her face with her blanket when coming out of her longhouse."

We do not know whether her father also died during this epidemic, but the child "was still very young when her father died", after which she lived "under the authority of her aunts and the influence of her powerful uncle who was the main leader of his village."[6]

Notes

1   L. Campeau, GANNENTAHA, Première mission iroquoise (1653-1665), Montréal, Maison Bellarmin, 1983, p.7

2   C. Chauchetière, La vie de la B. Catherine Tégakoüita dite à présent La Sainte Sauvagesse (1695), Archives ASJCF, Saint-Jérôme, no.343, p.11-2 - Indiqué ci-après par l'abbréviation VBCT.

    P. Cholenec, La Vie de Catherine Tégakoüita. Première Vierge Iroquoise, Ms. Archives du Monastère de l'Hôtel-Dieu de Québec, (1696) p.1, indiqué ci-après par l'abbréviation VCT.

3   P. Cholenec "Lettre et vie de Catherine Tekakwitha" par le P. Cholenec, au Père Michel-Ange Tamburini, Général de la Compagnie de Jésus, 1715, Doc. XIII, p.283, dans: Beatificationis et Canonizationis, Servae Dei, Catharine Tekakwitha, Virginis Indianae, Positio super virtutibus, Romae, Typis Pont. Universitatis Gregorianae, 1940. - Indiqué ci-après par l'abbréviation PO.

4   R.G. Thwaites, The Jesuit Relations and Allied Documents, New York, Pageant Book Company, 1959, vol. 43, p.214. - Indiqué ci-après par l'abbréviation JR.

5   VCT, p.2

6   F.X. de Charlebois, Histoire et description générale de la Nouvelle-France, avec le journal historique d'un Voyage fait par ordre du Roi dans l'Amérique Septentrionnale, Paris, Giffart, 1744, tome I, p.573. Indiqué ci-après par l'abbréviation HDNF.

2
Her Early Youth

Ever since the smallpox epidemic, as treacherous as a snake, had crept into Ossernenon, the Mohawks feared the "okis", or demons, who had brought sickness and death into their midst. In order to move away from these evil spirits, they chose a location one mile to the west, on the left bank of a small stream named Auries[1], and built a new village. They built it on a hill where they could watch the river and the entire countryside in case of an attack.

On one occasion, when they were visited by a group of Dutch envoys from Fort Orange*, the Mohawks asked for their help[2]. Would they not lend them a few horses, or better still, would they not come themselves and hitch the horses to tree trunks to haul them up to the top of the hill? The Dutch were more accustomed to this type of work than the Mohawk warriors. The proposal did not appeal at all to the white visitors. "Don't you see how tired we are?" they said. "We have been travelling through the forest, we are very few, and what is worse, you have no roads for the horses to pass! You must excuse us. You will surely succeed in building the palisade yourselves. On the other hand, as a sign of our friendship, we are leaving you fifty new axes." With such smooth talk, they bid farewell to the Mohawks and headed back home.

The ravages of smallpox continued. Toward the end of summer, the Mohawks of the Turtle* clan finally completed the palisade and built their longhouses inside. As village chief, the uncle of the little orphan girl had to set an example and work eagerly at the construction. According to Iroquois custom, the oldest woman, who exercised matriarchal authority in the clan, had appointed him chief after the death of his brother. As Fr. de Lamberville* wrote, he was "the most highly considered man in the village."

During this year and a half of suffering and bereavement, the little one with her sight impaired and her face disfigured by smallpox felt a great void around her. No more mother to love her, no more father, tall and strong, to pick her up in his arms or to bounce her on his lap, no more little brother to caress; only a corn doll* with no features. Luckily, her uncle and her two aunts were there. Never would Mohawks, or natives of any other nation, abandon children whose parents had passed to the Land of Bountiful Hunting. Girls were well accepted in Mohawk families; as they grew up, they would perform housekeeping chores and work in the fields; if they married a good hunter, the entire household prospered. The chief had no children; he therefore acceded to his wife's desire to adopt another little girl older than their niece and who would later be called Kateri's "adopted sister."

The family felt sorry for the younger girl, so disadvantaged and alone, and still so frail as a result of this terrible illness. She could not stand bright lights; the brightness of the sun blinded her and she would stretch her little arms forward to feel her way as she walked. One day, seeing her groping about, they named her Tekakwitha, which means "Here She Comes" or "She Moves Something in Front of Her". Poets have translated her name as "The One Who Puts Everything in Order." Perhaps they were not far wrong.

The Turtle people did not move to their new location until mid fall. First of all, in Ossernenon, taking in the harvest was the task of women and girls who were old enough. At four and a half, Tekakwitha helped out in many small ways. There was corn to pick in the fields as well as sunflower, squash, pumpkins and beans. Since many of those who had worked at the harvest in previous years had died, the survivors had to work twice and three times as hard. Every morning at dawn, carrying baskets on their backs, they hurried to the fields. They broke off ears of corn one by one and threw them into their baskets. Hundreds and hundreds of barrels of corn were transported to the new homes before they set fire to their old village.

The new village was named Caughnawaga*, meaning "By the Rapids." Near the steep hill on top of which stood the rampart, the small stream of Auries flowed into the Mohawk River. Tekakwitha had to get used to her new surroundings. The smell of the fire that had consumed the houses of Ossernenon had not yet completely dispersed; she could still smell it very strongly in the air she breathed. Looking out from the terrace above the river, one could behold a truly splendid scene. Maple trees had turned red by now, while oak, elm and birch trees were clothed in hues of topaz, contrasting with the emerald of the pine trees, to the delight of those who could admire them. As for Tekakwitha, she could only guess how beautiful they were.

In an environment where so much was unknown to her, the child lived one day after another as did all the other Mohawk girls. Since this was the fall season, she followed her aunts and adopted sister to the neighbouring forest to pick the roots needed to prepare medicines and dyes. For example, the dried leaves of the edible red and purple shadberry fruit were used to make herb tea which helped to cure diarrhoea. There were also cultivated mushrooms, such as the puffball, which her aunts cooked. Also, wild onions and golden garlic which they ground or minced, and then mixed in with nut or sunflower oil. This was always a valued seasoning even after the use of salt, so prevalent among the white people, had been introduced to them.

Tekakwitha's uncle, a domineering character, was interested mainly in hunting and war. He hated the Onseronni Onwe*, who lived in the north, with their Black

26

Robes like Isaac Jogues, whom he considered a dangerous sorcerer who had brought pestilence to the village some ten years earlier. Yet, many Mohawks had taken kindly to the missionary. One of the women elders had even adopted him as a nephew, but a handful of discontented men had struck him down along with two of his companions. The old uncle had no regard for the Christian faith. Faithful to the tribal religion, he practiced all its rites, believed firmly in dreams and took part in the strange dances organized by the shamans.

Kateri's aunts, the chief's wife and the unmarried one, who seem to have been Christians already, demonstrated a rather good disposition at first. Indian women rarely punished their children; oftentimes, they spoiled them excessively. The upbringing of the little ones was always left to the mother, even that of the boys, until they were twelve. She would perform this duty through word and example. Little boys and girls were made to bind faggots for the fire, to clean the dishes and the mud floor and to supervise their younger siblings.

When she reached the age of seven or eight, Tekakwitha was taught the more difficult tasks involved in housekeeping. She went out to collect dry wood in the nearby forest and piled up a good supply of it at the entrance of the longhouse in anticipation of rain or snow. Every day, she went down with a bucket to the stream which flowed down the hillside, to draw water. She ground corn and prepared sagamite*, the favourite dish of the Iroquois people.

At that time, her aunts took great pains to persuade the child to make herself beautiful, hoping to marry her off early, according to Mohawk custom. As did every mother concerned about her children, they made her wear buckskin clothes and ornaments worthy of her rank as daughter of the chief of the Turtle clan. Her mocassins were adorned with dyed porcupine quills arranged with artistic taste. She wore an elegant necklace, bracelets, ear and finger rings and a wide sash, all of white or purple wampum*. Her aunts, no doubt, spent much time carefully combing her hair and tying it in a knot at the back of her head with an eelskin ribbon dyed red. To put the finishing touch, they painted up her poor little face.

According to Fr. Chauchetière, the idea of marriage held by the Iroquois was that of a contract between "two people claiming to live together, while they may, in fact, be quite far from each other. They also use the term marriage for certain agreements they make simply out of friendship and which they firm up by giving away a child who is often still in the cradle; for example, they may marry a girl to a little boy."[4]

This is what happened to Tekakwitha when she was scarcely eight years old. The boy was not much older. Both of them were smart enough to make nothing of it. "Thus the marriage was in name only and not what Catherine's family pretended it was," concluded Fr. Chauchetière, who wrote about this incident.

Fr. de Lamberville, close to whom Kateri lived in her early years, said that she was a "good-natured and peaceful child, naturally inclined to do what is right, with an extreme repulsion for any kind of evil. Not only could she not stand the impurities of those of her nation, she also loathed the other sins which are ordinarily committed, such as drunkenness, the fascination for dreams and the superstitious feasts."[5]

All these years, the Mohawks had gone plundering French settlements and attacking the Algonquins in their own lands or during their travels along the Saint Lawrence River. They had burnt their farms and taken captives away to their villages, either to burn them at the stake or to keep them as slaves. Tekakwitha could not stand seeing anyone hurt, not even slaves, and she also felt strongly that it was wrong to go and watch a man die at the stake.[6]

The Onseronni Onwe had long had enough of these assaults and captures. Moreover, in June 1655, Tracy* had arrived in Quebec with long awaited military aid from France: the Carignan-Salières Regiment. The French built a number of forts along the Mohawk River and posted garrisons there. This worried their enemies who, on December 2nd, sent six ambassadors to Quebec, one of whom was the famous Garakontie*, to ask for peace on behalf of their tribe and of the Goyogouins* and Tsonnnontouans*. As proof of their good faith, they released their prisoner, Charles Le Moyne. A peace treaty was signed December 13th, 1665. It was to be ratified within "four moons" by those who were absent. However, as skirmishes continued to occur on both sides and the only way to pacify these nations was to overpower them, "preparations were made for a military expedition against those with whom no peace had been agreed upon",[7] i.e. the Mohawks and the Oneidas.

Governor de Courcelle* set out from Quebec on January 9th, 1666, at the head of three hundred soldiers of the regiment and two hundred recruits from the colony accustomed to the Canadian forest. On the third day, many of them suffered severe chilblains and others were so numb with cold that they would have died in the snow had they not been carried away. Clumsy on their snow-shoes, the French regulars stumbled constantly and this considerably delayed the march of the small army. When they reached Trois-Rivières on January 25th, a wave of arctic cold swept across the entire country and a large number of soldiers, unable to keep going, had to be carried to people's homes.

These losses were replaced when the small army reached Fort Saint-Louis* and Fort Sainte-Thérèse*, where the troops had agreed to rally on the 30th of the month. The whole column having been reassembled started marching courageously; they crossed Lake Champlain which was covered with snow, up to four feet deep in some places, and went through the small valley which opened onto Lake Saint-Sacrement.

On the southern end of this lake, they waited in vain for the Algonquins who were to guide them, and then they ventured into unknown territory, not knowing where they were going. They captured a few men on the way and learned from them that most of the Mohawks and Oneidas had gone to war against the Wampum Makers tribe. The only ones left to watch the villages were the elderly, the young boys and the women.

After this, the Governor ordered his men through various passages and trails and, on February 9th, had his troops set up camp in the middle of the woods. That same evening, his soldiers found themselves face to face with a Mohawk detachment and, for this reason, thought they were in the vicinity of Caughnawaga. Sixty fuseliers gave chase to these one hundred Mohawks who fled as fast as they could. But this was only a deceptive maneuver: an ambush had been set up for the Onseronni Onwe. Hiding behind trees, with one volley of gun shots, the Mohawks killed eleven soldiers and wounded several others, while the French military only killed three Iroquois and wounded six. Actually, Mr. de Courcelle was three days walk from Caughnawaga and, being completely lost, bivouacked two miles from the Dutch settlement of Schenectady*!

Following their victory, the Indians carried four French scalps to the leaders of this village, who spread the news to the people of Fort Albany*. These in turn sent three delegates to Mr. de Courcelle to ask him what he had in mind in coming this way "into the lands of His Majesty the King of England without notifying the local Governor?"[8] This is how the French Governor learned, to his great surprise, that New Holland had passed over to British rule since September 6th, 1664. How discomfited he would have been, however, had he known - the Dutchmen, now British subjects, didn't know either - that France and England had been at war with each other for two weeks!

After explaining everything, Mr. de Courcelle requested food for this soldiers and care for the wounded, which, for a price, was granted to the extent possible. On Sunday, February 12th, Mr. de Courcelle was on his way again, empty-handed, back to Quebec, which he reached on March 17th, 1666, leaving behind on the way the bodies of more than sixty men who had died of hunger and cold.[9]

We may assume that Kateri rejoiced at her nation's victory. Her uncle was one of two hundred warriors who had halted the white army. How secure she must have felt when she saw her "father" again as he sat near the fire, quietly smoking his calumet! The threat of a return of the Onseronni Onwe announced by two prisoners hardly worried the chief. The defeat of the French army had only served to enhance the prestige of the Mohawk Turtles, Bears* and Wolves*.

New ambassadors were added to those who had come to Quebec in December 1665: the Seneca delegates in May 1666 and later, in July, the Oneida* delegates.

The latter claimed to speak on behalf of their own people and of the Mohawks. The treaty was ratified, but before the end of the month, the same Mohawks killed seven young Frenchmen. Despite further attemps to make peace, the Lieutenant General of the Americas had had enough.

Upon the instigation of Intendant Talon, the Marquis de Tracy left Quebec September 14th for another expedition.[10] Mr. de Courcelle escorted him with six hundred soldiers of the Carignan-Salières Regiment, six hundred French settlers and approximately one hundred Huron and Algonquin allies. Their heaviest equipment consisted of two small cannons, which they hauled all the way to Iroquois territory to knock down the palisades.

According to Mother Marie de l'Incarnation,[11] the army reached the vicinity of Caughnawaga, the Turtles' village, on October 15th, the feast of Saint Teresa. The weather was the worst it could be: it rained relentlessly, one storm after another. Mr. de Tracy, though he was well on in years, was not discouraged; he ordered his troops to walk all night.

The Iroquois were not aware that French forces were at their gates. No doubt they would have been caught by surprise had not a few of them been attacked and beaten on the way by some of the Algonquins. This gave rise to a general alarm in the villages. In order to take their positions of defense, the warriors sent the women and children away with instructions to hide in the forest. Tekakwitha and her aunts also left, under heavy rain, to hide.

The soldiers marched to the beat of their drums. At the sight of these troops marching in order and without fear, the Mohawks became so frightened that, without waiting for the assault, they fled hastily to the village of the Bears, which was nearby, and asked for refuge. The army broke into the place, encountering no resistance, and after setting fire to it, pursued the enemy into the village where they had fled.

The chief of Andagaron* had been warned by the Turtles that the aggressors were more than four thousand! When he heard the first sounds of the twenty drums and caught sight on the horizon of the huge column marching against him, his throat tightened as if it were gripped by the hand of death. He was the first one to take to his heels, followed by Tekakwitha's uncle and the other warriors of both villages.

The French officers thought they would find nothing in this canton but miserable huts or shanties, but "they found everything so beautiful and pleasant that Mr. de Tracy and those with him were amazed. They saw wooden longhouses twenty-six feet long and proportionately wide, housing eight or nine families each (...) The houses and storage spaces were so full of food that it was estimated there was enough to feed all of Canada for two full years."

All this time, Tekakwitha and the women of Caughnawaga were waiting in the forest still damp after the rain, for the chief to return. Defeated, the uncle went in search of his family and found them hiding in a makeshift shelter. One may wonder if they were close enough to Andagaron, the morning of October 17th, to hear the solemn Te Deum of the French army after its victory and to see the cross it put up in front of every fort with a sign bearing the Act of Possession[12] of the country in the name of the King of France? Little Tekakwitha may have heard "Vive le Roy!" shouted three times by the military.

After this ceremony, the army helped itself to all the food it needed for its sustenance and then set fire to the palisades, the longhouses and all the food stocks: corn, beans and other produce from the land. Finally they went back to the other villages and ransacked everything in the same manner, pillaging the countryside as well.

On November 5th, 1666, Messrs de Tracy and de Courcelle and their army, loaded with victuals and booty, returned to Quebec in triumph. Soon afterwards, the entire city knew the details of the invasion, but also the amazement of the French soldiers at the beauty and fertility of the Mohawk* country. They spoke of a vast stretch of cleared land and rich prairies where the grass was as tall as men. They were astonished at the sight of the corn growing twelve or thirteen feet tall, with cobs one foot long carrying more than four hundred grains, and of many other vegetables which grew in abundance!

When Tekakwitha and her family returned to Caughnawaga, there was nothing left but smoking ruins. In a hastily built shack, the child suffered cold and hunger most of the time, despite the berries and roots they could find and the few heads of game her uncle managed to hunt. As a result of such devastation, a major shortage of food was bound to occur. The "Three Sisters"* were missing: there were no more comfortable longhouses with braids of corn hanging from the posts, no more squash or beans. This was going to be a harsh winter.

31

Notes 2

1. T. Grassman, The Mohawk Indians and Their Valley, Schenectady, J.S. Lischynsky, 1969, p.210.

2. E.H. Walworth, The Life and Times of Kateri Tekakwitha. The Lily of the Mohawks, Albany, N.Y., J.B. Lyons Company, 1926 p. 40

3. Lettre du P. Jacques de Lamberville, dans Lettre du P. Claude Chauchetière touchant la mission des Iroquois du Sault St-François-Xavier proche Montréal, 14 octobre 1682, Ms. Archives de la Compagnie de Jésus, Province de Paris, Vanves, p. 8

4. VBCT, p. 19

5. Lettre du P. Jacques de Lamberville dans LCC, p. 6

6. VBCT, p. 18

7. JR, vol. 50, p. 130ss.

8. E.H. Walworth, work previously quoted, p. 72. Translated by the Author.

9. MV, P. 250-2

10. JR, vol. 50, p. 140ss.

11. G. Oury, Marie de l'Incarnation, Ursuline (1599-1672), Correspondence, Solesmes, Abbaye Saint-Pierre, 1971, p. 773-4.

12. MV, p. 257; L. Lamontagne, à "Prouville" dans: Dictionnaire biographique du Canada, Les Presses de l'Université Laval (Québec) et University of Toronto Press, 1966, vol. 1, p. 568-9.

3

First Encounters

Things had become relatively calm between the two nations and Mr. de Courcelle sent two or three Mohawk and Oneida prisoners back home, enjoining them to relay the demands of the French to their cantons. It seems that this peacemaking actions was understood, for, on July 5th, 1667, a Mohawk delegation arrived in Quebec with a few Oneida friends. Three days later, they offered presents to Mr. de Tracy and Governor de Courcelle and, among other requests, asked for Black Robes: two for the Mohawks and one for the Oneidas. After two days of reflection, their wish was granted, on condition that they release their French and Algonquin captives and leave their wives and children behind as security.[1]

Those three Black Robes were Frs. Jacques Frémin, Jean Pierron and Jacques Bruyas, Jesuits. Two lay assistants* went with them: Charles Boquet* and François Poisson. Father Frémin* was thirty-seven years old; having come to Canada in 1655, he had been part of the unfortunate foundation of Sainte-Marie de Ganentaha* in Onondaga*. He was such a vigorous man that many thought he was a former soldier. Better still, he mastered the Iroquois language. His companion, Father Pierron*, had just arrived in Quebec in June and was one year younger. Father Bruyas*, who was the same age, had already spent two years in New France.

On July 17th, they set sail up the Saint Lawrence and Richelieu Rivers; from there, they headed to Fort Sainte-Anne* at the entrance of Lake Champlain. They had to stay there more than a month, until the feast of Saint Bartholomew, August 24th, on account of some sixty Mahicans*, or Wolves, who had set an ambush for the ambassadors.

Having reached the far end of Lake Saint-Sacrement, the missionaries and the ambassadors only had approximately thirty leagues to travel by land before reaching their destination, Tionnontoguen*, the most important village of the Mohawk canton. They were met by fourteen Mohawk warriors and other scouts posted a little farther to make sure the French army was not returning to invade the country once again. Meeting these Iroquois was a boon to everyone: "Most fortunately for them and for us", wrote one of the Fathers, "instead of enemies, we were angles of peace to them, and instead of the lions they once had been, they became our servants, acting as porters for us at the appropriate time. Divine Providence had sent them to help us with our baggage, for we could hardly have carried them ourselves overland all the way to our destination."[2]

In such company, the three Fathers and the two lay assistants walked for short periods at a time until they were at three quarters of a league from the new Caughnawaga, which had been set up temporarily until the new village was built on the north shore of the Mohawk River. They stopped over in this village where they were received quite ceremoniously, according to customary politeness. They were finally led to the longhouse of the chief, the uncle of young Tekakwitha. Everyone gathered round to have a leisurely look at "these Frenchmen who were so peaceful after being in such a fury a short while before, setting fire everywhere."[3]

The chief and the aunts charged the eleven year old child with the care of the travellers. Small and frail, her face speckled by smallpox, she performed her duties to perfection: at the morning meal - the only one served among the Iroquois - the girl served the Fathers generously and with such modesty and gentleness that they were impressed and remembered this for a long time afterwards. The rest of the day, there was a pot of meat and vegetables simmering over the fire, from which they could help themselves any time they were hungry.

Tekakwitha was able to watch the visitors quite freely. She "was impressed by their affable manner and by their regular prayers and other practices throughout the day."[4] She noticed how diligently they reached out to meet old Christians. "God prepared her in this way for the grace of Baptism, which Fr. Cholenec feels she would have requested had the missionaries stayed longer in her village."[5]

Fr. Frémin's first concern was to visit the longhouses to seek out the Huron and Algonquin captives who made up two thirds of the population. Tekakwitha may have heard her aunts talk about the ten Huron children baptized by the priest, to the great joy of their parents.

The missionary had another opportunity to administer the Sacrament of Baptism, a real gift of divine mercy. He discovered in an Iroquois longhouse a poor woman soaking in blood, having been scalped shortly before by Wolf warriors.[6] Seeing her more dead than alive because of her wounds, the missionary had no hesitation; he spoke to her of the afterlife, of the pains of hell and of the blessings of heaven. The dying woman turned a deaf ear and Fr. Frémin went out to his companions who began to pray for the salvation of the unfortunate woman. He returned to her but a new obstacle stood in his way, an elderly woman who pushed him away and encouraged the wounded one in her resistance. The hour of assent had not yet come and the Black Robe went away. A third visit was just as fruitless. The entire French party was losing hope of saving the dying woman since they had to leave the village very soon.

Yet Fr. Frémin made a final attempt while the other four Frenchmen raised their arms to heaven to implore divine mercy. This time, Fr. Frémin found the woman quite changed; she listened and repeated the prayers with fervour. "She was so well disposed", he wrote, "the Holy Spirit having been her Master and Instructor, that we gave her holy Baptism before she died..." This was his first Mohawk convert.

The five Frenchmen were forced to stay longer in Caughnawaga because the warriors had gone in pursuit of the Mahicans who had assulted this woman. The official welcoming of the Black Robes was intended to take place in Tionnontoguen. Fr. Chauchetière explained later that the missionaries had arrived in the canton "during a period of drinking parties; therefore the people being in no condition to receive them as they should, had made them stop in the village of Caughnawaga..."[7]

During their short stay in this place, Fr. Frémin assembled the Christian Hurons to regulate the religious practices they were to observe. A Mohawk woman twenty-five years old had slipped in among them. When the missionary had finished speaking, she declared to him that she wished to become a Christian. The Black Robe replied that he would judge her sincerity by her perseverance. He promised to instruct her and to explain gradually to her the great happiness which awaited her. For her part, she never failed to conduct herself as an Indian of the prayer or to attend all the assemblies with the same fervour as the early Christians.

Fr. Frémin then selected a longhouse to be used as a chapel where all should meet morning and night for community prayers. He appointed one of the Christian women to notify the faithful of the time of these meetings. The Mohawk woman proposed herself instead for this charitable and, one might say, humble service. Fr. Frémin himself attested that, with the most heroic courage, she overcame the shyness which was natural to Iroquois women and went from longhouse to longhouse extending these invitations.[8] In fact, she hardly ever showed up without being taunted and insulted by non-Christians.

When the priest was about to leave, realizing that she could not yet be baptized, she said to him: "At least, baptize my only son; he hasn't committed any sins like I have to become unworthy of this grace." The missionary granted her request and encouraged her by promising to return within two weeks to instruct her.

After spending three days in Caughnawaga, the missionaries first went to another village, Andagaron, located approximately two leagues away. From there, they set out for Tionnontoguen, the chief village of the canton, rebuilt one fourth of a league from the site which had been burnt down by the French the previous year.[10]

Two hundred men escorted them, all marching in order with an admirable gravity. The Fathers walked last, in front of the white heads, the most considered men in the land. Having reached the outskirts of the village, the entire party came to a stop. The best speaker of the nation came forward, surrounded by his ambassadors, and gave the Black Robes a congratulatory speech. He assured them that the Mohawks were pleased to see the French in their midst and that they hoped the white men would "dissipate the fog in the air, i.e. the troublesome interference of the Wolves, and that they would temper their spirit so as to guarantee peace", which the French had come to bring. After this the Mohawks led them inside the palisade where they were received with a salvo of honour from the entire artillery, each man firing from his house, plus two artillery men who fired from both ends of the place.

A banquet was served, which consisted of a dish of boiled corn with a little smoked fish, actually sagamity, and for dessert, a basket of pumpkins.

It was customary among the Iroquois and their neighbours to let some time elapse before responding to a welcoming speech or to a proposal made in public. Therefore it was on September 14th, the feast of the Exaltation of the Holy Cross, that the men, women, children and elders of the six Mohawk villages assembled in Tionnontoguen, where Fr. Frémin explained to the whole nation why the Black Robes had come.

The three Jesuits and their two lay assistants opened the meeting with the song of the Veni Creator, playing between verses "a small musical instrument" - not doubt a Jew's harp or a fipple flute - which delighted the crowd. Fr. Frémin then harangued his listeners in the Iroquois manner, i.e. using gestures as well as words. He stressed the advantages of peace and the disadvantages of war, which the Mohawks had sorely experienced the previous year.

The priest then reproached them for their treacherous and cruel treatment of the True Axe Makers, from whom they had received no ill-treatment. After this he declared plainly that he was here with his friends to change their warlike disposition and to teach them how to live like human beings and become Christians. Then the great Onontio* (Governor de Courcelle) would accept them as subjects in the name of the King and grant them royal protection. However, they were not to practice any kind of hostile activity against the True Axe makers nor their allies.

To convince the Mohawks of the importance of maintaining peace, Fr. Frémin had a long pole, some forty or fifty feet long, planted in front of them with a wampum necklace hanging from the top. Everyone wondered what the Black Robe had in mind. After a few minutes of silence, he solemnly declared that the first Iroquois who would kill a True Axe Maker or one of their friends would be hanged like this. Let them remember the public execution of their compatriot Agariata* who had killed Mr. de Chasy!

The astonishment caused by this unexpected gift was almost unbelievable. Everyone remained head down, not daring to look up at the swaying necklace or to make any comments.

The same speaker who had welcomed the Fathers at the entrance of Tionnontoguen finally rose as though recovering his spirits and began to walk around the pole with gestures of amazement. This man who was more than sixty years old feigned not to comprehend the meaning of the wampum necklace. He went through a series of exclamations and gestures until he finally seemed to have understood its meaning. Then he grabbed his throat with both hands several times, dramatically tightening his grip to impress upon the multitude surrounding him the horror of this kind of death. After this, he launched into a long and very eloquent speech interspersed with the most surprising quips, at the end of which he released into the hands of the Fathers the captives they had requested, among others a French man whom the Mohawks had been detaining for some time. Moreover, he willingly released twelve Algonquins, more precisely Nez Percés and Ottawas. He also offered the Jesuits the choice of site where they could build their chapel and promised his people's help in building it.

Everyone said goodbye to each other, as was the custom, and went home. What did Tekakwitha understand of the speeches of the Black Robe and of the great Mohawk speaker? This little eleven year old was no fool and her eyesight had somewhat improved, enough not to have to feel her way around any more. No doubt she understood the essential message of each of the two men. As a true daughter of her people, she certainly found the demands of the True Axe Makers quite stiff.

Fr. Frémin remained in the chief village of the Mohawks. Fr. Bruyas, along with Charles Boquet, left for Oneida* before the end of September. This is where Catherine Gandeaktenha* and her husband, François-Xavier Tonsahoten*, a Christian Huron, lived; they were the future founders of the Saint Francis Xavier Mission in La Prairie, where Tekakwitha was to reach one day the heights of holiness. Fr. Frémin decided to send Fr. Pierron back to Quebec with François Poisson to inform the Governor and the Intendant of what he felt was the best way to maintain peace with the Iroquois.

Having returned to her village, Tekakwitha resumed her every day life. She had several occasions to meet the young woman whose child Fr. Frémin had baptized. This woman continued inviting the Christians, including Tekakwitha's aunts, to meet morning and night for prayer. Fr. Frémin had promised to return within two weeks to instruct her, but he was unable to get away from some urgent business and he failed to keep his word. The young mother went to Tionnontoguen to see the Black Robe.[12] The priest was delighted to see his neophyte again and told her he would begin in earnest to teach her the prayers and the most important mysteries of the faith, but she knew them already thanks to a friendly Huron woman. Nervertheless, as the missionary did not know her well enough, he delayed her Baptism once again and commanded her to return home, where he would come shortly after to fulfill her desire.

The Jesuit was, in fact, in Caughnawaga a short while later. He inquired from a few Christian Huron women about how the catechumen had been doing. Everything had gone beautifully in his absence; she had even been an example to the whole population. Finally he spoke to her directly. "I found her to be a woman of rare innocence, sound mind and good memory", he wrote. "She had accustomed herself to recite the Rosary five or six times a day and I can attest that, from morning to night, she was continuously in prayer." For all these good reasons, the Father felt he must give her Baptism.

Immediately after this, a number of trials fell upon her. Two days after her Baptism, her son fell seriously ill; but she was not shaken. She continued with her usual devotions, thus deserving the healing of her child. Shortly afterwards, her husband was killed by the Wolves near the village. She loved this man more than her own life. As the missionary noted, she was a normal human being with a good mind and came from one of the best families of the region. All these wonderful qualities had produced, in the last eight or ten years, a marriage filled with mutual love; it was considered the most successful marriage in the land.

Instead of demolishing her faith, this illness and this death made it even stronger, which she certainly needed in order to face the attacks of her husband's family and her own. She had killed her husband by becoming a member of "the prayer", they howled a thousand times for eight days, inflicting on her every ill-treatment one can imagine. This was more than she needed to be discouraged. She then sent for Fr. Frémin. He was amazed at her solid faith and at her fidelity to her devotions, which were a haven of peace and sweetness in the midst of her heavy trials. The story goes that one day the donkey of the great Saint Teresa of Avila threw her into the river. As she emerged, soaking wet, she cried out: "Lord, no wonder you don't have many friends; you treat them so badly!" This Mohawk woman, a contemporary of Tekakwitha, could have used the same language for, twenty days later, she developed such swelling of her eyes that she could no longer see.

Once again her family as well as her husband's persecuted her: "Isn't it bad enough that you killed your husband?" they said. "Do you also wish to kill yourself? Don't you see that the Faith is causing all these evils? If you want to let yourself be a prey to all this misery, at least spare your child and the rest of your family..."

For one more week her relatives harassed her; they even brought in the local jugglers to heal her through superstitious foods and rituals. She absolutely refused and, as soon as she was free, she went to a Christian Huron who knew a good remedy for her illness. Three months later, she had recovered her sight and her body was restored to health. All through this period of affliction, she taught her four year old son his prayers. Fr. Frémin likened her to the Christians of the first centuries of the Church.

38

In 1667, Tekakwitha was only eleven years old, but, in all likelihood, she was impressed by the testimony of this fervent woman. Despite her good disposition, the hour of Christianity had not yet come for her. Now aware of the kinds of persecution that came after a conversion, this timid child had not yet understood what "the prayer" was all about. Her uncle's hostility did not help in any way. Of course, she had been fascinated by the Black Robes and their companions, whom she had hosted when they first arrived in the canton. She remembered how gentle they were, like a beautiful day at the end of summer, and how they spent hours praying to the Great Spirit in the peacefulness of the longhouse. She was deeply impressed by these memories. Yet was there not another image also persistently coming to her mind: the spectre of a wampum necklace swaying in the wind atop a long pole?

Notes 3

1. MIC, p. 789, note (2).

2. JR, Vol. 51, p. 184.

3. Ibid. p. 186.

4. PO, Doc. XII, p. 249.

5. Ibid.

6. JR, vol. 51, p. 186-8.

7. VBCT, p. 15.

8. JR, vol. 51, p. 192.

9. Ibid.

10. Ibid. p. 200-8.

11. Ibid. p. 194.

12. Ibid. p. 192-200.

4

Her New Home

Faithful to the promises made to Fr. Frémin on his arrival in Tionnontogen and with incredible ardour, the Mohawks built a chapel dedicated to Sainte Marie. The Huron captives, who were fervent Christians in spite of having been deprived for many years of the Sacraments and of religious instruction, came to the chapel to attend holy Mass and practice their devotions.

The missionary[1] admitted being unable to hold back his tears of joy at the sight of these poor slaves so constant in their faith. Each day, he had to spend eight consecutive hours leading them in prayer, reserving the rest of his time for other pastoral duties. Mothers brought their ebony-eyed little ones to him that he might trace the sign of the Cross on their foreheads, a gesture which they quickly accustomed themselves to do before putting them to bed at night. It was quite common for people to talk about heaven and hell at home, for the Black Robe frequently spoke about these topics to his flock as well as to the old Christians of the other villages of the canton.

Fr. Frémin was invited to Caughnawaga, which was approximately fifteen miles from Tionnontoguen. The first thing he did was to look after the old Christians. Young Tekakwitha saw the tall silhouette of the Father going from longhouse to longhouse. He found in this village forty-five fervent Christians whose "devotion far surpassed that of ordinary Christians, even though they had had no assistance from their pastors for such a long time." Among them, "a few Iroquois drawn by the fragrance of their good example and convinced of the truth of our holy Faith," continued on the right path.

In the spring of 1668, the chiefs of the Mohawk territory delegated a handful of men to the Governor of New France.[2] Tekakwitha's uncle had a say in the choice of the envoys, of the presents to be given Onontio and of the requests to be presented to him. What these ambassadors requested most of all was help against the Wolves. At the same time, to soften Mr. de Courcelle, they requested more Black Robes to assist Fr. Frémin, who was overworked. The Governor and his Council received these representatives graciously.

On October 7th of the same year[3], Fr. Pierron, who had been away for a year, returned from Quebec and joined Fr. Frémin in Tionnontoguen. Three days later, as superior of the Iroquois missions, Fr. Frémin gave his place to him and left for the Seneca canton. Tionnontoguen, as Fr. Pierron found it, was quite different from that which Mr. de Tracy had known! "These people live in such poverty", he said, "that they hardly eat any meat or fish; but, by the grace of God, the missionaries live quite happily in such deprivation." "Our Mohawks are the poorest of the poor," said the priest in one of his letters; "but, with that, I love them more than myself, seeing how well disposed they are to Christianity."

The missionary began immediately visiting the villages of the canton every eight days. He spared himself no effort or fatigue, walking long distances for fear of hearing that a sick person had died before he was able to baptize him or her. This is how Tekakwitha got used to his presence and numerous activities. The priest made a number of excellent paintings to illustrate the mysteries of faith, and the success of his depiction of a happy and unhappy death was quite phenomenal. Up until then, those who could not be bothered often covered their ears and said: "I don't hear." These two scenes enable the missionary to explain to them the immortality of the soul. No one, after this, dared to say: "I don't hear."

In Caughnawaga, [4] the fidelity of the new Christians under the leadership of a fervent catechist, consoled the Jesuit. The example of the brave young woman who, in spite of mockery and trials, had deserved Baptism for herself and her son, had borne fruit. "We bow our heads in the face of these insults", the catechist confided to the priest, "and when we are gathered together, we pray God to open the eyes of those who make fun of us that they may see what we see." Tekakwitha lived in this contradictory environment, in which some turned to a new religion and others opposed it.

Fr. Pierron found these neophytes as far advanced as the French in piety and the service of God. "They know all the most difficult things about the mystery of the Holy Trinity", he said, "and they distinguish the two natures in Jesus Christ; they know what the Church teaches about the immortality of our souls, about the judgment, mortal sin, venial sin and original sin; and since we take special care to teach them the ordinary prayers and the commandments of God and of the Church, which they sing every Sunday in Iroquois verses," they know everything they absolutely need to know in order to receive Baptism. The missionary was convinced that the blood on Isaac Jogues was bearing fruit.

One day, probably in the fall of 1668, the Turtles moved their belongings to the second Caughnawaga, on the north shore of the Mohawk River, where the town of Fonda, N.Y. is today. At this place, the river splashed against large rocks. A small pool of clear water, known today as the "Tekakwitha Spring," supplied the whole village with drinking water; it sprang halfway down a hollow surrounded by trees, near the Cayadutta which flowed into the Mohawk River. Above it, from a narrow strip of land between the river and the spring, Tekakwitha could see the warriors building a strong palisade around the site where longhouses were under construction.

Inside, other brave people, helped by younger men, were putting the finishing touch to a few kanonsote*. These structures⁵ were between eighty and two hundred feet long and twenty-five feet wide and could house six or eight families. Along the center, hearths were set up, one for every two families. In the rounded roof, an opening was provided above each hearth; to this aperture, which served as a chimney, a moveable sheet of bark was attached to close it in case of rain or snow. Along the walls of the longhouse, approximately ten feet above the floor, there was a light platform on which to put various things. Underneath it, at one or two feet above ground, they built much sturdier platforms, approximately twelve feet long and six feet wide, to sit on in the daytime and to sleep on at night. On the framework of the longhouse built with logs and poles, the warriors, temporarily transformed into carpenters, installed large overlapping squares of elm or walnut bark. They had lifted this bark from trees in the early days of spring and flattened it under heavy rocks. Now that it was properly dried, it supplied the material for the walls of the kanonsote.

All these comings and goings went on before the fascinated eyes of Tekakwitha. At the end of the day, she would hastily return with the rest of the family to the longhouse which her uncle had helped build. The women had divided their dwelling according to the position of the hearths. This was the place where the family members met each morning, at least during the cold season, for the only meal of the day. Tekakwitha, her adopted sister and her aunts soon began to weave rush mats to cover the mud floor. They laid the hides of wild animals on the lower platforms to be used as blankets. On the poles overhanging the family area, they hung pieces of smoked meat, long strings of corn made with twelve to twenty ears braided together, and dried tobacco leaves. Any time of the day, whenever they wished to satisfy their hunger with corn meal, there were lovely little bark dishes and wooden bowls on hand, which they had brought from the old Caughnawaga. No doubt the heavy mortars and wooden pestles were soon ready to grind the whole wheat, which was a basic ingredient of their ordinary food.

Before the end of fall, the kanonsote, being in fact quite attractive, were ready to be lived in. In addition, the men of Caughnawaga lent a hand in building a longhouse to be used as a chapel dedicated to Saint Peter. Tekakwitha did not dare enter it.

Fr. Pierron, as a good pastor, tried hard to bring "the prayer", i.e. Christianity, to the level of the Mohawks. He quickly noticed that they loved playing games - this was their only pastime when they were not at war. He invented a game especially for them and called it "From Point to Point," i.e. from the point of birth to the point of eternity. The Iroquois called it "The Road to the Place where one Lives Forever, either in Heaven or in Hell."⁶

This game conveyed an eloquent message through the use of coulour and taught some powerful lessons through symbols; besides, it was easy to master. The seven Sacraments were presented, the three theological virtues, the commandments of God and of the Church with the most common mortal sins and even the most usual venial sins. Then came original sin in its own box, followed by all the evils it generates. The priest had also included the four last things, the fear of God, indulgences and the works of mercy. Moreover, in four different boxes were grace, conscience, individual freedom to choose salvation or perdition and, finally, what is hardly in tune with XXth century thinking, the small number of the elect. These religious card games surely had a positive influence in Caughnawaga and Tekakwitha may have often watched them with a few of her friends, for it seems that women had to be content with looking on!

Fr. Pierron, always an innovator, did not stop there; he kept coming up with new initiatives in the same vein. He actively opposed jugglery, i.e. the art of healing through superstitions which he considered criminal. This practice was truly a hindrance to the conversion of the Mohawks. He was considerably successful in outwitting it by providing the sick with something better than jugglery, i.e. health for their bodies through medicines sent from Quebec and, often, health for their souls through his moral and spiritual support.

Another evil which he did not fail to attack was drunkeness and debauchery, which go hand in hand. The old and the new Christians supported him in this struggle. They had noticed that a demon from outside was seriously impeding the conversion of the majority of their compatriots and weakening the entire canton in the war against the Wolves: this demon was Dutch liquor sold to them in New Orange, now known as Albany. Inspired by the Iroquois Christians, a public council searched for the most effective way to fight off this curse. On the suggestion of Fr. Pierron, they wrote a petition to Governor Francis Lovelace of Manhatte, who very politely answered[7] with a promise to punish severely anyone who would contravene his orders forbidding the sale of liquor to the natives.

Tekakwitha was now twelve years old, but she looked barely ten. Yet she was already considered an adult and expected to do all the work women did. She spent long hours all summer picking wild strawberries, blackberries, raspberries, elderberries and, later in the season, bilberries or "blueberries", as Fr. de Charlevoix called them.[8] Three baskets were used to pick these fruits: two small ones held at both ends of a strip of leather slung over the shoulder and a third one, fairly large, held in the hand. When the two small baskets were full, she would empty them into the large one. She would return home in the evening with her three baskets full of delicious berries, to the great delight of her aunts and of the other women of her longhouse. When late autumn came, it was time to shake down acorns, walnuts and hazelnuts from the trees. Finally, in nearby fields, the "Three Sisters," i.e. husked amber corn, jade coloured beans and plump golden squash were harvested.

Notes 4

1.   JR, vol. 51, p. 208.

2.   JR, vol. 52, p. 134.

3.   Ibid. p.116-20.

4.   Ibid. p. 132-4.

5.   William N. Fenton, "Northern Iroquoian Culture Patterns," in Trigger, B.G., Handbook of North American Indians, Smithsonian Institution, Washington, 1978, vol. 15, p. 303.

6.   JR, vol. 53, p. 206-212.

7.   JR, vol. 52, p. 138-40.

8.   HDNF, vol.II, "Description des plantes principales de l'Amérique septentrionale.", p. 52.

5

War and Death

For the first time, the harvest in the new fields was not as abundant as usual. The fear of the Wolves hiding in the bushes and watching for opportunities to attack, caused Mohawk women to be extremely careful in their comings and goings. Too many of their friends had been struck down and scalped on the outskirts of their villages.

The Mahicans, who were not properly identified by the French, were of Algonquian stock. They lived along the Hudson River and had been overpowered by the Mohawks for many years. After 1660 they began fighting with their oppressors again and, once more in the summer of 1669, they attacked their hostile northern neighbours.

At dawn on August 18th,[1] Tekakwitha was awakened by war cries and by the whistling of bullets cutting through the palisade and through the bark of her home. The warriors jumped to their feet and took up arms: muskets, tomahawks, clubs, bows and arrows.

Then, with a deadly howl, they ran to the ramparts. Before them, hundreds of feathered Wolves with streaks of paint on their faces were rushing forward in attack. (Fr. Pierron said three hundred; some Boston reports mentioned six or seven hundred.) Their Chief, Chekatabutt, "House on Fire," a wise and sturdy middle-aged man, led them valiantly. Tekakwitha along with the other Mohawk women prepared bullets for the warriors and armed themselves with knives and other defensive weapons in case the enemy erupted in the place.

At the very beginning of the combat, four Mohawks were killed and two wounded, one of whom died soon afterwards. Warned of the attack, the warriors of Andagaron, the neighbouring village, hurried to Tionnontoguen. They shouted on arrival "that the whole country was lost, that Caughnawaga was besieged by an army of Wolves, that all the young men had already been cut down and that the fort of Andagaron, which was next to it, was about to perish." Fear had caused them to magnify the truth.

Without going into a panic, the men of Tionnontoguen streaked their faces with the hot colours of warriors in combat. They dressed up in their best looking attire and hastily set out for Caughnawaga. Fr. Pierron joined them at once in the hope of being of assistance to the wounded and the dying. They learned on arrival that, after two hours of bitter fighting, the enemy had already retreated. One Wolf had fallen in front of the ramparts and his hands and feet had been cut off to be eaten. Wailing cries rose up inside the palisade for the death of the brave men of the village who had courageously given their lives to defend the place. This was most likely the day when Togouiroui*, whom the Dutch knew as Kryn, distinguished himself by his bravery and earned the name of Ganeagoua, "Great Mohawk". He was soon to play a wonderful role at the Mission of Saint Francis Xavier in La Prairie, where Tekakwitha would go for refuge after her Baptism.

The brave men of Tionnontoguen decided with the warriors of Caughnawaga to continue pursuing the enemy. They had provisions of flour prepared and they sailed down the Mohawk River in their canoes. The water flows very rapidly at that time of year. They moved as quickly as they could, but as night came upon them before they had caught up with the invaders, they sent scouts to find out exactly where the enemy had pitched camp. Having reached the place, the scouts tried to get even closer, but the Wolves' sentry sensing danger let out a resounding "Koue, Koue!," Indian for "Who is there?" The query was answered by a dead silence and no alarm was sounded.

Following the scouts' report, the Mohawks decided to lay an ambush for the Wolves. They would attack them on their way home instead of trying to force their way into the temporary redoubt where they had taken shelter. To carry out their plan, the Mohawks went hurriedly to Kinaquariones, today Wolf Hollow, north of the Mohawk River, and positioned themselves at this most advantageous site along the road leading to the Dutch settlement. They counted on seeing Chekatabutt and his men pass by this place the next day.

Early the next morning, the Wolves broke camp. When the first twelve of them began making their way through the Kinaquariones pass, not suspecting the danger, they were hit by a volley of gun shots. In the midst of shouting, yelling and the hissing of bullets through the air, those who managed to remain unhurt turned back to rally at the camping site where they had spent the previous night. The Iroquois, who where on their heels, delivered a furious attack on them. The combat lasted till evening. Many Mohawks were wounded or killed; the others captured four of the twenty-four enemy women and six warriors in the heat of hand-to-hand fighting.

At the crack of dawn on August 20th, the Mohawks returned to resume the combat, but the enemy had fled by night. As was the custom, the victors cut off the heads of those left behind to scalp them at leisure and they buried their own dead. That evening, Fr. Pierron, who had remained in Caughnawaga, rejoined his Mohawks. They said that the enemy had lost approximately one hundred men. "I have always doubted," confided Fr. Pierron, "that such a large number had been killed, for the Iroquois only brought back nineteen scalps." Besides, the Wolves claimed to have lost only fifty men and to have killed forty Mohawks. Chekatabutt died on the battle field, to the great chagrin and deep regret of his people.

The missionary diligently went about, looking after the wounded Mohawks. He then obtained permission to talk to the Wolves. He instructed the captives immediately, as best he could, for fear of not being able to do so if he waited until their return to Caughnawaga.

Two days later, the warriors accompanied by a large number of their compatriots made a triumphant re-entry to their village. They carried the hair of their victims carefully painted and fixed to the tips of sharp rods while the prisoners, divided into several bands, walked to the beat of the death song. The priest spotted a captive woman carrying a sick infant sucking her breast. As they came by a stream, he baptized the baby who died shortly thereafter.

In Caughnawaga, the Jesuit continued to prepare the Mahicans for Baptism. There were a few among the Mohawks who said to one another: "Don't you see how he loves our enemies?" Others added that the Black Robe should let these people, who had done so much harm to them, burn in hell. Many, however admitted that the priest was doing the proper thing in instructing them and that the vengeance of man should not extend beyond the limits of the enemy's life. The grace of God was doing its work. Although the Indian woman who served as interpreter for the Black Robe did not know all the truths being taught, all the captives, men and women, asked Fr. Pierron for Baptism before their execution.

As they were about to celebrate the victory, Tekakwitha grew tense at the thought of the tortures which would be inflicted on the captives. She refused to attend the carnage. Sitting in the family area of her longhouse and busy sewing beads on a buckskin mocassin, she was overwhelmed by the doleful chanting of the condemned prisoners, the horrifying shrieks of the women being burnt alive and the glorious howling of the victors intermingled with the smell of roasting flesh.

The hours went by till evening. The teenage girl stretched out on her mat, but sleep was a long time coming for the impressions of the last few days played havoc with her mind. Gradually, however, the voices and chaos of the outside world grew silent. She finally heard, two or three times, the chirping of the nightjar on the edge of the forest and, soon afterwards, she fell asleep.

* * *

Not satisfied with their victory, the Mohawks decided to take revenge on the Mahicans for the affront they had inflicted upon them[2] by attacking them in their own fortress in Caughnawaga. With the strong support of four other Iroquois nations, they rallied four hundred warriors to go and fight the Wolves in one of their forts near Manhate. They first attempted an ambush, which failed to fool the enemy. Forced to engage in open war, they came up against an impenetrable fortress and had to turn back in confusion. A small band of five warriors rejoined them with one captive and one scalp.

This capture somewhat concealed the failure of their expedition and they made preparations to execute the Wolf. Fr. Pierron, who was making the rounds in the other villages, was not on hand to prepare the prisoner for Baptism. A fervent catechist named Marie Tsiaouentes*, who was also an oyander*, i.e. one of the most highly considered women of the nation because of her noble rank, went to visit the unfortunate man. To her utter amazement, she found him praying in the manner of the Algonquins baptized by the Black Robes. She instructed him at once concerning the Christian mysteries and the poor fellow thanked her for her charity in this place where he thought he would find nothing but death and hatred. A few days later, he died a cruel death at the stake, but he died in peace, resigned to his fate, after receiving Baptism. As one may suspect, the conduct of Marie Tsiaouentes was not appreciated by all of her compatriots.

Fr. Pierron had been so devoted to the Mohawks that the elders showed their esteem for him by inviting him to their ritual of the dead.[3]

The assemblies of mourning for and replacement of chiefs killed at war were occasions for the most important council of the five Iroquois nations. This gathering took place in the village of the mourning nation, Caughnawaga in this instance.

The missionary accepted this honour and was quite impressed by finding himself among the top leaders of the Onondagas. Oneidas and Mohawks, each group remaining separate from the others according to custom. While waiting for the address of the Onondaga chief, the Mohawks talked among themselves about their fables and superstitions. "I joined them," said the missionary, "cleverly introducing a few words of truth into their falsehoods; I showed them clearly how ridiculous their superstitions were."

The reaction was quick. One chief, a friend of the priest, tried to silence him using his authority, as he did on occasion with his own people. The priest protested: "What wrong did I say for you to make me stop talking? And if I am telling the truth, why don't you want them to hear it?" The old man replied that it was the custom for them to talk about their fables on such occasions. The altercation continued even louder so that, when the time came to sing - hymn singing was the essential element and the most solemn moment of the Iroquois assembly - the same chief ordered the missionary to leave. Fr. Pierron went for refuge to the Onondagas, where the famous Garakontie received him very warmly.

This was not the end of this affair. After the ritual, which lasted five hours, the priest returned to Caughnawaga and made known his displeasure to the population. The chief in question came to apologize and admitted to him with great sincerity: "My brother, I can well see what is at the bottom of this quarrel: the fact that we are not Christians yet; but if you trust me with this great concern, I promise there will be a successful outcome." This sixty-five year old chief informed the Black Robe,

48

calmly this time, of the manner in which he should address them; then, he personally went about inviting the leaders of the Mohawk villages.

Fr. Pierron received all these important people in his house where, following the advice of his guide, he was able to pour out his heart in a long tirade, Iroquois style. At the end of his address, the missionary threw three armfuls of wampums in front of his attentive listeners. The first one to ask them to worship the true God and to follow His law, the second one to urge the jugglers no longer to invoke demons for the healing of the sick, and the last one, to eliminate superstitious dances. Each of these three requests was received with acclamations, after which the guests cautiously added that an answer would be given at a future council.

There were two councils. One in the presence of the Onondagas who had just returned from the Dutch settlement where they had gone trading; the other with the Mohawks elders, at which the chief who was referred to above spoke in these terms: "My brother, we are now dealing with an important matter. You are asking us for things which are very hard for us to agree to; indeed, is it not most awkward for us to break suddenly with habits in which we have been nourished and to give up absolutely things that have been ours since the beginning of the world (...) We are asking you to instruct us and to believe that you will find our minds submitted to everything you command. (...) Set up your chapel in such a way that we may go there to receive your instructions, which we know are the explanation of the will of God."

After this address, they presented to the priest as much wampums as he had given them, which meant that their hearts were sincere and the agreement was sealed.

Shortly afterwards, the medicine men of Caughnawaga threw their turtle rattles and other juggling instruments into the fire, the women no longer called jugglers when they were sick and the people performed no other dances than those approved by the priest. Finally, everyone openly declared allegiance to the faith. This manifestation of good will toward the religion of Iesos Christos* called an end to much prejudice, gave the Jesuit more freedom and fostered the conversion of many people in Caughnawaga.

From then on, Tekakwitha saw young people as well as old making their way to the little chapel, which was once unattended by those of her nation. What happened there...?

Notes 5

1. JR, vol. 53, p. 136-48.

2. Ibid., p. 156ss.

3. Ibid., p. 212ss; E.Tooker, "The League of the Iroquois: Its History, Politics and Ritual" dans: Trigger, B.G., Handbook of North American Indians, Smithsonian Institution, Washington, 1978, vol. 15, p. 418-41; Hale, Horatio, The Iroquois Book of Rites, D.G. Brinton, Philadelphia, 1883, p. 59-66.

6

He Was Handsome

At the dawn of Christianity in Caughnawaga, there was no shortage of women of outstanding character. Marie Tsiaouentes,[1] who dared to thrust her way through the warriors to prepare an enemy Wolf for Baptism, combined boldness with prestige and on numerous occasions, gave proof of her faith and courage.

While visiting in the neighbouring Dutch village, she defended her new faith against Calvinist "heretics" in their own temple. Deeply devoted to the Blessed Virgin Mary, she explained so well the reasons for this devotion to the Mother of God that some of them, filled with admiration for such piety, insisted that she sell them the statue of Our Lady. She replied that, even at the peril of her life, she would never part with this little statue which had been sent from Quebec by Mother Marie de l'Incarnation. Her example, said Fr. Pierron, was such an encouragement to other Christian women in Caughnawaga that no insult or violence could shake their determination. No doubt the two aunts of Tekakwitha were touched by her influence.

Within a short time, this little group of Christian women became the talk of the Dutch Protestants and of the Mohawk traditionalists, who went so far as to warn them that "their zeal might very well cost them their lives." The answer came swiftly: life was no object to them for they had consecrated it to Rawennio* (God) in Baptism. Marie even added that, even if she were to have her hands and feet cut off, she would rather have her life than her faith taken away from her. Her courage was soon to be put to the test.

Four scoundrels decided to intoxicate her. They deceitfully invited her to a feast without telling her that liquor would be served. She went to it not suspecting the trap. Seated on mats, the guests began to drink. When her turn came, she flatly refused the cup being presented to her. "I have made a fool of myself enough times before my Baptism", she said. "I am determined to behave myself better on this point than I have done in the past." They insisted; she pushed the drink away with a strong resolve. They threatened to mistreat her. She firmly declared that she was afraid of nothing in the world except sin. At this the four ruffians grabbed her, one by the arms, another by the head and a third one by the waist, while the fourth one tried to forcibly pour the liquor into her mouth. They failed, however. Marie held her teeth together so tight they could not get her to swallow even a drop!

On another occasion, while sorcery was still prevalent in the village, Marie and her friends were invited once again to a feast at the house of an elderly Christian woman. They realized, to their complete surprise, that a medicine man was presiding over the festive meal prepared for the healing of the sick. Marie stood up there and then and said in a loud voice: "Let whoever is a true Christian stand up and walk out of here with me. As for those who are Christians in name only, they may remain for this superstitious feast." Four or five guests walked out after her.

The others admired them, amazed that they would act in this way. It was unthinkable that well known women and particularly an oyander would allow themselves this kind of behaviour.

"As for the customs of our country, they said, we don't object to those that are in agreement with reason and the law of God, but we cannot accept those that are offensive to either one of these."

In a completely different setting, Tekakwitha, who had not yet been converted, also showed her ability to paddle against the current. As soon as she became of age, her family began, for the second time, to look for a husband for her. This was not without personal gain. According to custom, the game hunted by the newcomer was brought in for his wife and the members of her family.

Tekakwitha[2] was now fourteen years old. As her face was disfigured by smallpox and outsiders looked upon her as a misformed slave - which caused some to say, after her death, that God took her away because men didn't want her - young men were not interested in her. Yet, she had the qualities that would have made her an ideal wife.

She had a pleasant disposition and a great sense of humour. She devoted herself faithfully to the daily tasks customary to Mohawk women. She crushed the corn, prepared the soup and the bread, filled everyone's plate and, despite her dim vision and halting gait, was always the first one to set to work. Besides, her nimble hands created artistic wonders with porcupine quills and moose hair; she made head straps used for carrying wood and more elegant necklaces with wampum beads used by the elders to negotiate the affairs of the nation. She also knew how to sew the European way, like her neighbours who had learnt it from Dutch women or from Huron captives who had lived among the True Axe Makers. She would cut thin strips of eel skin dyed bright red with sturgeon glue and use these ribbons to tie her jet black hair in a knot at the back of her head. Finally, what others didn't know how to do she did with great skill. For example, she made baskets, crates and buckets for drawing water. Sometimes she softened bark used in making mats and sometimes she cut poles on which to hang ears of corn.

She had other qualities which were less valued by her people. From her earliest years, she refused to attend dances and games. Her prudence as well as her shyness were also noticed on several occasions, for she was reluctant to appear in public.

According to those who knew her at a very young age, she was not one to go about visiting or running from place to place; she was no gossiper, nor was she lazy, arrogant or fascinated by her dreams. She was not eager to dress up in fancy clothes as were most young Iroquois women; on occasion, however, she would let her aunts adorn her. Later on, she judged this condescension to be one of the greatest faults of her life and made up for it by her tears and penance. Her most admirable trait, however, was the repulsion she felt, even in those days before she became a Christian, for anything that had the faintest scent of impurity.

As she grew older, her aunts, who were concerned about her future - for there was a time when they would send her away from one longhouse to another - resumed their efforts to get her married. Not only did a husband look after the needs of his wife, he also provided the entire longhouse with the game from his hunt. One evening, as Tekakwitha returned home from the field or the forest, she was made to dress up in her loveliest apparel and to slip on leggings and a finely embroidered skirt. Clearly, they were expecting visitors, but this did not trouble her. Seated on the lower platform facing the family area, she waited patiently. The flame from the wood shavings lighted up the white and purple beads decorating her mocassins and the Indian pearl necklace which brought out the great sweetness of her maiden face.

The dull tread of an approaching stranger and the welcoming voices of her aunts and uncle signaled to her that it was soon time to serve the meal. Dressed in his finest buckskin kilt with a fringe and porcupine quill embroidery, a handsome young man walked towards her. He wore a bonnet adorned with a bunch of small white feathers topped by a long eagle feather. A handwoven sash decorated with white wampum beads hung from his shoulder and around his waist. Beaded mocassins emerged from his high buckskin leggings, which were decorated at the bottom and on the sides with porcupine quills of many colours.

Tekakwitha eyed him placidly, which was no surprise to him. Her reserved attitude came from her being so shy, he thought. He sat near her, reassured by the kindly welcome of the young girl's parents. She was taken aback, not knowing what to do. So, one of her aunts passed the sagamity to her. "Serve it to our visitor", she said. The young maiden stood up, took the smoking cup and hesitated. What was the meaning of these restrained smiles on her aunts' faces, of this air of solemnity on her uncle's and of the expectant look in the eyes of the brave young man? A moment passed, she felt it was an eternity, then it all became clear to her. Her mind was made up; as quick as lightning, she dashed through the longhouse, lifted the bear hide which closed the entrance, threw the cup of sagamity to the ground and fled to the nearest corn patch.

Her aunts angrily went after her and attempted to bring her back, but it was all in vain. Baffled, they had to return and awkwardly apologize to the suitor, who went home empty handed. What an embarrassment for the uncle, before the entire village! He had to force Tekakwitha to obey him at once! The stratagem was tried again, to no avail. Tekakwitha fled, once more, and hid behind a crate of corn. She continued ingeniously to evade the traps that were set for her by her aunts.

Tekakwitha paid dearly for her firmness, which was regarded as intolerable insanity and obstinacy, an attitude which was unheard of among the Iroquois. "Insanity, they shouted, insanity!" and they resorted to violence. They made her a slave and imposed upon her the harshest and most unpleasant chores. They maliciously interpreted the most innocent things she did, constantly accusing her of lacking attachment to her loved ones, even charging her, on account of her Algonquin blood, with a secret hatred of the Iroquois nation.[3]

This little one endured with almost superhuman patience a veritable hell: insults, angry looks and high-handed heckling. She remained even-tempered and allowed nothing to alter her natural gentleness. Every day her heroism was admirable indeed. More than that, she continues with care and docility, and with a smile, rendering her aunts all the services they required of her. Thus she succeeded, despite everything, in regaining their favour. Deep down they loved her. Tekakwitha never heard any more talk in Iroquois land about her getting married.

In 1670, Fr. Pierron was replaced by Fr. François Boniface,* who came to live in Caughnawaga. As soon as he mastered the difficult Iroquois language well enough, he began taking over the work of his predecessor. First, he established regular services, among which the holy sacrifice of the Mass was reserved of neophytes, but other activities such as catechism classes, hymn singing and the explanation of the paintings of Fr. Pierron were attended by anyone interested.

Day after day, the new missionary presided over the morning and evening prayers in the small chapel dedicated to Saint Peter. As soon as he realized that his Mohawk people enjoyed the hymns from France, he began having the Christians sing at the end of the common prayers. He even founded a children's choir with seven and eight year olds to celebrate God's praise, "which the angels never cease doing in heaven". All the children vied for the honour of being admitted to the choir and the parents were rightfully proud to see them join.

The preaching of Fr. Boniface, combined with that of Fr. Bruyas, finally produced a harvest of believers. In 1671, the young missionary baptized more than sixty Mohawks. In the spring, there was a major upheaval in Caughnawaga. Surely, Tekakwitha was impressed by it. Fifteen of the most fervent Christians, catechists and catechumens set out for Quebec to settle among the Hurons of Notre-Dame-de-Foy in order to practice their religion without hindrance.

More than fifty other Christians had made the same plan and their canoes, already filled with supplies for the long trip, were ready for departure. However, the well-founded fear of displeasing their families and even more so of giving rise to further attacks by the Wolves once the village was deprived of so many valiant warriors, forced them to put off their departure until a more propitious time.

Among those leaving was Marie Tsiaouentes and her two young sons. Her husband had perished recently; the circumstances of his death are unknown. When the news of her upcoming departure began to spread from longhouse to longhouse, her angry relatives gave her a row. How could an oyander, a high-ranking lady, leave her native land and abandon her people to go off into exile among the Hurons?

They convened a council which accused Marie of betraying her people. To culminate a crescendo of violent heckling, shouting and yelling, they stripped her of her title of oyander and gave it to another. There was nothing left for her to do but leave! The humiliating assembly had in no way shaken her purpose and, with her little Ignace Tokakion and his elder brother, she boarded the canoe which was to take her to Quebec. There, she would be appreciated by the Natives and by the True Axe Makers, who would nickname her "La Prétieuse" (sic).

A widow named Anastasia was among the travellers. For two years, she had refused to marry an Iroquois of good reputation and an excellent hunter, but hostile to "the prayer". According to Fr. Boniface,[4] God tried the virtue of this woman. She saw three of her relatives agonize and die and would never allow the "false faces" to come near them. Anastasia acted in the same manner when her own children became dangerously ill. She would have preferred to see them die assured of their salvation rather than healed as a result of the jugglers' incantations. This extraordinary woman was doubtlessly Anastasia Tegonhatsiongo* (Tekonwatidionko), the friend of Tekakwitha's mother.

The repercussions of this exodus were immediately felt in Tekakwitha's home. Her uncle was not at all happy to see fifteen Mohawks of Caughnawaga leave the village. Nor was he pleased at the thought of the fifty other deserters ready to take off, but who had changed their minds at the last minute. Who knew if the same fancy would not get hold of them once again? Sullenly, he brooded over his anger. Hadn't the nation's manpower been decimated already by the numerous wars fought from Hudson Bay to the Atlantic coast? Hadn't a smallpox epidemic left a trail of death in their midst some twelve or thirteen years ago? Who could say there wouldn't be others? Three to four hundred Mohawks to defend the nation were a very small number; the other four Iroquois nations had to be called upon to wage war against the Wolves, and with no great success at that...What would happen the next time danger struck without these good warriors tempted to go into exile? The migration had to be stopped at all cost!

Notes 6

1. JR, vol. 53, p. 185-95.

2. VBCT, p. 16-22; VCT, p. 1-4.

3. PO, Doc. XVII, p. 319.

4. JR, vol. 57, p. 98.

The Church Takes Root

While the leaders of the Mohawk nation interpreted the departure of the Christians for the north as a catastrophe, another disaster was about to strike the canton. Owing to a relative calm followed by a final peace signed on December 5th, 1671 between Iroquois and Mahicans, the road was now clear and free of danger to Fort Orange,[1] where the great lovers of alcohol could go and binge at will.

In 1672 and 1673, Fr. Bruyas complained about the goings on at Sainte-Marie of Tionnontoguen. Nothing prevented the Natives any longer from getting drunk during the hottest season. Previously, they only drank from time to time, for they always had to be prepared to fight off the attacks of the Wolves. Now, there was no more control; drunkenness was so rampant that the only times they stopped drinking was when they went out of the village. There were even some who took their small cask of liquor with them on their fishing trips, some twenty-five leagues away.

Fortunately, and thanks no doubt to the influence of the Christians, a much smaller number of Mohawks in Caughnawaga than in Tionnontoguen slipped into excessive drinking. There were enough, however, who went belching and staggering from longhouse to longhouse to darken the days of Tekakwitha.

Another misfortune made its appearance shortly afterwards and caused new losses. A type of plague broke out at the beginning of June 1672 and lasted until September in Tionnontoguen before reaching Caughnawaga. "It was a fever so malignant, noted Fr. Bruyas, that in less than five days, one had to either get better or die, a victim of its virulence..."[2] Most of those afflicted suffered so much that they lost their minds. In Caughnawaga, Fr. Boniface, as well as his confrere in Tionnontoguen, devoted himself to the sick and dying, enduring great fatigue and continuous night watches. He was able to baptize fourteen plague victims who were still in their right minds before seeing them breathe their last breath. Impressed by the missionary's devotedness, Tekakwitha felt increasingly drawn to "the prayer" of Iesos Christos. Yet she dared not confide her desire to the Black Robe because of her uncle who constantly fumed against the Christians who were becoming more and more numerous in the village.

Fr. Claude Dablon*, who edited the letters of Frs. Bruyas and Boniface for the "Relation des Jésuites" of 1672-73, declared that "it was in Caughnawaga that people embraced the faith more constantly than in any other Mohawk country; this was the place where a Church in the proper sense was first seen to take form, the place where the Christian generosity of its members was seen to blossom the most...

We, therefore, consider it as the first and most important mission we have among the Iroquois,"[3] He adds: "since the Mohawks were the first to shed the blood of the missionaries who brought them the faith, so were they the first to receive the fruits of their merits and in greater abundance than the other Iroquois nations: this is how the words of Tertullian concerning the martyrs of the primitive Church prove to be true in New France as well as in other parts of the world, i.e. that the blood of martyrs is a seed which gives birth to new Christians."[4]

At the end of August 1672, Fr. Bruyas wrote from Tionnontoguen to his superior in Quebec: "I hope that next year will be more fruitful and that the good example of the Mohawks of the mission of Saint Peter being converted every day will impress those of Sainte Marie so much so that they will finally do likewise."[5]

Indeed, in the village of Caughnawaga, the faith surrounded and invaded every house like a rising tide. Tekakwitha could see more and more of the people she knew embracing Christianity. That year alone, in addition to those who has asked for the saving waters of Baptism on their death beds, thirty adults had solemnly received the Sacrament of regeneration in the Chapel of Saint-Pierre.[6] Discreetly, but tenaciously, Fr. Boniface used every means suggested by this zeal to reveal to his people the beauty of the Christian faith.

For Christmas, he set up a small creche - the first one in Iroquois land - and surrounded the figure of the divine Child with numerous vigil lamps and he decorated the crib with sweet-smelling pine branches. It was very simple, yet it was enough to stir the devotion of the faithful, both old and new. They were in rapture and their enchantment reached its highest point when the small choir of adults and children began singing old French carols in their own language. The missionary could not resist the entreaties of those who were not yet Christians to be let in to contemplate this delightful sight at leisure. Despite the bitter cold, the service lasted longer than usual.

Surely, the two aunts of Tekakwitha were not without finding a place in front of the heavenly Infant. Back at their home, in the absence of the chief, they talked about this in the presence of Tekakwitha. Did the young girl go and roam around the church afterwards? Maybe. One thing we know for sure is that she did not beg the priest to be admitted near the creche.

An old Church custom imported from France by the missionaries became well established in Caughnawaga: the ceremony of the blessing of the bread. Every Sunday during holy Mass, this Sacramental reminded all present that they were brothers and children of God and this bread was the symbol of the eternal happiness in store for them; it soon became a precious token for the Mohawks "of the prayer," (This tradition is still observed in Kahnawake* and Akwasasne*, but only on Christmas day.)

The devout woman who distributed the holy bread in the chapel served "a little lunch" afterwards at her longhouse for all the Christians. They, in turn, repaid the courtesy and everything went smoothly, with fervour and charity, and everyone kept growing steadily. Unfortunately, Tekakwitha was not one of them.

Those were baptized got into the habit of wearing the crucifix, medals of Our Lady and of the saints, and a rosary, which they considered as their most precious jewels. They even dared to present themselves with these adornments at the small Protestant church of Albany, where no one ever succeeded in taking a single rosary bead away from them.

These symbols of her mother's religion challenged Tekakwitha. They were also a sign beckoning several other people, among them, a courageous woman nicknamed Satekon*. She was baptized and, six months later, abandoned by her husband, Togouiroui,[7] following a misunderstanding which they had concerning their only daughter. This adventurous spouse was one of the most prominent chiefs of the village, the one who had earned for himself the title of Great Mohawk during the war between his nation and the Wolves. Saketon's only consolation was her little one whose cheerful character delighted the entire village. Shortly after this event, however, the little girl died and the grieving mother found herself all alone, in addition to the fact that everyone blamed her for adopting the customs of the True Axe Makers by becoming a Christian. They claimed that "the prayer" had caused her child to die. All their efforts to persuade her to give up her faith were to no avail. On the contrary, she disregarded the calumnies levelled at her and was more faithful than ever to the common prayers in the chapel, morning and evening, and to the Sacraments. Her life was so exemplary that even unbelievers judged her to be without reproach.

Despite her faith and spirit of resignation to the will of God, poor Satekon must have felt that the future held very little happiness for her. This is when God gave her back her husband, once a declared enemy of "the prayer" and now a Christian at heart, to whom the only thing lacking was Baptism. What had happened?

His face hardened by anger, Ganeagoua had gone away accompanied by another chief. Some time later, both of them happened to be in the vicinity of Chambly for the great winter hunting season. There, they met a catechumen and his wife, both of whom spoke to them of the happiness of their existence in La Prairie. The woman, who knew her prayers well, would recite them aloud every day. The Great Mohawk was impressed by these prayers. "The one who thought them", he said to his new friends, "has a lot of common sense: these prayers are very well thought out!" He had found out by then that they had been composed long before the Black Robes were born, which made him value them so much that he memorized them perfectly.

In the spring of 1673, he along with his companion and the catechumen accompanied by his wife , reached the village of La Prairie, called Kentake* in Iroquois. As was the custom of Christian hunters, they presented themselves to the church of St. Francis Xavier to thank the Lord for the bountiful hunt He had given them. Fr. Frémin, superior of the Mission, whose watchful eye never missed a thing, wanted to meet the newcomers. He had heard that one of them was the Great Mohawk and the other also a chief from Caughnawaga. The two men confided to the Black Robe their desire for Baptism. The Jesuit explained to them for several weeks the truths of Christianity and the immense love of the Creator for each one of us. To the Great Mohawk, who had admitted to him the circumstances of his departure from Caughnawaga and how he had abandoned his wife and daughter, Fr. Frémin promised Baptism as soon as he returned to La Prairie with Satekon and his child. He made the same promise to his companion, provided he brought his family back with him.

Reassured by this story and filled with the joy of the reunion, Satekon listened to the Great Mohawk telling her about his plan to go and establish himself at St. Francis Xavier of Kentake and to bring with him everyone who wished to follow. He succeeded in persuading forty-two Mohawks from his village and from the neighbouring village of Andagaron to join his group. His young nephew, Martin Skandegonrhaksen*, of whom Tekakwitha would hear later, went along with him. A young couple living in Tekakwitha's longhouse - her adopted sister and her husband - most probably joined the convoy. Fr. Bruyas also ordered Fr. Boniface, exhausted by his labours and the hardship of his existence in Caughnawaga and Andagaron for the last three years, to board the small fleet. The Great Mohawk felt deep sorrow at not being able to bring his daughter whom he had loved so much. In mid-June of 1673, early in the morning, the voluntary exiles bid farewell to their country, their longhouses and their fields, and headed for the Iroquois village on the great northern river.

The Mohawks of Tionnontoguen who were not yet completely won over to "the prayer", complained bitterly to Fr. Bruyas.[8] What were the Black Robes trying to do? Were they determined to turn their country into a wasteland and to ruin their villages by emptying them of their most valuable inhabitants?

The Jesuit showed them, with the use of a wampum necklace, that he felt for them in their dismay. He stated clearly to them that neither Fr. Boniface nor himself had suggested to the Mohawks of Caughnawaga to leave. The one responsible for this unprecedented exodus was their bravest warrior. He concluded by assuring the assembly that there was nothing to fear, for Mr. de Frontenac, the new Governor, would inform the king of the good faith of the Mohawks. They themselves had once said, through one of their ambassadors, that the French and the Mohawks were like two bodies animated by the same soul, or two brothers acknowledging the same father. This winsome answer, wrote Fr. Bruyas, averted the oncoming storm.

The Mohawks of both villages were so distraught by this exodus that the missionaries thought they would soon imitate their compatriots. At Tekakwitha's longhouse, her uncle flew into a fury when he found out that his adopted daughter and her husband had gone away. He then retreated in grim silence at the thought that Togouiroui, though he was the Great Mohawk, had surely gone out of his mind. Therefore, even if she was attracted to "the prayer", the young maiden felt stranded, incapable of making a move.

At the Huron settlement of Notre-Dame-de-Foy, near Quebec, Marie Tsiaouentes was thinking of her former compatriots and commended them each day to the Lord, but this did not satisfy her. So she asked Fr. Chaumonot, superior of the Mission, to write her nation a message, which she dictated to him.[9] As a former oyander, she strongly urged her people to listen to the Black Robes, to do away with their old habits and to become Christians. Tekakwitha wanted to follow her advice, but when...?

Notes 7

1. JR, vol. 57, p. 80.

2. Ibid.

3. Ibid. p. 88.

4. Ibid. p. 90.

5. Ibid. p. 86.

6. Ibid., p. 90-6.

7. H. Béchard, The Original Caughnawaga Indians, Montreal, International Publishers, 1976, p. 79-106.

8. JR, vol. 57, p. 108-10.

9. JR, vol. 55, p. 262-6.

8

A Christian at Last!

Fr. Bruyas was the only missionary left among the Mohawks after the departure of Fr. Boniface, who passed away in Quebec at the end of 1674. His wish to see the Indians of Saint Marie follow the example of those of Saint Peter came true in the course of 1673. Many adults embraced the faith with great fervour in Tionnontoguen. He also had to look after the Turtles of Caughnawaga and the Bears of Andagaron. He would never succeed by himself in improving all these new Christians, perfecting the old ones and properly initiating the catechumens to the mysteries of the faith. Being overworked, he wrote to Fr. Claude Dablon, his superior in Quebec, asking for help.

Tekakwitha had never dared approach Fr. Boniface; she thought even less of going to Fr. Bruyas when he came to the village. There can be no doubt, however, that she was moved by a major event which happened in Tionnontoguen: the conversion and Baptism of Assendasse,[1] one of the most renowned Mohawk elders, who, as a result, also contributed in giving the missionary extra work.

This elderly man of approximately sixty-five, exceptionally intelligent and experienced in administration, was the head of one of the most prominent families of the canton. Very proud, underhanded and sly, he was not an easy subject to convert. According to Fr. Dablon, (who could only have known this through the correspondence of Fr. Bruyas), self-interest and the fear of ridicule kept this man in his infidelity. Indeed, he profited by the superstitious practices of his people and, were he to renounce them at his age, he would inevitably become the target of sarcasm on the part of the whole population. Nothing was more unbearable to an Iroquois than being sneered at and turned into ridicule.

For two years, he had been obstinately resisting the powerful attraction of grace which prompted him to adhere to "the prayer". During a trip to Montreal, a speech of the Count of Frontenac engaging the Iroquois delegates to embrace Christianity decided him to ask for Baptism upon returning to the cantons.

Feelings and words were not enough to satisfy the fervour of the new Assendasse.* He immediately and effectively renounced all the superstitions of his people. Fr. Bruyas was impressed by such generosity. In order not to prolong the trial period, the missionary granted him Baptism at once.

On the day following his Baptism, the elderly man offered a great feast. During this friendship meal, he stood up and announced to the guests his total and final rejection of the superstitions of his country, especially the dream cult. Besides, he fearlessly stated his inviolable attachment to the Christian faith. He said: "I have concluded an eternal brotherhood with the one who baptized me; if the French ever start a war again and come to kill us, I shall not abandon my affection for him and I shall always distinguish the one who takes away the life of the body from the one who gave us the life of the soul and will always preserve it in me as long as I shall obey him."

Fr. Bruyas noticed later that he had kept this promise and that he performed all the practices of Christianity with such fidelity that he was a model for all believers. Prompted by a sort of holy rivalry, he strove to surpass Chief Garakontie of Onontague in the practice of the faith. He tried to get the people of the Mohawk country to value "the prayer" as much as that great Christian had done in his own canton.

The faith of the chief had the missionary in awe. I can guarantee, wrote the Jesuit, "that of all the Christians, none is more obedient, none is more docile than Assendasse..." However, it was necessary that his faith be tested and tested it was, quite severely.

After his Baptism, Assendasse wanted all his loved ones to join him.[2] They did as he wished, but shortly after, sickness and death overtook his longhouse. His family accused him of attracting these scourges by adhering to the religion of Iesos Christos. This once proud man remained unaffected by these reproaches. By acting in this way, he could have become the first Iroquois martyr. A relative of his who deeply resented his being a Christian purposely got himself intoxicated, grabbed him by the neck, pulled his rosary and crucifix off him and angrily threatened to kill him if he did not give up all this hardware. Assendasse remained unshaken. "Kill me, he said; I'll be happy to die for such a good cause. I feel no regret in giving my life in testimony of my faith."

The elders had been the chief antagonists of Christianity, but were they not, now, in the process of establishing it? The missionary was of the opinion that the devil feared so, judging by the efforts exerted by the evil spirits to stop the progress of this foreign religion. Some people had been taunting the priest for some time. An elderly man publicly accused him of ruining the country by attacking the dream cult and the other superstitions. He denounced him violently and declared that if he did not leave the village, he would have him chased away by the whole canton.

Fr. Bruyas also suffered abuse on the part of the Dutch Calvinists,[3] who violently resented him. They even forced him to evade them and to hide so as not to fall victim of their harsh treatment.

In Caughnawaga, at the beginning of summer 1675, Tekakwitha's journey towards the light was given new direction by the unexpected visit of a close relative of the Great Mohawk, Martin Skandegonrhaksen.[4] He had come from La Prairie de la Madeleine in the hope of bringing to the faith one of his friends of his native canton. Alas! his former comrade had become a notorious drinker. After numerous efforts, Martin acknowledged that nothing could be done. Failing to convert the great guzzler, he turned to unbelievers. Using a very courageous stratagem and going against the old tribal custom, the young man spoke in public to a crowd in which there were several elders.

He went to the chapel of Saint Peter where his mellow voice drew a crowd of people to hear the singing of hymns in Iroquois which he had learnt on the shores of the Saint Lawrence River. Having won over his listeners, he took the opportunity to speak to them of the splendour of the Christian faith as it was practised at the Mission of Kentake.

As he went about visiting homes, Martin vigorously attacked impurity and drunkenness and spoke with glowing enthusiasm of Iesos, Wari and Sose*. It was amazing to see this young man speak even in front of the elders, contrary to tribal custom. The awareness of his presence, words and conduct spread all across Caughnawaga like sparks running through stubble. The eagerness of this young Christian undoubtedly warmed the heart of Tekakwitha. The visits of Christians from La Prairie were a comfort to her, but their departure left her in extreme sadness.[5]

In mid summer, Tekakwitha saw Fr. Jacques de Lamberville appear at the gates of her village. He was the helper requested the previous year by Fr. Bruyas. Born in Rouen, the capital of Normandy, on March 24th, 1641, Jacques de Lamberville had entered the Jesuit novitiate in Paris on October 20th, 1661, preceded five years earlier by his brother Jean. Ordained to the priesthood in 1674, he embarked for New France ten or twelve months afterwards. Shortly after his arrival, he went over to the Iroquois land.[6]

Fr. Bruyas was happy to entrust Caughnawaga and Andagaron to his care. Like the Turtles' village, the Bears' was on the north shore of the Mohawk River since the invasion of the Marquis de Tracy. It was protected by only one palisade, had four gates approximately four feet wide and contained some sixteen houses built on a small plain at a rock's throw from the river. The other village, Caughnawaga, could boast a double palisade also provided with four gates of the same width protecting approximately twenty-four longhouses.

The young priest was delighted to find in this place a generally fervent mission, thanks to the efforts of his predecessors. Most of the chiefs and elders respectfully attended the services in the small chapel. There were even several young men who did likewise. Had it not been for the ravages of alcohol, all of Caughnawaga, or almost all, would have been Christian. The only ones left were a handful of stubborn individuals, such as Tekakwitha's uncle.

Fr. de Lamberville had certainly studied Iroquois in France before coming to the New World, for he very soon began instructing his flock. In late summer and early fall, all the women of the village went to harvest corn and all the men went fishing or hunting, therefore the missionary had to interrupt his teaching. He then took advantage of his free time to visit the longhouses and instruct the old and infirm.

One September afternoon, he was doing the rounds of the deserted village in the sun which was still quite hot in this autumn season. As he passed by, a few dogs barked without upsetting him, for he had already made friends with them. When he came to Tekakwitha's longhouse,[7] he remembered that the women, who were never lazy and seldom idle, were certainly busy in the corn fields. He continued on, but pressed by an interior impulse, he turned back, lifted the bear hide covering the entrance of the longhouse and walked in. After a few moments, his eyes adjusted to the dim light coming in from the roof through the openings where the smoke from the fires escaped.

To his great surprise, the house was not empty. He found Tekakwitha lying on her mat and two or three elderly women too weak to work in the fields. The young maiden was suffering from a sore on her foot which made her unable to walk; her companions with wrinkled faces stared at the man of "the prayer" with piercing eyes.

Delighted to see the priest a few steps away from her, the young woman smiled. For nineteen years, she had been living in infidelity; out of timidity and fear of her uncle, she had never dared to approach a Black Robe. Today however, she could not hide her joy at being able to talk to the ratsihenstatsi*! Now, there was nothing hindering her and, mindless of the elderly women, she revealed her heart's feelings to the missionary. She spontaneously confessed her desire to become a Christian. The priest "spoke to her about Christianity" and found her so docile that he exhorted her to "take instructions and attend chapel services, which she did most assiduously after she was cured."[8] She then realized that it wouldn't be easy , but despite major obstacles to be overcome, and at all cost, she declared herself ready to surmount them. These words fell from her lips like precious white and purple wampum pearls. More deeply moved than he would allow himself to show, Fr. de Lamberville whispered a prayer of thanksgiving.

The Jesuit admitted later having been convinced at this very first encounter that God had great plans for Tekakwitha. The Holy Spirit, he thought, had enlightened her that she might see the truths of faith more clearly and had touched her heart to inflame it with love. He did not, however, hasten to baptize her, but he took all the usual precautions for admitting unbelievers to Christianity.

Concerning this intuition of Fr. de Lamberville, Fr. de Charlevoix*, who regarded him "as one of the holiest missionaries of New France," added this comment: "God undoubtedly creates between those whose hearts He has especially set apart for Himself a sort of spiritual sympathy which bonds them, even in this life, in a union which is to endure in the home of eternal glory."[9]

As soon as Tekakwitha got better, the missionary gently invited her to come and pray in the chapel. Her aunts, who alone had authority over Tekakwitha, made no objection. Once harvest time was ended, regardless of frequent rains and even snowfalls which had stripped the trees of their magnificent and colourful foliage, Tekakwitha went to the chapel every day and took advantage of the teaching given to the Christians. In addition, the Jesuit visited her and explained to her in detail the precepts of the faith and the mysteries of Christianity. With all her heart, Tekakwitha cooperated with the grace of this preparation for her Baptism, the value of which became clearer to her as time went by.

One of the great joys she derived from instructions was getting to know about the Blessed Virgin Mary. This orphaned girl found in her a mother, the ideal Mother, much better and much more beautiful than she could ever have imagined. Fr. Chauchetière wrote that "she had a tender devotion to the Mother of God from the moment she was told of the qualities, power and glory of Our Lady and how she is to be honoured."[10]

Towards the end of the year, news came from Tionnontoguen which made Tekakwitha very happy. Fr. Bruyas had received from Belgium a miraculous statue of Our Lady called "Notre-Dame-de-Foy."* He unveiled it as ceremoniously as possible on the feast of the Immaculate Conception with the singing of the Litanies of the Blessed Virgin in Iroquois. After December the eight, he unveiled it every Saturday evening while the same Litanies were sung. It remained exposed every Sunday for all the faithful to see, and they assembled three times to recite the Rosary in front of the image of their heavenly Mother. The effects of her presence were not long in coming. The old Christians regained their initial fervour and the number of new converts increased from day to day. Even the unbelievers said that, since the Mother of Iesos had come to their village, they were no longer afraid of anything.[11]

The people of Caughnawaga thought these events were quite extraordinary. It was amazing to see such an influx of piety in Tionnontoguen, where the majority of people had been so hostile to "the prayer." Many Christians and other sympathizers went to the main village to recite the Rosary before Our Lady. In all likelihood, Tekakwitha, who had such a tender devotion to Mary, took part in this pilgrimage of approximately fifteen miles, despite the cold of winter and her impaired eyesight which was blinded by the brightness of the sun shining on the snow.

Christmas, and the Circumcision of Our Lord which was celebrated on New Year's Day, filled the heart of this devout catechumen with joy and gratitude. She remained in front of the crib for hours in thanksgiving, in her ardent love of Jesus to whom she prayed with all her soul. Considering her rapid progress, Fr. de Lamberville gave in to her entreaties and anticipated the date of her Baptism. For other catechumens, two years of preparation were necessary, but not for Tekakwitha. Wouldn't such a delay be a hindrance to the journey of a soul already so dear to the Creator? The priest thought that one fine Sunday in the spring, maybe Easter Sunday, would be quite appropriate for the Baptism.

However, to make even surer that he had made a wise decision, he undertook a careful scrutiny of the life and morals of the Christian-to-be. He first spoke to those who lived in Tekakwitha's longhouse, not only those of her own hearth, but everyone living under the same roof. He then took his inquiry out into the village. Nowhere was there a discordant voice, not even among those who had once hurt her the most. The missionary was amazed, even more so as he knew backbiting was very common among the people of these areas.

The Jesuit expected great advantages to result for his young Church from the Baptism of a young woman of such character. He chose the most important day of the Christian year, Easter Sunday, April 5th, 1676, to administer this Sacrament to her; she was given the name of Catherine. It is not known which Catherine was the patron saint, but since Saint Catherine of Sienna is the only one mentioned in the best known biographies, we presume she was the one.

The news of her upcoming Baptism gave Tekakwitha tremendous joy. She memorized all the usual prayers in order not to delay the desired event. She also learnt how to recite the Rosary, which became a favourite prayer of hers, and spared no effort to assure that she received the eminent grace she so ardently anticipated.

During Holy Week, Tekakwitha kept herself in close union with the One she loved more than her own self. She was ready to receive the Creator of her soul. All the faithful were invited to the ceremony to which the young woman presented herself along with two other converts. The bark chapel had been made beautiful for this festive occasion. Magnificent beaver, wildcat, otter and bear pelts decorated the walls and covered the mud floor. There were no flowers. None could be found in this cold, early spring season.

Just about every Christian responded to the Black Robe's invitation. Several young mothers were present, most of them with their latest newborn in a gaoseha*. Young maidens also, in their most attractive wampum-beaded dress, aware of the looks of young men close by, and, finally, devout old men and women completing the assembly. All eyes were turned to the three Christians-to-be, especially the chief's daughter.

Wearing his white surplice and purple stole over his black cassock, Fr. de Lamberville walked to the door of the chapel. Tekakwitha's modesty, peace and piety were reflected in her bearing and delighted all those who surrounded her,

"Catherine," the priest said finally, "what do you ask of the Church of God?"

- "Faith," she answered with a firm voice.

- "What will faith give you?"

- "Eternal life."

- "If you wish to enter eternal life, observe the commandments, love the Lord God with all your heart, with all your soul and with all your mind and your neighbour as yourself."

After the first prayer casting out Satan and invoking the Holy Spirit, the ceremony went off quickly. The priest placed on Catherine the end of the stole which hung from his left shoulder and led her into the church.

Deeply moved by the words of the priest, she opened her heart wide and recited the Creed and the our Father on her knees among the Christian people and in the company of the other two candidates.

The missionary then went to the corner of the church which served as a sacristy, changed his purple stole for a white one, as a symbol of purity, and put on the white cope, which was the custom for adult Baptisms.

Having returned to the Baptismal font, he asked:

"Catherine, do you renounce Satan?"

- "I do," she said.

- "And all his works?"

- "I do."

These words filled the church and remained with her all the days of her life.

God's great moment had come. Catherine bowed her head and the priest poured the Baptismal water on her forehead, saying: "Catherine, I baptize you in the name of the Father, and of the Son, and of the Holy Spirit."

The new Christian stood up again. They covered her head with a white veil and gave her a lighted candle to hold in her right hand. The children's choir, founded by Fr. Boniface, sang a hymn in Iroquois. Joy abounded in all hearts, but none more than in Kateri's,[12] the new child of God inhabited by the Holy spirit.

Notes 8

1. JR, vol. 58, p. 170-4.

2. JR, vol. 59, p. 236-8.

3. JR, vol. 58, p. 178.

4. OCT, p. 107-14.

5. VBCT, p. 42.

6. JR, vol. 60, p. 320-1.

7. VBCT, p. 31-2.

8. Narration of Lamberville in LCC, p. 7.

9. HDNF, vol. I. p. 575.

10. VBCT, p. 99.

11. Jr, vol. 59, p. 238.

12. Soon in Kahnawake, on the St. Lawrence River, Kateri will learn that her new name was known and appreciated. The remains of Catherine Gandeaktenha, whose account will be reported in Ch. 10, were venerated there. Also, another Catherine had passed away at the Sault St.Louis, at the age of 13, "immaculate virginity"; unfortunately no more is known about her. These two Catherines served as stars to guide their own people, but Kateri will shine as the sun, illuminating the whole scenery.

9

The Tomahawk Trick

Ratsihenstatsi had already noticed that many converts went no further than being baptized and, shortly afterwards, no longer practised their faith. "They hardly perform any of the functions of Christianity", [1] he declared, in the style of the XVIIth century. But he had greater expectations of the results of grace in Kateri for, "even before receiving this great Sacrament, her good nature, her vivacious mind and her naïvety and candour gave the missionary reasons to believe that she would, one day, make great progress in virtue".[2]

The hopes of Fr. de Lamberville and of fervent Christians were not disappointed. Kateri even surpassed their expectations by the fervour she showed in the following months. All her wonderful dispositions to virtue, which, heretofore, were hidden in the confines of her longhouse, came out in the open from the moment she had to go out and attend Christian services along with the other neophytes. She gave the example of perfect fidelity to the common exercises: Mass, prayer, instructions, fast and abstinence, which were mandatory in those days.

Kateri was not content with the usual practices. The Holy Spirit was beckoning her and she responded with all her heart. She asked the Jesuit to direct her in this new way which was being opened to her. Her prayers, devotions and practices of penance were submitted to obedience. She was so docile in observing the plan of perfection proposed to her by Fr. de Lamberville that, within a short time, she surpassed all the other Christians. Her compatriots found in her a model of humility, devotion, gentleness, charity and all the other Christian virtues. Even those who felt no attraction to religious practices silently admired her and held her in high esteem. Her director at that time adequately described the months that followed her Baptism: "Since then, I can say that I have found nothing in her suggesting any relaxation of her original fervour."[3]

Kateri lived in peace. Her soul sang in the joy of meeting the Lord. Even her family didn't seem to mind her new lifestyle. Yet, both history and the Scriptures teach us that the faithful one who begins to grow in union with God must prepare to be tested. The words of Christ which so radically changed the lives of the Apostles have proven to be true century after century: "If anyone wishes to follow me, he must deny his very self, take up his cross and follow me." (Mt 16, 24). On first sight, this is not an attractive prospect. True, Saint Teresa of Avila often repeated: "Either to suffer or to die." Not everyone is at that stage. Kateri was. What is meant here is not morbid suffering or a journey down the dark tunnel of annihilation, but rather an eminently positive gesture, that of walking in the bloodstained footprints of Jesus as He ascends Calvary in anticipation of His glorious Resurrection. Therefore it was not long before the extraordinary virtue of Kateri brought persecution upon her on the part of the very ones who could not but think highly of her. Was not the great purity of her conduct a tacit reproach to them for their disorderly conduct?

Her purity was the first target of her persecutors. Fr. Pierre Cholenec*, who later became her spiritual director, said that they tried to attack her purity by using various tactics. "The confidence which the neophyte had in God, her distrust of herself, her perseverance in prayer, the sensitivity of her conscience, which made her fearful of the very appearance of sin, gave her complete victory over the enemies of her modesty."[4] Later on, they would realize how special to the Lord was the one He had thus favoured. Indeed, it was in confirmation of her virtue that the first healing of the sick took place after her death, especially the healing of souls, as witnessed by this other quote of Fr. Cholenec: "I have found more than thirty people whom she helped to get back on the right road; among others, she delivered several from violent temptations of the flesh and obtained for them the gift of chastity. It is mostly in this area that she has worked wonders for souls."[5]

She also had to overcome obstacles related to her life in the community;[6] no novitiate, old or new, was ever harder on its novices than Kateri's own village was on her. The people of her longhouse began to pressure her because her faithfulness to go to the chapel on Sunday prevented her from working in the field with her aunts. The latter, who seem to have been rather mediocre Christians, became increasingly aggravated. They came to the point where they had nothing but bitter words for her. Had Christianity softened their niece? Had it not made her lazy? This kind of talk was soon turned into action. Kateri noticed that her aunts left no food at the longhouse on the days when she did not do her share of gardening. This is how, in Caughnawaga on the Mohawk River, they went about getting Christians to abandon their Sunday practices. In this way, Kateri's aunts hoped to force her to go along and help them with their work.

The young woman still preferred to go to the little chapel of Saint Peter every Sunday and holy day. In addition to the Mass, she loved the recitation of the Rosary in two alternating groups, a favourite exercise of Christian Indians. They would sing hymns between decades; "they enjoy singing and do so perfectly in tune," said Fr. Cholenec; "they have sharp ears, beautiful voices and a rare taste for music."[7]

Kateri endured everything: reproaches, insults and hunger. She preferred to go without food rather than transgress the law which commands to make holy the day of the Lord and His feast days; she declared herself ready to die rather than break it.

Her firmness profoundly angered her family. When she went to the chapel, they would have her followed by drunken people or people feigning to be drunk, who would throw stones at her.[8] She would protect herself from these attacks by using roundabout ways to go and pray before the Tabernacle.

Like the waves that spread around a stone thrown in the water this mean disposition of Kateri's family soon spread to the entire village.[9] Even little children pointed their fingers at her, taunted her and derisively called her Christian, "meaning the same as if they said bitch", wrote Fr. Chauchetière. She soon came to be known only by that name and counted herself happy to bear it.

Moreover, all the enemies of "the prayer": mockers, jugglers and drunkards united against her. Her uncle went as far as to bribe a young warrior to go into Tekakwitha's longhouse with a tomahawk. The young man performed his strange task. His eyes glittering with anger, he suddenly irrupted in the longhouse and, having come close to Kateri, he raised his tomahawk over her head as though to smash it. Remaining calm, Kateri simply bowed her head. Her courage so disconcerted the aggressor that he fled at once, as though driven by an invisible force.

When the frost and snow of winter came, the young woman found a certain kind of peace. Thus she reached the feasts of Christmas, the Circumcision and Epiphany. For the first time of the year. Then came Lent of 1677 and Easter, the first anniversary of her Baptism. How she wished she could receive in her heart, in holy Communion, the Lord Jesus who was the centre of her life! But the Black Robes did not allow neophytes to receive communion until four or five years after their entrance into the Church so as to be reasonably sure they understood what the Eucharist was.

The end of winter was drawing near, though the ice still had a tight grip on the Mohawk River. Kateri soon surpassed all other Christians and became a model of humility, devotion, gentleness and charity. Despite public opposition, the esteem the practising Christians had for her kept growing.

One of her aunts, however, who had a sly and treacherous spirit, bristled at the sight of such perfection and constantly censured the most innocent words and actions of the young Christian.

One spring day, while Kateri's family was out hunting in the vicinity of the Dutch settlements, an Iroquois custom gave her an unexpected pretext for uttering a horrible calumny against her niece. It was customary for uncles to call their nieces daughter and, conversely, for nieces to call their uncles father; similarly, first cousins called each other brother. On one occasion, Kateri inadvertently happened to speak of her uncle, calling him by his name instead of by the name of father. The minute she returned to the village, her aunt went to see Fr. de Lamberville. She thought she would thus give the Black Robe the proof that his young convert was not the miracle of holiness she was claimed to be.

"Well!" she said, addressing the priest, "Kateri whose virtue you think so highly of, is nevertheless a hypocrite who is deceiving you; just a moment ago, in my very presence, she solicited my husband to sin."

The missionary, who was no fool, asked the mean woman on what she based her accusation. On hearing what had given rise to such a hateful suspicion, he reprimanded her severely and sent her away ashamed.

Out of prudence, however, he questioned Kateri afterwards regarding her conduct, after giving her a rundown on sin and the pains of hell. The neophyte answered all his questions peacefully. It was on this occasion that she revealed something which might have remained unknown had she not been tested in this manner. Thanks to the mercy of God, she had not been a victim of incest, neither on this occasion nor at any other time; nor did she remember ever defiling the purity of her body; moreover, she had no fear of being damned on this account. She was afraid, however, not to have the courage to let herself be knocked on the head for refusing to work in the fields on Sundays and holy days.

No sooner had she admitted to this fear than a wonderful example of bravery came to strengthen the courage of the young Indian woman. A good Christian woman of the Mission of Lorette*, who was on a visit to Mohawk land, refused to get intoxicated with a group of heavy drinkers. Incensed by her refusal, the latter decided to force her to drink by laying her on the floor and pouring liquor forcibly into her mouth. This valiant woman did not give in; she kept spitting in their faces until they let her go. Kateri, for her part, never had to extricate herself from such traps, but she felt the need for the gift of fortitude.

The aunt with a deceitful tongue had not amended her ways. When she harassed her niece, the young woman would go to the priest and tell him about all her troubles. He was awed by her candor, her obedience, her profound humility and the simplicity with which she walked on her way to God. He finally suggested two things to her: first, to go into exile at the Mission of the Sault to practice her Christian life in peace; second, to have recourse to prayer constantly, which she already did.

Notes 9

1. PO, Doc. XIV, p. 305.

2. PO. Doc. XII, p. 252.

3. Letter of Fr. de Lamberville in LCC, p. 7.

4. PO, Doc. XII, p. 253.

5. VCT, p. 83.

6. VBCT, p. 37-8.

7. PO, Doc. XII, p. 253-4.

8. Ibid, p. 254.

9. VBCT, p. 37-8.

10

A Land of Refuge

The advice of Fr. Jacques de Lamberville to go and live at the Mission of Saint Francis Xavier had appealed to Kateri for a long time. Up until now, however, the disapproval of her family, her lack of experience of life and, perhaps, the fear of the unknown had kept her in her native land. On the very day of her Baptism, she had watched with sadness thirty Iroquois[1] go into exile, led by Togouiroui. On the 14th of July, the Great Mohawk had returned once again to Caughnawaga accompanied by two dogiques*: a Mohawk named Kinnouskouen* and a Huron named Etienne Tegananokoa, both ardent preachers of the Gospel. Kateri had seen them; she had even heard Etienne teach hymns to the Christians at twilight. The two men set out for the north again, taking along several Mohawks[2] whom they had persuaded to turn away from the war path. What was this promised land where converts voluntarily went into exile?

In 1667, Fr. Pierre Raffeix*, procurator of the Collège de Québec, went to the fief of La Prairie-de-la-Magdeleine to see that it be properly farmed. This concession had been given to the Jesuits by François de Lauzon in 1647 and the authorities of the colony insisted that they exploit it. The Jesuits established a residence there, which was to serve as a place of rest for the missionaries, "those of Iroquois land as well as those serving among the Upper Algonquins, also called Outaouaks, and to supply them more easily, from this place, with the things they needed for their subsistence". At the same time, they invited a few French settlers to take possession of a few tracks of land. It was in this context that the providential encounter of Gandeaktenha, Francis Xavier Tonsahoten and Fr. Raffeix took place.[3]

Gandeaktenha,[4] an Erie woman captured by the Iroquois when they destroyed the nation of the Cat in 1655, was brought with her mother to the Oneida village as a slave. There, she won the hearts of all around her and was given in marriage to Francis Xavier Tonsahoten, a Huron turned Iroquois and a Christian. She also succeeded in taming this proud warrior who had a quarrelsome and difficult character. Together, they made plans to go hunting in the vicinity of Montreal and, from there, to go on to Quebec to find the Black Robes. This would also be the occasion to get medical treatment for Francis's leg.

When Fr. Bruyas, accompanied by his interpreter and assistant Charles Boquet, arrived in the Oneida canton, Gandeaktenha's heart was inflamed with love for the religion of the Christians, about which her husband had been telling her for a long time. She met the missionary, who chose her to translate his words into Iroquois when Boquet went out hunting or fishing. This was the opportunity of her dreams to learn the Christian principles from the priest in the Huron language, which she knew well. These marvellous conversations fostered the neophyte's good disposition, so much so that she soon "had to suffer intense persecution on the part of her family and even of the whole village."[5]

One day, Charles Boquet had to return to Quebec, and the assembly of elders decided to send a small group of people to escort him on this long journey. Tonsahoten volunteered to go and took along his wife, his mother-in-law, his father and two or three other Indians.

When they reached Montreal, Francis Xavier went to the Hôtel-Dieu Hospital to get treatment for his leg. Meanwhile, a few Mohawks who wished to be converted joined them and, in the middle of November,[6] they all set out for Quebec.

Fr. Chaumonot, who worked among the Hurons and also spoke Iroquois fluently, gladly gave them instructions and Bishop de Laval baptized these eleven catechumens on December 3rd, 1667, in the Chapel of the Infant Jesus at the Jesuits' College. Governor de Courcelle, Intendant Talon and a few officers served as godfathers. Gandeaktenha received the name of Catherine and, shortly after, she was confirmed and married in the Church. From that moment on, her desire was to share her faith as a baptized Christian with all her people far away; moreover, Francis was determined to return to Oneida. However, on their way back home, through Montreal, they met Fr. Raffeix.

The missionary invited them to spend the winter in La Prairie, where they could eat well, for the game was excellent in those areas. They spent the winter under the same roof as the priest, with a few French people. A short time later, Catherine's aunt and five or six other members of her family came to join them and, at the beginning of April, Charles Boquet showed up with thirty Oneidas who wished to become Christians. This meeting was the occasion for a joyful family reunion at which Catherine told everyone how happy she was to be a real Christian at last and encouraged them to go to Quebec. They hesitated, however, for they didn't know anyone in the capital city[7] and they remained in La Prairie some time longer. Finally, Catherine offered to lead them herself to Fr. Chaumonot, who completed the catechetical instructions begun by Fr. Raffeix. Bishop de Laval baptized them at the beginning of summer.

They were all invited to stay among the Hurons to protect their new-found faith, but Francis insisted on going back to the Iroquois canton. Catherine persuaded him, however, to pass through La Prairie, where her heart was calling her. Fr. Raffeix was delighted to see her again and proposed that they share his dwelling until they built their own longhouse, if they wished to stay. They lingered on till the winter hunt, during which their conduct as Christians was irreproachable. When they returned from hunting, they found fields ready for sowing, which the priest had ordered to be ploughed for them.

The women got down to work immediately. Some forty Frenchmen had already settled in the area and Francis Xavier decided to build a hut for himself near the Rivière de la Tortue. Three other companions soon did likewise; one of them was Ateriata*, the godson of King Louis XIV.

The foundations of the Indian Mission of La Prairie were laid and Catherine was the first leader of this new Christian community. Her universal charity towards both French and Indians was a haven of peace for the bodies and souls of the neediest of the poor and, from the slave she once had been, she became mistress of the hearth in the longhouse of faith.

In 1670, the new village had five longhouses and Fr. Raffeix had a small church built. The following year, the Indians decided to settle there for good and chose two Huron chiefs to govern the village: one war chief, François-Xavier Tonsahoten, and one religious chief, a layman, Paul Honogenhag.[8] Everyone agreed that from then on, whoever wished to join them was, first, to give up once and for all, polygamy, drunkenness and any superstitious belief in dreams. The villagers planted "ten memorable trees" at the entrance of the village; "on one of them they hung drunkenness, and on the other, impurity, both subdued by faith".[9]

For a while, Catherine provided accommodation for Fr. Philippe Pierson* who had come to live among the Indians to learn the Iroquois language. This Jesuit Father distributed rosaries of the Holy Family to the most fervent villagers, without being able to explain it. One day, Catherine wanted to find out more about it and, thanks to her, the fellowship of the Holy Family took root in La Prairie. The purpose of this group was to lead its members, both men and women, to the heights of holiness. Finally, Fr. Raffeix left for Nundawao and was replaced by Fr. Frémin, one of the three Black Robes Kateri had met in Caughnawaga in 1667.

As early as 1672, there were native people of many nations[10] living at the Mission. They were a strange mixture resulting from the fact that the Iroquois had gone warring against a multitude of nations from which they had brought home captives and "it was those captives," says Fr. Cholenec, "and the Iroquois, their conquerors, who came to live here with their prize so that they might all become fervent Christians." The Iroquois group included those from the Five Cantons, plus Hurons, Neutrals*, Eries and Conestoga; in the Algonquin group were Mahicans, Montagnais, Nipissirinians and Socokis. They had four chiefs governing them: two Hurons and two Iroquois.[11] Paradoxically, among all these people of various origins, where disagreements could easily have arisen and resentments resurfaced, "charity and union reigned, beyond anything one could imagine"[12] These Indians became exemplary Christians and lived in harmony with the French, acting as one body, rejoicing together and doing small favours one for another. Some bad weeds grew in the midst of the good seed, however, when a few Frenchmen who traded with the Indians wanted to "establish a cabaret in la Prairie". Fr. Frémin complained to the Count de Frontenac, who had come to the seigneury to thank the Jesuit for "supplying him with flour for Fort Cataracoui.*" Thus cornered, the Count agreed to the priest's request and issued "an ordinance expressly forbidding to trade alcoholic beverages in La Prairie."[13]

The village of "the prayer" came to be renowned throughout the colony and, in 1672-73, more than eight hundred travellers were accommodated, which caused a shortage of the two-year food supply which the villagers had accumulated. Famine had become a prospect. Most visitors returned to their countries, but they left behind two hundred new Christians[14] who had to accept the rules of the Mission or else, leave: no more shamanic beliefs, no more sacrifices to pagan gods, no more prostitution nor drunkenness...

The Great Mohawk, who had gone hunting in the vicinity of Chambly, was deeply impressed when he met the Indians-of-the-prayer. These Christians put their zeal into action in all things and everywhere, especially during the hunting season, when they informed and exhorted the infidels they met. This is how the Great Mohawk was converted and how, on his return from the hunt, he came to ask Fr. Frémin for Baptism. The priest laid the condition that he have a wife! The proud warrior immediately returned to the cantons to get his wife and brought back, in addition, "some forty people, men, women and children." So many Indians sought refuge in this new village that, in less than seven years, the warriors of Mohawk land had become "more numerous in Montreal than in their own country," which infuriated "both the elders of the villages and the Flemish of Manate and Orange."[15]

In addition to being infiltrated, once more, by the liquor trade in La Prairie in spite of the ordinance, the Mission was to be tried by two other unfortunate events: first, a rupture of the Hurons, and then the death of Catherine.

Three predominant nations: the Iroquois, the Hurons and the Onondagas, wanted to have their own respective chiefs. The Indians met in council for this purpose, but dissension set in. The Hurons had long deliberations while the other two nations immediately elected their chief. "Deeply hurt by this, the Hurons broke away from the others and went to set up a new mission across the river. This separation was a hard blow, bound to cause disunity for a while. Finally, however, finding the same faith and the same Gospel everywhere, and especially unity among all the missionaries of Canada,"[16] the efforts of the devil to destroy the faith in this village were in vain.

In the fall of 1673, Catherine fell seriously ill and Francis Xavier gathered his friends for a meal, according to custom. However, this was a Christian feast at which they prayed to Jesus and Mary and recited the Rosary for the dying woman.

She passed away on November 6th, leaving her husband and all the villagers with the unforgettable memory of her detachment from earthly goods, of her purity of heart and of her limitless dedication. She was called "the mother of the poor, the good Christian and the pillar of faith."

In organizing the funeral, Francis called the elders together and told them that the time had come for him to abandon a few ancestral customs, such as giving relatives and friends some of the belongings of the deceased person and burying the rest with the body in the grave. "For my part, he said, I decided to dress Catherine in her most beautiful clothes in anticipation of the Resurrection and to give, as would have been her wish, all her belongings to the poor." Most people at the Mission adopted this new custom from then on, except that they preferred to give the most beautiful clothing to the poor.

In 1674, the impoverished soil of La Prairie was no longer adequate for raising corn; therefore many Indians spoke of returning to the Iroquois cantons. Moreover, the liquor trade in the outskirts of the Mission continued to aggravate the missionaries, who thought of a new refuge for their flock in a location protected from harmful contacts with the white men.

Fr. Antoine Dalmas*, who had replaced Fr. Pierson, visited Isle-Jésus for this purpose, but this plan was soon discarded by Fr. Claude Dablon, superior of the Jesuits of New France, when he heard, through Fr. Dalmas, that this place too would be easily accessible to the liquor trade. They looked for another solution.[17]

In 1675, Fr. Cholenec, who had recently come from France, replaced Fr. Dalmas, who left for Sillery. Under Fr. Frémin's leadership, the Confraternity of the Holy Family developed considerably; this association still exists today in Kahnawake, Quebec.

That same year, the Mission was honoured by two important visitors: Bishop François Montmorency de Laval and Intendant Jacques Duchesneau.[18]

The first Bishop of New France docked at the village of La Prairie on May 25th, 1675. Everyone awaited his visit with pomp and cheer. They had prepared a beautiful Indian style reception for him. After cleaning the entire village, the Indians formed a green archway going from the church to the river. Along this tunnel of branches, they built three leafy bowers in which the Bishop was to stop to receive complimentary speeches. A small raft linked this avenue with the river.

The moment the episcopal canoe came in sight, Fr. Dablon, who was then visiting the Mission, paddled his way to meet him. At the sound of the bell, all the villagers assembled on the shore. Fr. Frémin stood on the right with his Indian people, Fr. Cholenec on the left with the French settlers, and the captain of the

Hurons with the elders of that nation stood on the small raft. Before the prelate came to shore, Tonsahoten shouted to him: "Bishop, stop your canoe and listen to what I have to say to you"; then he delivered the first complimentary speech. The Bishop disembarked accompanied by his assistant, Mr. Dudouyt and by Fr. Gabriel Souart*, P.S.S., Pastor of Montreal. Everyone followed them in procession to the little church, stopping at the first bower to listen to the speeches of the two captains, one Onondaga and one Oneida; at the second bower, it was Paul's turn, the dogique, who stood on a tree trunk which served as a pulpit.

The next day, the Bishop baptized, married or confirmed eighty Indians and a few French people. During his homily, which was translated by Fr. Frémin, he declared that he had come especially for the Indians. After the ceremony, a banquet was served at the longhouse of Paul Honogenhag*. During this meal, the prelate announced that he was going to visit every family and every person in their own longhouse. Therefore, all of them began to decorate their homes with the most valuable things they had.

Bishop de Laval left the Mission on the third day, blessing the assembly and assuring the people that he was taking their hearts with him and leaving them his own.

One month later, on the 27th of June, the fourth Intendant of New France, Jacques Duchesneau* de la Doussière et d'Ambault landed in La Prairie with an escort of approximately fifteen canoes, in which were François-Marie Perrot*, Governor of Montreal, Fr. Souart and some fifty prominent men of the colony. Like Bishop de Laval, he conversed at length with the Iroquois, Huron and Wolf Indians assembled in council, and then offered them a banquet. The population was impressed by the piety, gentleness, integrity and zeal of the illustrious visitor. Both the Jesuits and the Indians were grateful to him for granting them a track of land one league and a half long, which was named Sault Saint-Louis*. This concession was approved by Louis XIV only four years later, on May 29th, 1680.

As this was the eve of the feast of Saint John the Baptist, after a ceremony at the church, the villagers marched in line towards a heap of firewood where the Intendant lighted the traditional "feu de la Saint-Jean" in the midst of musket salutes fired by French and Indian youths.

The visit of the Bishop and of the Intendant of New France affixed the official and spiritual seals to the Indian village founded by Catherine and Francis Xavier in 1667.

In July 1676, the Indians and their missionaries moved[19] a few miles upstream to the place called Sault Saint-Louis or, in Iroquois, Kahnawake (by-the-rapids), a land of about two square leagues. F.X. Tonsahoten offered his field to build the chapel. Now separated from the French of La Prairie, the new converts were able to practice their devotions their own way more freely, which increased and confirmed their piety.

In His divine Providence, the Lord had provided and prepared this place of refuge for Kateri. Her adopted sister was already there with her husband. Stimulated by the daring apostolic activity of the Great Mohawk and his friends, the "big sister" decided to make her desire known. How happy Tekakwitha would be if she could come and live here in peace, in the village-of-the-prayer! She discussed it with her husband, who decided to go and get his sister-in-law. Hot Ashes*, one of the most prominent of the Oneida converts volunteered to help him and so did a Huron from Lorette. Shortly afterwards, these three brave men set out on the path leading south.

Notes 10

1. PO, Doc. XII, p. 257.

2. JR, vol. 61, p. 64.

3. JR, vol. 55, p. 32.

4. VBCT, p. 58-72; JR, vol. 61, p. 194ss; JR, vol. 63, p. 148ss; OCI, p. 5-55.

5. JR, vol. 52, p. 22.

6. The different narrations accuse divergences.

7. JR, vol. 52, p. 24.

8. JR, vol. 55, p. 36.

9. JR, vol. 63, p. 166.

10. JR, vol. 58, p. 74; vol. 55, p. 34, vol. 61, p. 194.

11. JR, vol. 60, p. 276.

12. JR, vol. 55, p. 34.

13. JR, vol. 63, p. 174.

14. JR, vol. 58, p. 80-6, 252; vol. 63, p. 166; vol. 61, p. 238-9.

15. JR, vol. 63, p. 178.

16. JR, vol. 63, p. 180. These small renewed schisms formed gradually the Mission at the Mountain directed by the Sulpicians of Montreal. See also JR, vol. 60, p. 286.

17. JR, vol. 58, p. 112.

18. JR, vol. 59, p. 268-90.

19. JR, vol. 63, p. 190.

11

The Escape

Hot Ashes,[1] Ogenheratarihiens in Iroquois, had been one of the most influential chiefs among the Oneidas. After receiving Baptism from Fr. Frémin along with his wife, Marie Garhio, and his children, Louis Garonhiague was now going to serve as an escort of Kateri's brother-in-law with the Huron friend and a few neophytes. To camouflage the purpose of their journey, they would go and trade beaver pelts with the British of Albany.[2] In the manner of the Great Mohawk, they would stop on their way at all the Iroquois villages in the hope of persuading their compatriots to become Christians. Of course, they would begin with a tour of the Mohawk villages, which were the eastern gateway to the Iroquois cantons.

As soon as they reached Caughnawaga, Hot Ashes and his companions entered the longhouse of Fr. de Lamberville.[3] Immediately, a crowd of people came to greet them, as was the custom, and among them was Kateri Tekakwitha.

Hot Ashes spoke of "the prayer" and of the happiness of the Iroquois now established in Kahnawake, on the great northern river, to all the Mohawks assembled before him. Among other things, he reminded them that he had once been, as his audience knew well, a chief in Oneida, a warrior, and that he had behaved in the past as they did. He went on to say that, in those days, he was a dog and that he had begun only a few months ago being a man.

As he spoke, the elders began to walk out, one after another, and then the rest of the crowd followed. Kateri was the only one who had been moved by his words. She felt as though God spoke to her through his mouth. Soon afterwards, she went to the missionary and told him that she was finally determined to follow his advice and she begged him to prevent her family from putting any obstacles in the way of her departure. She would escape, she said, even if it cost her her life![4]

Against all hopes, her aunts did not express too much opposition; but her uncle's anger was to be feared, for he had so strongly condemned these departures which benefited the Mission of Kahnawake.

As soon as he could, Kateri's brother-in-law went to meet her secretly. He revealed to her that he had made this trip with his companions for the purpose of bringing her back to Saint Francis Xavier. He added that his wife wanted very much to have her near her in his longhouse and spoke very highly of the Mission on the Saint Lawrence River, opposite Tiotiake*, known today as Montreal. The speckled face of his sister-in-law, turned up towards him, lighted up with joy.

Fr. de Lamberville entrusted her to Hot Ashes, who confirmed her in her decision. The missionary was pleased to find out the real purpose of his three visitors.

As soon as the young chief was able to meet Kateri, he promised to facilitate her departure and explained to her how. As he was planning to go and preach in his canton of Oneida and even further, he would give her his place in his red elm canoe. She could then leave with her brother-in-law and the Huron companion. The occasion was all the more propitious since her uncle had gone trading with the British and the Dutch of Schenectady.

Before the great departure, Fr. de Lamberville encouraged Kateri to place all her trust in God; he gave her some additional advice and letters for the Fathers of the Saint Francis Xavier Mission, where she was going to find refuge.

All three of them, the brother-in-law, the Huron and Kateri, left at once while Hot Ashes went away to Oneida. The fugitives paddled quickly and silently, following the curves of the river without decreasing their speed, careful to avoid pursuit. It was surely near the place where a small stream, the Chuctanunda, runs down a beautiful hill and flows into the Mohawk River that they abandoned their canoe on the shore and disappeared into the great forest. The Mohawk River flows towards the southeast, which would have taken our travellers away from their destination if they had continued; had they left it sooner, they would have had to go through very rough and difficult terrain. Besides, in case of need, the brush through which the northward path ran was safer for the fugitives.

For the long journey awaiting them they needed food. The brother-in-law decided to go and buy a few loaves of bread at the Dutch house of Schenectady, which had become British territory after the capture and recapture of Orange* in 1664 and 1674.

Meanwhile, in Caughnawaga, Kateri's escape was soon discovered and a messenger was sent to notify the elderly man. The messenger quickly found the chief among the merchants of Orange. He went into a fury on hearing the news of his niece's escape. Out of spite, he loaded his gun with three bullets and set out in pursuit of the abductors. With all the skill of an experienced warrior, he took every path, one after another, to retrieve his possession. Kateri's brother-in-law, for his part, came across the dreaded uncle on his way to Schenectady, but the chief passed by his prey without the least suspicion.

Hidden under leafy boughs, Kateri and the Huron of Lorette, a brave Christian who had been living in continence with his wife for years, awaited the return of the brother-in-law. He finally rejoined them with a good supply of bread and told them what had happened. The Iroquois maiden saw in this a manifestation of Providence and felt the desire to abandon herself completely to Rawenniio - the true God. She decided from then on to use every occasion available to her to work for her salvation.

After resting a while, the fugitives got on their way again, heading north. The best road to Lake Andiatarocte crossed the area known today as Galway in Saratoga County. It went down into the valley where a small river named Kayaderosseras flowed, and turned eastward around the long mountain ridge on top of which laid Desolation Lake, and headed directly to the landing place now called Jessup's Landing on the Oigue* River. A short distance from this place, above Palmer's Falls, the river was shallow enough to be waded through. Across it , a good path ran along the eastern shore up to Luzerne, at which point it broke away to head northeast; finally, after crossing a very beautiful valley, it came to the rough shores of the Andiatarocte. Here they found a canoe, probably the one Hot ashes had hidden in tall grass when he went down to the land of the Mohawks.

After a short halt, our three travellers sailed off to the north. They were almost certain that the vindictive uncle was no longer after them. Yet they did not slow down, and once in a while, they glanced at the high banks decked in their autumn splendour. Like a song of joy, the lake mirrored the carmine red, dark green, light gold and milky white of the maple, pine, birch and vinegar trees.

At the place where the Andiatarocte opens into Lake Champlain, Kateri and her companions had to prepare to portage through the woods for a distance of half a league. The rest of the trip looked promising. Within a short while their canoe glided smoothly on the lake, also called "the great sea of the Iroquois". Three quarters of a league from the shore, they came to Ticonderoga*, the place where Kateri's father had stopped with his young wife and his warriors, twenty years before, to offer a sacrifice of tobacco leaves to a nation of invisible men believed to live in the depths of the waters. The three fervent Christians, who had rejected these superstitions, simply prayed Rawenniio to enlighten the hearts of all the Mohawks.

Five or six days of travel went by. Kateri's voyage "was a continuous prayer and the joy she felt as they came closer to Montreal cannot be described,"[5] wrote Fr. Chauchetière in 1695. At last, they caught sight of the fleurs-de-lys flag floating on the ramparts of Fort Sainte-Anne built on an island at the northern end of Lake Champlain. A few hours later, they rowed down the Richelieu River, which was approximately one hundred and fifty feet wide almost throughout its course. After about thirty miles, in the vicinity of Saint-Jean-sur-Richelieu, they abandoned their canoe near Fort Saint-Louis*, where they could see the fortified gate and the three bastions. From here they took the path that went through the thick of the forest to Sault Saint-Louis, which is known today as the Lachine Rapids.

The small Indian village was built on high ground from which one could see the Saint Lawrence River right across to the opposite shore. In the distance, smoke rising from the houses of Montreal vanished in the northern skies. At the bottom of the high cliff, the rapids crashed with a terrifying noise and the water spumed as if it were under the wheel of a windmill.

Notes 11

1. OCI, p. 115-24.

2. PO, Doc. XII, p. 258; VCT, p. 9.

3. Narration of Fr. Lambreville in LCC, p. 7 on PO, Doc III, p. 9-10.

4. VBCT, p. 55.

5. VBCT, p. 57.

PART TWO

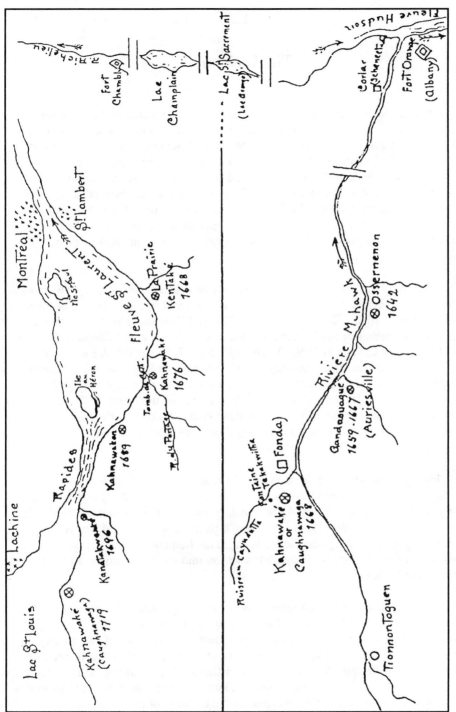

Iroquois Mission on the banks of the St-Lawrence.
Iroquois Mission on the banks of the Mohawk River.

12

The Welcome

Fr. Frémin[1] had been presiding over the life of the Church of the Sault for six years. This Jesuit Father had been a missionary in the Iroquois cantons as early as 1656, among the Onondagas of Saint Marie of Ganentaa, and then among the Souriquois of Richiboucto. Having returned to France for his "third year," he came back to new France in 1660 and worked in Cap-de-la-Madeleine among the Algonquins and Montagnais. After 1667, he was sent to the Mohawks, Senecas, Onondagas and Cayugas. In 1671, he was sent to the Mohawks, Senecas, Onondagas and Cayugas. In 1671, he was appointed superior of the Mission of Saint-François-Xavier-des-Prés. Fr. Pierre Cholenec[2] came in 1674 to give him a hand.

This priest was born in Léon, Brittany. He had surely heard in his youth about Marie-Amice Picard, a mystic whose body was interred in the Cathedral of Saint-Pol-de-Léon in 1652. This fellow-citizen of his had lived many years with no other food but the Eucharist, like Theresa Neumann of our time. Pierre Cholenec entered the Jesuit order in Paris in 1659. From 1664 to 1667, he studied philosophy at the Royal College of La Flèche, the city in which Jérôme Le Royer de la Dauversière, founder of Montreal, died in 1659. Pierre Cholenec was then appointed prefect of His Most Serene Highness Prince Rinaldo d'Estre, an indication of his amiable character, not at all reminiscent of the harsh coast of Lower Brittany. He later completed his theological studies at Collège Louis-le-Grand in Paris and, from there embarked for Canada.

Finally, four months before the arrival of Kateri,[3] Fr. Claude Chauchetière came to the Mission from Quebec, where he had become fluent in the Huron language. He was filled with wonder by the spectacle which unfolded before his eyes. He wrote: "We are in a place located on a very high level, beautiful and pleasing to the eye, sixty leagues from Quebec, and it is called the Iroquois Mission. It is the finest mission in Canada and its piety and devotion make it very similar to the best churches of France."[4]

Fr. Chauchetière had been marked as a child by the death of a priest who was about to embark for America. "This gave me a taste of how good it is to give oneself to God," he said. At eighteen, he entered the novitiate of the Society of Jesus in Bordeaux. During the long years of study proper to the Jesuits, the conviction that he was to devote himself in Canada kept growing in him - there would be more to endure out there than in France - but he was careful not to go to New France until he was seriously entrenched in the work of his sanctification.

Despite all his good will, he felt that his efforts were useless. "It seemed to me that all I did was sew and rip up the seam...Then I figured I could supplement what I lacked through humility. This virtue was the source of all my happiness." He looked for the most obscure tasks, which his superiors assigned to him all the more willingly since they considered him incapable of doing better things.

His extraordinary humility soon gained him some exceptional graces. He experienced trances and mystical raptures. During his prayers, which reached the heights of ecstasy, the mysteries of the Saviour unfolded before his eyes. He thus attained an almost uninterrupted union with his Creator, a union of heart and spirit which never ceased, even at night.

His vocation to New France became clearer to him in his years of teaching at La Rochelle. In 1673, he came into contact with Fr. François Le Mercier* who had come from Canada. He immediately began studying Huron under his tutorship. He would recite the Rosary in this language because of the spiritual consolation he felt in praying to God in this way. After his ordination, he embarked for Canada.

Those were the three zealous missionaries who welcomed Kateri when she arrived at the Mission in October 1677. The young Indian maiden handed them the letters of Fr. de Lamberville. Fr. Cholenec who was in charge of the spiritual direction of the Mission's flock, received this revealing message: "Catherine Tegakoüita will live at the Sault. I ask you to please take charge of directing her; it is a treasure which we are giving you, as you will soon realize. Guard it well and make it bear fruit for the glory of God and the salvation of a soul which is certainly very dear to Him."⁶ Her face was even more revealing than the letter, said the missionary.

When Kateri met this Ratsihenstatsi for the first time, he was thirty-seven years old. It is thanks to him that we know something of the interior life of Kateri during the winter of 1677. "There is one", he wrote, "who walks with a limp; she is the most fervent of the whole village, I believe, and though she is cripple and always sick, she does some amazing things."⁷ Fr. Cholenec noted on many occasions the role of the Holy Spirit in her life. Within a few weeks, the young woman distinguished herself among all those of the Mission to the point of drawing the esteem and admiration of all. "It can be said truthfully that she was never a novice in the practice of virtue," he said, "that she was learned in this regard from the very beginning and that she had no other master than the Holy Spirit, so rapidly did she stride towards perfection."⁸

All introductions being made, the brother-in-law took Kateri to his home where she was welcomed with open arms. She immediately felt as though the land of Sault Saint-Louis was her native soil. The longhouse in which she entered was no different from the one she had lived in Iroquois land. At least two families lived in it, that of the adopted sister of Kateri and that of the owner of the place, Anastasia Tegonhatsiongo, who had known Kateri as a little child and also her deceased mother. This woman was one of the pillars of the Mission. She had a rare talent for instructing her people in the Christian faith and the new refugee became attached to her as though she were her mother.

There were, in the new village, twenty-two Huron and Iroquois longhouses.[9] For the moment, they had to make do with a small bark chapel. Hanging above the altar was a "challenging necklace"* which was a reminder from the Christians of Lorette to those of the Sault to take their faith seriously and to build a chapel as soon as possible. It also exhorted them to fight the various demons striving to bring on the ruin of both missions."[10] Kateri "gave free rein to her devotion"[11] in this chapel. Fr. Frémin had named the new location "Mission Saint-François-Xavier du Sault". The faithful of this mission were so fervent that they were later compared with the Christians of the early Church.[12] The Indians-of-the-prayer had no other topic of conversation but the Lord; their only concern was to serve Him well and they were not content with observing the commandments of God, but they also practised the evangelical counsels. Everyone, young and old, valiantly tried to walk in the footsteps of Christ. Almost every longhouse was a school of virtue.[13]

The first Mass was celebrated "at the crack of dawn for those most in a hurry to go to work".[14] After sunrise, a second Mass was said for everyone and there was no one who would not attend either one of the Masses, and most people went to both, even in the coldest weather. They would then go about their usual occupations, coming and going with their rosaries in their hands. Many of them lived in continual union with God.

Finally, Kateri found what she had long been looking for without knowing it: to be a Christian without incurring a cultural shock. Within this kind of earthly paradise, she thanked the Lord every day for transporting her into the land of light.

The young Indian woman soon realized that the existence of the first Iroquois Christians revolved around the day of the Lord.[15] There are two Iroquois words for Sunday: Niiohne, the day of the Lord, or Enta, the great day, the feast day. The newcomer was able, at last, to enjoy this custom, after spending her Sundays in Caughnawaga without food or drink rather than not sanctifying the day of the Lord.

Before dawn, on Sunday, many Indians came together before the Blessed Sacrament to prepare themselves more adequately to sanctify the day of the Lord. Kateri was there before them all. She would sit on the left-hand side, reserved for women, and would remain there until the eight o'clock Mass celebrated by Fr. Frémin. After the Gospel, the celebrant, or quite often Paul Honoguenhag, preached a long and admirable sermon. Then the dogique intoned the Creed in Iroquois and everyone joined in the singing. The crowd continued singing during most of the

Holy Sacrifice until the Tetsitewanonwera ne Niio, the final Deo gratias.

At ten o'clock, the bell called everyone back to church for the recitation of the Rosary, during which they recalled the mysteries. Saint Catherine Labouré had the remarkable privilege of kneeling before the Blessed Virgin, who sat in an armchair, and of actually seeing her. Kateri meditated upon her Rosary without the help of apparitions, but her faith penetrated any shroud of mystery that might stand between her and the Mother of the Saviour.

At one o'clock in the afternoon, Anastasia went to the meeting of the Confraternity of the Holy Family, of which she had been a member ever since she had gone to Quebec. Kateri joined her at three, when the bell rang for Vespers. The men and the women took their respective places, as was the custom; Fr. Frémin, the dogique and two altar boys put on their surplices on the Epistle side. After genuflecting before the Blessed Sacrament, the dogique sang the Deus in adjutorium, which everyone joined in two choirs and continued until the Gloria patri of the last psalm. Actually, they did not sing the psalms themselves, but the prayers they knew. Kateri immediately memorized the prayer to the Guardian Angel, the morning and evening prayers, those of the Elevation and of thanksgiving for the gift of faith, plus the Ten Commandments. At the end of the Office, they sang the Ave Maria to the tune of the Gregorian Magnificat.

The afternoon ended with the Benediction of the Blessed Sacrament, after which everyone went home. These public devotions, which divided the times of day and week at the Saint Francis Xavier Mission, filled the heart of Kateri with sweet joy.

After a short while, Anastasia Tegonhatsiongo took a growing interest in the interior life of her protegée. She inquired from her how she had behaved, since 1671, when she herself had left the canton to come and settle in La Prairie with her family. The young woman answered that she had lived no differently since then than at the time when Anastasia lived in her neighbourhood in Caughnawaga.[16]

Another time, Anastasia questioned her concerning the white and purple wampum beads she wore around her neck and in her hair. She also inquired whether she was thinking about marriage. Was she not of age and had she not even passed the age when young Iroquois women started a family? This drew a smile from Kateri who, deep down, was already determined not to marry. Anastasia sounded out the young woman again to find out if she had any tendency to spread malicious gossip, a rather common fault among her peers. Her young friend did not even know what this word meant; not only could she not define the word, but what is better still, no word against anyone, not even her slanderers, had ever come out of her mouth.

One day, as these two women were engaged in such a conversation, a young man entered their longhouse and noticed Kateri obediently seated near her instructor. "They say that this one has sore eyes," he said in jest, and pulled one end of the young woman's blanket to look at her face mottled with light, whitish spots. Kateri blushed at having her head thus uncovered, but she picked up her blanket without any anger. Her patience made her invulnerable and incapable of hurting anyone or complaining about anyone.[17]

Kateri became strongly attached to the good Anastasia. She made it a rule of conduct for herself to accompany her in the fields and in the woods, while softly reciting her Rosary to avoid being distracted from thinking of the God of love. Throughout the day, as they felled trees or picked corn, the two Indian women talked to each other about God and about the ways to please Him and to make progress in His service. Anastasia told her companion about the lives of the saints, about their aversion to sin and the many acts of penance they had performed to atone for their faults. Kateri learned more while working with her instructor than she did anywhere else.

Kateri went even further. She sensed that there were things she did not know and that were being hidden from her because of her fragile health, but her ardent desire to always do more soon made her discover many things.

Some women of the village had a peculiar behaviour and practised very harsh forms of penance.[18] The first one who had indulged in these kinds of penance, around the feast of Christmas 1676, had taken off her clothes in freezing weather in front of the cross of the cemetery. It was snowing at the time, and since she was pregnant, the snow falling on her had caused her such pain that she thought she would die, along with her child.

Four of her friends had acted similarly after her example. Two of them had dug a hole in the ice and immersed themselves in the water for the time it took to recite the Rosary in Iroquois, which was twice as long as in French. One of the two, fearing to be found out, had not dared warm herself upon returning home, but had gone to bed with ice on her shoulders.

Many other forms of mortification were practised by men and women in a spirit of penance, until such time as they were instructed to abandon what was excessive in those austere practices. Kateri Tekakwitha undoubtedly decided to follow these good examples.

The young Mohawk woman who had embraced perfection in all things, contributed significantly to this atmosphere of fervour. She was powerfully drawn to the altar by the presence of Christ, the divine Magnet, even outside the hours of regular devotions. She would go to church barefoot in the dark, at four o'clock in the morning, and converse with the good Master, far from noise and distractions. She would attend the first Mass at dawn, and the next one at sunrise, return to the chapel several times during the day and in the evening after work, and remain there quite late at night; it could be said that she was the first one in and the last one out. On Sundays and feast days, she spent the whole day in the holy place, coming out only to have something to eat.

Her love of Jesus blossomed in her prayers. Scarcely one month after her establishment at the Mission, the Holy Spirit blessed her with a "sublime gift of prayer accompanied by such heavenly sweetness that she would often spend several hours in succession in these intimate communications with her God."[19] She prayed mostly with her eyes and heart. The words that seethed deep in her heart poured out in sighs and tears. So many tears that it can be said she had the gift of tears, a gift which seems to be quite rare today. They were tears of joy which flowed spontaneously under the touch of divine sweetness and love.

Despite her eagerness to spend as much time as possible before the altar, she never went to church when it was time to work. Her spiritual father noted that "her devotion was all the more to be valued since it was not the idle kind in which there is usually nothing but self-love, nor was Kateri one of those stubborn devotees who are at church when it is time to clean the house."[20] Her work very quickly became a means of union with God. Was this not what He was asking of her?

Kateri saw those who had been Christians for a long time, such as Anastasia and her first Oneida companion, Jeanne Gouastraha*, who later became her faithful imitator, [21] receive holy communion fairly often. She told Fr. Cholenec of her desire to make her first communion the following Christmas. She even insisted, for custom had it that the newly baptized were not permitted to approach the holy Table until many years afterwards. Pope Saint Plus X had not yet recommended daily communion, although Saint Ignatius had already encouraged frequent communion in the Spiritual Exercises*. Around the beginning of December, convinced that this Mohawk woman was indeed the "treasure" Fr. de Lamberville had mentioned in his letter, Fr. Cholenec granted her the desired permission.[22]

The good news filled Kateri with joy, and with the help of the missionary, she disposed herself the best she could for her First Communion. On Christmas day 1677, she received the Lord Jesus in her heart. What went on between Him and her on this occasion is not known to us. Fr. Cholenec reports the following concerning this first sacramental union: "The matter was too well disposed and only required coming close to the divine fire to receive all its warmth; she came to it, or, better still, she threw herself into this furnace of sacred love burning on our altars." It can be said that from this day on, the life of Kateri blossomed; she came out of her shell and began to look quite different as she remained so filled with God and His love.

This fact was so well known among those around her that the most devout women were eager to sit near her in the church. Her mere presence helped them to prepare for holy communion.

Notes 12

1. Kateri Quarterly, nos: 50-51-53-55-56-57-58-59, 1972-1974.
    Indicated hereafter by the abbreviation K.

2. JR, vol. 59, p. 315, note 50.

3. VBCT, p. 10; Autobiographic notes of Father Claude Chauchetière (1695).
    Archives ADJCF, Saint Jérôme, No. 390, p. 14. Indicated hereafter by the
    abbreviation NA.

4. JR, vol. 62, p. 166.

5. NA, p. 15.

6. VCT, p. 11.

7. LCC, p. 51.

8. VCT, p. 13.

9. JR, vol. 60, p. 276.

10. JR, vol. 63, p. 192-4.

11. VCT, p. 58.

12. VCT, p. 8.

13. VCT, p. 12.

14. JR, vol. 60, p. 284.

15. Ibid., p. 276-85.

16. VBCT, p. 75.

17. Ibid., p. 107.

18. JR, vol. 62, p. 174-6.

19. VCT, p. 15.

20. Ibid.

21. OCI, p. 159.

22. VCT, p. 17-8.

13

Her Last Hunting Trip

After Christmas and the Epiphany, everything returned to normal. It was the season of the great winter hunt. The Indians "take their wives and children along on their hunting trips," wrote Marie de l'Incarnation in 1668, "and it is the women who skin the game, tan the hides, smoke the meat and the fish, cut the wood and, finally, do all the chores."[1] The time had come, and even if Kateri's heart held her back near the real Presence in the little chapel of the village, she could no longer put off going; her adopted sister and brother-in-law were pressing her.

Life was much more pleasant in the woods than at the Mission. There was plenty of good food. Women, especially, were not tied down to house chores and work in the fields. Their main occupation was to prepare meals; they spent the rest of the time in recreational activities.

This is not to say that, because of this, the life of the soul was completely forgotten. Fr. Chauchetière said that when the Indians of the Sault lived in the woods,[2] they brought along small notebooks in which the days of the week were indicated by lines on which the priests had marked with a cross every Sunday and feast day, which they observed quite faithfully.

Kateri did not allow herself to be influenced by this easy life; she observed the customary religious practices and added some of her own, as if to compensate for the church services of the village, which she missed.[3]

Every morning, she prayed to God with all the others, as was the excellent custom of those who went hunting. Then, while they ate together the only meal of the day, she left the hut at about the time the Holy Sacrifice was being offered for the faithful at the Mission. She went silently to an oratory which she had arranged in a cluster of trees, having carved a small cross in a tree trunk on the bank of an icy brook where the people went to draw water. In this living chapel, she united herself in spirit with the Masses being celebrated in the village. We know how devoted to the holy angels were Theresa Neumann and Padre Pio in our time. Kateri had a similar confidence in her Guardian Angel. She would beg him to attend Mass in her place and to bring back to her the merits thereof.

When the men had gone hunting, around nine o'clock, she returned to the women and worked the rest of the day. Her main task was to bind the firewood into faggots, which she gladly accepted to do because it was a service to the whole community and because, since it was a solitary job, it enabled her to converse freely with the Lord Jesus. This therefore was her favourite occupation. Sometimes, she would go out to cut wood even before the sagamity was ready, and only come back in the evening. If someone compelled her to eat in the morning before going to work, she would secretly add soil or ashes, filched out of the nearest hearth, to her food.

On other days, she prepared the soup, or when the weather did not permit outdoor activities, she sat near the fire and made beautiful necklaces from moose hair. She would then encourage those around her to sing hymns or tell stories from the lives of the saints, which they had heard in church. She did all this quite naturally, to facilitate intimacy with God and avoid frivolous or uncharitable talk.

Occasionally, she would also go with the other women some two leagues or more away, to fetch stag, moose, beaver or marten meat from the game which the men had hunted down. If the little group happened to go in the direction of Fort La Mothe*, as the Great Mohawk and her relative, young Martin Skandegonrhaksen[4] had done less than two years before, she undoubtedly recalled the three apparitions of Our Lady to Martin in the middle of the woods, a few days before he died on December 22nd, 1675.

One day during one of those trips, a few women whom Kateri had joined, came to a frozen marsh. Letting the others walk ahead of her, Kateri strolled for a long time barefoot on the sheer ice.[5] The women not seeing her any more, waited for her. Fearing she might be in trouble, her adopted sister walked back to her in case she needed help. This is when she saw her on the icy pond with her bare feet.

Once she had completed her daily tasks, Kateri sometimes went to her small oratory during the day and in the evening before going to bed. Despite the almost arctic cold, several times a week she would end her last visit by flagellating herself with a switch. She was not yet familiar with the instruments used for this purpose. In the same way as she slipped away to pray, she also performed these acts of penance quietly, without the knowledge of those around her, just as she had done in the village, solely under the impulse of the Holy Spirit. Finally, regardless of her extreme fatigue and natural frailty, she spent a considerable part of her nights in prayer.

Kateri was not happy with this life in the woods. Her heart's desire was to return to the village where the Saviour in the Blessed Sacrament waited for her in the little bark chapel. She also missed the Mass, Benediction and exhortations. A rather serious misunderstanding brought to a head her dislike of the hunting season.

Late one evening, one of the men who had hunted moose all day, came back to the hut.[6] The last flickers of fire wrapped in smoke left every nook in the dark. Exhausted, this man who had had nothing to eat or drink, slumped down in the first

Kateri all absorbed in God while working.

available space and immediately fell asleep. He was one of the oldest Christians of the Mission, and never, in twenty years since his Baptism, had he given rise to any suspicion of wrongdoing. He and his wife got along so well that he could rightfully boast of never having had a quarrel with her.

When she woke up the next day, his wife was surprised not to find him near her. She was even more surprised, when she looked around for him, to see him lying near Kateri's mat. What had happened? Could it be that he had sinned with the young woman? Was she having secret dates with her husband? Despite her scarred face, could she have seduced him by her sweet and pleasing manner? What made things worse, the same day, her husband talked about a canoe which he had built in anticipation of their imminent return to Sault Saint-Louis, and had added that he needed an able woman to help him haul it to the forest. "Kateri will come", he said quite simply. He knew how willing she always was to help. One can imagine the dismay of his wife!

However, this Iroquois woman being a good Christian, did not expose her suspicions to her companions. She waited until the end of the hunt and the return to the village to go and tell Fr. Frémin all about the affair.

The hunting season sometimes gave rise to many different experiences. Here is the most unusual adventure which happened to Mary Theresa Tegaiaguenta,[7] who would soon become Kateri's best friend.

She had been baptized in 1669 by Fr. Jacques Bruyas, S.J. in her native canton, Oneida, after two years of catechumenate. Some time before her Baptism, she lost her only son. In those days, her country was flooded with alcohol from Fort Orange, and though she had resisted the temptation to drink for several months she finally succumbed.

Around 1674, she settled at the Saint Francis Xavier Mission with her husband, who was not a Christian. In spite of the fervour of most of the people, she continued leading a mediocre life. Then she was struck by another great misfortune. When the days started getting shorter towards the end of autumn 1675, Mary Theresa, her husband and a young nephew left for the winter hunt, heading west along the Ottawa River. Other Indians gradually joined them, until there were eleven of them altogether - four men, four women and three children. Mary Theresa was the only Christian in the group.

As the weeks went by fraught with hardship and uncertainty, the northern wind swept through the forest, covering the ground with shrivelled, reddish maple leaves and yellow birch leaves. Not a single flake of snow fell from the sky. Yet there had to be snow for a good hunting season. Not a wild animal came into sight, not even the cotton tail of a frightened rabbit. The food supply went down quickly, and the whole group faced the terrible threat of hunger. Mary Theresa's husband managed to kill a moose, which was avidly eaten in no time. Two sunsets later, they were reduced to eating a few pieces of the hides they had brought to make moccasins. Then they had to eat the moccasins themselves. Finally, these famished people got to the point of munching the bark of trees and the few autumn weeds which still held up in spite of the cold.

The group was about to starve to death and Mary Theresa's husband fell ill. A Mohawk and a Seneca decided in desperation to go and hunt some distance further. They promised to return within ten days. One and a half weeks later, the Mohawk came back empty-handed and alone. He said the Seneca had also failed to catch anything and had died of starvation. Our Nemrod however was quite healthy, which made him suspicious. Had he killed and eaten his companion? The band, utterly bewildered, made an about-turn and went in the direction of the Algonquin villages and the French settlements. Lost in grief, the poor widow of the Seneca and her two children followed them, disconsolate. They took Mary Theresa aside and pressed her to leave her husband to his fate. She firmly refused and found herself alone with her sick husband and her young nephew. Two days later he died with the deep regret of not having received Baptism. His grieving wife, faithful to the end, buried him with great difficulty in a shallow grave. In tears, she heaved the little boy up on her shoulders and walked wearily in the direction in which the other eight had disappeared.

When she caught up with them, these unfortunate people had been wandering about for almost three weeks, completely exhausted. This avalanche of misfortune had unsettled their minds and they had come to a strange decision: they would kill a few of their group so that the others might survive. Cannibalism was extremely rare among the Iroquois; they were farmers, and usually knew how to stock enough food to last them the whole winter. Besides, the people of the Five-Cantons lived close enough to white settlements to call for their help in case of famine. Even though their decision was made, they nevertheless questioned Mary Theresa to find out what was the Christian law on this matter. Is it permissible to take the life of a few people to save that of many others? Mary Theresa did not dare answer. She was ill at ease in the maze of Christian morality and fearful not only of co-operating in manslaughter if she approved their plan, but also of eventually risking her own life.

First an elderly man accepted to die for the others, convinced that he would be too much of a burden on the way. After strangling him, they ate his flesh. Then came the turn of the Seneca widow and her children.

The feeling that she might soon die enlightened the conscience of Mary Theresa. The sins of her past, especially those committed since her Baptism, haunted her like a frightening spectre. She was seized with a great horror of all the disgusting days of the past. Distressed at the thought that she had gone to the hunt without going to confession, she asked God with all her heart to forgive her, and promised Him to go to confession as soon as she got to the mission, if He saved her from this mortal danger. Better still, she promised to begin a new life and to do penance for her sins.

Her prayer was answered. In January 1676, after having suffered incredible tribulations, only five survivors tottered into the village of the Indians-of-the-prayer. Among them were Mary Theresa and her nephew. Faithful to her promise, she received the Sacrament of Penance shortly after her arrival.

The Indians of the Sault were, in fact, in the habit of going to confession upon returning from the hunt. Fr. Cholenec noted that some of them "live in the woods in the same innocence as they do in the village, and come back with the same purity of conscience as when they left. I am not exaggerating when I assure you that in many of them, we do not find sufficient matter for absolution upon their return".[8]

Notes 13

1. MIC, p. 828-9.

2. JR, p. 62, p. 180.

3. VBCT, p. 86-8; VCT, p. 19-22.

4. OCI, p. 107-14.

5. VBCT, p. 88-9.

6. VCT, p. 22-3.

7. VBCT, p. 77-8; VCT, p. 30-3.

8. JR, vol. 62, p. 180.

14

The Holy Family

On her return to the village, Kateri had no other thought but to make up for lost time. She therefore resumed all her devotions with fervour and went to meet her former instructor, Anastasia, to benefit once more from her valuable advice.

Since this was the beginning of Holy Week, Kateri decided to make the most of it to prepare herself for Easter, which fell on April 10th that year. This was the first time she took part in the celebrations of the holy Triduum at the Mission. The images of the sorrows and death of Jesus deeply moved her. Despite the persistence of the snow and cold, she felt such fervour, sweetness and consolation that her tears flowed abundantly, especially on Good Friday as she listened to the missionary preaching on the Passion of Christ. She kissed the Cross, and filled with gratitude and love, decided to bear in her body, for the rest of her life, the mortification of the Lord Jesus. She had the impression of having done nothing until then.

On Easter Sunday, Fr. Cholenec, her confessor, allowed her to receive communion for the second time, which she did with the same enrichment as on Christmas day. Her spiritual director also granted her another favour, that of being admitted into the Confraternity of the Holy Family and of the Slavery of the Blessed Virgin.[1]

The Association of the Holy Family was founded in Montreal on July 31st, 1663, by Madame Louis d'Ailleboust*, mother of Judith Brésolles*, R.H.S.J., the future Saint Marguerite Bourgeoys*, foundress of the Sisters of the Congregation of Notre Dame, Fr. Gabriel Souart, P.S.S. and Fr. Pierre-Joseph Chaumonot, S.J.,[2] for the renewal of Christian families. Two years later, Bishop François de Laval, then apostolic vicar of Quebec, raised its status to that of Confraternity and authorized it in all the territories under his jurisdiction. In La Prairie, the Confraternity was firmly established in the Iroquois Mission in 1675[3] by Fr. Frémin. The members met every Sunday at one o'clock in the afternoon for a brief exhortation.

A manuscript which I presently have in front of me, probably written in the XVIIIth century in Iroquois with French headings, mentions the programme of the meetings, gives a choice of prayers, such as the litanies and the rosary of the Holy Family and of the Marian Slavery - long before Saint Grignion de Montfort, - and lists some fifteen charitable services which the women were likely to render, for example, caring for the sick and keeping watch over the dying.

The rosary of the Holy Family quickly became popular. It was composed of three decades. Between each of them, the faithful were to meditate on the life of Our Lady. On the large beads, they recited the Our Father, and on the small ones, the invocation "Jesus, Mary, Joseph, Joachim and Ann, help us," to which they responded "Holy Trinity, one God, have mercy on us." At the end of each decade, they added a Glory Be.

Candidates for the Holy Family group were hand-picked among the most fervent women and men of a certain age. Once native people "have given themselves to God, they are capable of anything in matters of devotion, for they are naturally generous."[4] All those who were members of this group were considered by their compatriots with great veneration. To say that someone was a saint or that he or she was a member of this Confraternity was one and the same thing. Now Kateri, who was still very young and had been at the Saint Francis Xavier Mission only six or seven months, was already a member of this august assembly!

Far from being envious or critical, the entire village, and particularly the associates of the Holy Family, were delighted by this choice. She would be able to support this holy Confraternity on her own by her good examples, they thought. Kateri made the most of this favour. Her love of the Blessed Virgin increased so much that her entire spiritual life was coloured with it.

After being at Saint Francis Xavier for a few months, "an enlightened person" - who can only be Fr. Frémin - estimated that the new member of the Confraternity had reached the state of divine union, by reason of the "sweetness of this blessed state" which she experiences.[5] A good Christian wishing to become united with God here on earth must ordinarily go, first, through the so-called purgative and illuminative ways before reaching the unitive way. Under the special guidance of the Holy Spirit, who is quite unconcerned with books of theology, Kateri first went through the latter way, and then entered into the other two. In her contacts with God, she was constantly showered with new insights, so vivid that they enlightened her intellect and kindled her will like fire. She saw the beauty of Christian virtues incarnated in Christ, their Source, and her desire was to model her conduct on His, inasmuch as depended on her.

The great spiritual master of the time, Fr. Louis Lallemant*, S.J., was of the opinion that these insights sometimes cause souls already advanced in divine union to see all of their past life in a flash, as they will see it at the Last Judgment. These insights make all their sins visible to them, from the time of their childhood, and reveal to them God's plan for the government of the universe. Kateri thus discovered in her past life new reasons to love the Lord more tenderly, and to love Him to the extreme limits of her human possibilities, with the help of grace. Consequently, she hated herself, considering the slightest faults she had committed in the Mohawk land as crimes against the Most High. Hence her insatiable thirst for suffering.

A short time after Easter, an accident which could have been fatal, intensified Kateri's desire to live a life of penance. One day in the forest, she felled a tree which came down sooner than she expected.[6] She barely avoided the trunk, but could not stay clear of a huge branch which hit her on the head and threw her to the ground, unconscious. Witnesses reported that when she regained consciousness, she let out these words which they never forgot afterwards: "Thank you, Jesus, for coming to my help in danger." She later confided to her best friend Mary Theresa Tegaiaguenta* that from this moment on, she realized that "God had saved her life so that she might do penance for her sins."

This peaceful break in the village came to an abrupt end when the woman who had felt cheated by Kateri in the woods during the hunting season went to Fr. Frémin to lodge her complaint.[7]

Even if the priest knew Kateri Tekakwitha well and was aware of how she loathed impurity, he was not ignorant concerning human weakness. He therefore listened attentively to this aggravated woman, who was otherwise one of the most levelheaded and virtuous persons around. He also decided to question Kateri.

In the little corner of the church where the missionary received the faithful, he informed her of the story he had been told and exhorted her to avoid indecent behaviour at all cost. Kateri simply denied the accusation, without getting upset, knowing she was innocent. Surely her calmness should have justified her in the priest's mind, but it didn't. Shortly after, Anastasia Tegonhatsiongo joined in and strongly exhorted her to remedy the evil, if there was any, or at least to avoid it. The accuser, and a few other women who had, in some way, heard about the priest's stand on the matter, still regarded her as a loose woman.

In the land of the Mohawks, one of her aunts had once accused her falsely of committing incest with her uncle. Here however, in this land of faith, Kateri had never imagined that she would be implicated in such a fuss on account of allegations by fervent Christians. She had never felt so hurt. What was worse than anything was that the Father didn't seem to believe her, and even went as far as treating her as though she were guilty!

Kateri Tekakwitha had abandoned her family, her country and all the advantages she might have found in a good marriage. All she had left to sacrifice was her honour and reputation, and then she would have given everything to the Lord. She did so heroically, and thus became confirmed in her personal intent to vow her virginity. She kept this a secret however, and it was only at times of repeated persecutions such as this one that she felt compelled to affirm herself more and more.

The only revenge Kateri took on her accuser was to pray for her. Every one realized after a while that the accused had not complained about anyone and that she had only said what was needed to make the truth known. Her attitude finally persuaded those who had misjudged her and the honest hunter who had fallen asleep near her, to realize their mistake. The wonders which would occur after Kateri's death, a few years later, would provide all her accusers the opportunity to recall her charity, patience, devotion and good example. The overly suspicious wife wept over her fault for more than three years. She could not be consoled, thinking that Our Lord would never forgive her. The missionary had to use all his authority to free her from her mistaken belief and restore peace to her soul.

In the spring of 1678, Kateri came to know Mary Theresa Tegaiaguenta.[8] This first meeting was to mark the rest of their lives. Up until then, Kateri only had old Anastasia as a mother and mistress in the spiritual life. The woman, however, was getting on in age and could no longer do much for her. Besides, Kateri had outgrown her and needed a younger friend, eager to strive for holiness.

Mary Theresa was between twenty-eight and thirty years old. She had a fiery temper, prone to excesses in good as well as evil, as we have seen in the previous chapter. Her first contact with the Mohawk virgin would change her forever.

In replacement of the bark longhouse which had been used as a chapel since the Mission had moved upstream in 1676, the Jesuit Fathers had started building a chapel twenty-five feet wide and sixty feet long. After the spring showers had cleared the snow off the ground, they pressed on for the work to continue and had a carpenter finish the walls. One day, Mary Theresa went for a stroll near this spot and ended up entering the chapel. Kateri did the same and spoke to her for the first time. "Where will the women sit?" she asked. Mary Theresa replied by showing her the place where she thought they would sit. To this Kateri responded that "this wooden chapel was really not what God wanted the most, but that He wanted to live within us. She felt she did not deserve to be in the church with the others since she had very often driven Our Lord out of her heart and that she deserved to be expelled from the church with the dogs."

Mary Theresa, who did not yet know Kateri, was struck by the humility with which her future friend spoke to her, with tears in her eyes. These words of grace and life convinced her that God had sent her Kateri to transform her by her good advice and her admirable example. Little by little, they confided their most intimate thoughts to each other and, to be more at ease to talk, made their way toward the Cross which stood on the bank of the Saint Lawrence River.

Mary Theresa told the story of her disorderly life and of the traumatic experience she had suffered during the winter hunt, less than two years before. Kateri, in turn, told her about the visit of the three Jesuits in her village in the

107

Mohawk canton, in 1667, about her Baptism on Easter Sunday 1676 in Caughnawaga, and about her escape the following year. She also revealed her faults to Mary Theresa, especially her acts of vanity as a child, when she wore necklaces, bracelets, finger and ear rings, wide purple and white wampum sashes and oilskin ribbons. She then told her about the tree accident, which had made her especially aware that she must do penance for the sins of the past life. In response to this, Mary Theresa confided to her that she too had had a strange experience, one day, when she had climbed to the top of a birch tree to cut off bark, which she needed for her work. Looking down at a pile of rocks at the foot of the tree, she had been frightened, and at the same time, ashamed of fearing death more than hell. With tears clouding her eyes, she added that another time, filled with indignation against herself because of her sins, she had hit her hands with small branches.

This was the beginning of a friendship which was to last forever, a friendship based on their common desire to do penance for their past faults. "Since I directed both of them," wrote Fr. Cholenec, "they submitted their union to me and asked for my approval, which I willingly granted them, as I saw nothing but good coming from it for them."[9]

From this day on, they lived in union of heart and were inseparable. They were usually seen together working in the woods or in the fields. They hardly mingled with the other women, not because they didn't care for them, but because they didn't wish to be involved in their arguments or to listen to the village gossip, which would have distracted them from thinking about God.

Kateri was progressing with her new companion. She therefore went to the longhouse of the Oneida woman, one evening, to talk about spiritual things and prepare their weekly confession.[10] They decided to improve on it with a common penance. Mary Theresa, who had already invented a punishment for herself with small branches, suggested this means to Kateri,[11] who immediately went out to the cemetery to cut a handful of little sticks. Having returned to Mary Theresa's house, she hid her bundle of sticks under the mat on which they sat. At the sound of the bell, the two friends urged the other occupants of the longhouse to leave for the Benediction of the Blessed Sacrament. Alone at last, they shut the door and Kateri fell on her knees and begged Mary Theresa not to spare her. The Oneida woman refused, for fear that there would not be enough time left for her. But Kateri persuaded her to perform this act of charity toward her for she was too weak to do it herself.[12] This is how they scourged each other, "intermingling prayer and penance", after which they ran to the church, their hearts overflowing with joy. Vespers seemed to them shorter than ever. They had never felt happier in their lives.

After this experience, the two partners finding mortification most satisfying, resolved to choose a place where they could continue to scourge each other as Our Lord was scourged during His Passion. After looking around for a place, they found in the middle of the cemetery a wooden shelter with an open door. It belonged to a Frenchman who lived in La Prairie and used it for his dealings with the Indians. From then on, they went discreetly to this dismal place every Saturday to prepare their confession. Their preparation would begin with an act of contrition or another prayer which they had learnt from the missionaries, or else they would improvise one from their own hearts. Then Kateri would kneel down and expose her shoulders to be scourged.

She always complained that Mary Theresa did not hit her hard enough and begged her to exert more energy, even though blood came out after the third lash. When they had to stop because they were out of breath, they would begin reciting the Rosary of the Holy Family, interrupting it several times to give each other five lashes. "Towards the end, however, their devotion knew no bounds."[13] Their uncompromising love inspired Kateri to reveal the feelings of her heart. "My Jesus," she should say, "I must take a risk with you; I love you, but I offended you. I am here to satisfy your justice. Please, Oh my God, discharge your anger on me." Sometimes she could not say any more, but her tears would express her feelings. She would often add: "I am extremely touched by the three nails which fixed our Lord to the Cross; yet they are but an image of my sins." Such words would deeply affect her companion, who in turn would beg Kateri to chastise her. They did all these things in the greatest secrecy for about one year.

Mary Theresa Tegaiaguenta later assured the missionaries that in these moments, Kateri confessed her sins. Fr. Chauchetière reported that "she could find nothing more serious weighing on her conscience than the cowardly life she had lived since her Baptism, which consisted in not resisting those who drove her to the fields to work on Sundays and feast days, and in having a greater fear of death than of sin." These were the imperfections which led Kateri to become a great penitent.

A contemporary of Kateri, Mother Marie de l'Incarnation, was convinced that she was the dregs of the world, the most despicable person on earth, the weakest and vilest of all creatures. Similarly, Kateri considered herself the greatest sinner in the village. Jacques Maritain, the philosopher, explained that "the saints accuse themselves in this way, not so much out of a scrupulous conscience as out of a crushing ontological insight of human frailty in light of God's unfathomable grandeur and beauty, and of the abyss of sorrow into which His mercy has sent His Son to save us."

Notes 14

1. VCT, p. 26-9.

2. La vie du R.P. Pierre Joseph Marie CHAUMONOT, de la Compagnie de Jésus, missionaire de la Nouvelle France, écrite par lui-même par ordre de son Supérieur, l'an 1688. Nouvelle York, Isle Manate, A la Press Cramoisy de Jean-Marie Shea, M. DCCC.LVIII.

3. JR, vol. 63, p. 186-7.

4. VCT, p. 27.

5. VCT, p. 28.

6. VCT, p. 29-30.

7. VCT, p. 23.

8. VBCT, p. 77-9; VCT, p. 30-3.

9. VCT, p. 34.

10. VBCT, p. 92-5.

11. VBCT, p. 92.

12. JR, p. 62, p. 176.

13. VBCT, p. 94-5.

15

Montreal

Being well provided for by the spiritual guidance available to her in the village, by the support of the Confraternity of the Holy Family and by the stimulating companionship of Mary Theresa, Kateri was making rapid progress.

During the summer of 1678, the two new friends had the opportunity to visit the town of Montreal.[1] They crossed the Saint Lawrence River below the rapids and landed in Montreal. They went down to the commune of Pointe-à-Callières, known today as Point Saint Charles. Several times a year, four or five hundred Indians from the High Lands came to Montreal, bringing beaver and marten pelts, and rushed to the bargain booths where attractive goods were sold. At the time when Kateri set foot on shore, however, there was no trafficking going on. Fr. Cholenec would not have wished to expose her to the crowds of natives coming from everywhere, or to the whites who came from more than sixty leagues away to get some distraction from the hum-drum of their ordinary lives.

In those days, Ville-Marie was still in its very beginnings. The population of Montreal did not exceed six hundred. They all lived on the plateau which extended between the Saint Lawrence and the Small River (which later became Craig Street). Small houses stood in rows stretching along Saint Paul, Notre Dame and Saint James Streets, which were parallel to the river. A few cross streets enabled one to go from one street to another.

Kateri spent a few days on the island and was able to visit the French village. At approximately four hundred feet east of the dwellings, rose the chapel of Notre-Dame-de-Bon-Secours built by order of Marguerite Bourgeoys. The bell tower released the high-pitched tones of a one hundred pound bell, cast from the debris of a canon which had served to protect the French settlers against Iroquois attacks. Our two travellers most probably visited the sanctuary in which Our Lady of Montaigu* waited for her children.

Kateri visited the Hôtel-Dieu,[2] then on Saint Paul Street, next to the residence of the Sisters Hospitallers of Saint Joseph*, a congregation founded by Jérôme Le Royer de la Dauversière*, founder of Montreal. She prayed fervently in the chapel, the same one where the pioneer of the Indian village, Francis Xavier Tonsahoten and his wife, Catherine Gandeaktenha, had attended Mass on Christmas day in 1667.

In the wards of the hospital, among the ten sisters or so caring for the sick, were the first two Hospitallers who had come to Montreal in 1659, Catherine Macé and

Judith Moreau de Brésoles. The latter was one of the founders of the Confraternity of the Holy Family, of which Kateri was a member. Fr. Cholenec summarized as follows the young Mohawk woman's impression of the Hôtel-Dieu:

"Having spent a few days in Montreal, where she saw religious sisters for the first time, she was so enchanted by their piety and modesty that she inquired with great curiosity about the way these holy women lived and about the virtues they practised."

When they returned to the village, Kateri and Mary Theresa wanted to imitate in their own way the Hospitallers of Saint Joseph. Since they knew very little about their way of life, Mary Theresa suggested that they consult a Christian woman of old stock, a Huron of the Mission of Our Lady of Lorette. This Indian woman, named Marie Skarichions,[3] had been living at the Saint Francis Xavier Mission for a few years. She was a fervent Christian, who willingly accepted to join them.

These three women met soon afterwards near the Cross[5] where Kateri and Mary Theresa had talked when they first met. Marie Skarichions*, who was thought by the other two to be well versed in the ways of Christian perfection, was the first to speak. Once before, when she was sick in Quebec, she had had the opportunity to see the Augustinian Hospitallers at work; she may have known Sister Catherine de Saint-Augustin, the great mystic whom Bishop de Laval held in high esteem because of her virtue and discretion. Therefore she proposed to her new friends a few means of holiness borrowed from the Hospitallers of Quebec: these three companions were never to separate; they were to dress in the same manner, and if possible, live in the same longhouse.

While they were talking, their eyes wandered on the great river flowing at their feet. They caught sight of Heron Island*, which looked like a huge vessel anchored amid the rushing waters. They chose it at once as their favourite spot. Kateri saw it as a suitable place to fulfil her dreams of solitude.

This island, which can only be accessed from its lower end, forces those wishing to set foot on it to do so with utmost precautions, because of the tossing and spuming waters which have just passed the rapids. Back in 1611, Champlain and some of his sailors decided to go hunting on this island, which was then inhabited by herons. They had a fruitful hunt, but when they returned to their boat filled with game, the spuming waters sunk it and one of the sailors drowned.

The sight of this jewel of the Saint Lawrence stirred the imagination of our three fervent women. They were already, in spirit, building their little hermitage. The inhospitable shores of the island would serve them as a fence, and the thick brush would protect them from prying eyes. With tears in her eyes, Kateri thanked the Huron woman for initiating such a plan and begged her to continue helping her with suggestions.

All three of them decided to submit their plan of spiritual life to Fr. Frémin, superior of the Mission, in order to obtain his approval. Who was delegated? Probably Mary Theresa, who was efficient in carrying out business. The priest gently chuckled at this wonderful plan, but explained to Mary Theresa the reasons why he could not allow them to fulfill their beautiful dream. They were too young in the faith, this way of life was too unusual, Heron Island was too far from the Mission and the young men who canoed back and forth between Montreal and the south shore would constantly be in their house. He could have added another reason: since 1674, the Congregation of Notre Dame owned the island.[6] Mary Theresa returned to her two friends sheepishly and reported Fr. Frémin's decision; without grumbling they stopped thinking about their monastery on Heron Island, conceding that the priest was probably right.

From then on, Fr. Frémin realized that Kateri needed further instruction. One day, as the young Indian woman went to ask him if it was necessary to get married in order to be a good Christian - which is what Anastasia kept telling her - the missionary took the opportunity to explain to her the different states of life. When Kateri heard him say that God leaves to each one the freedom to marry or not, "she was overjoyed and had no further hesitation in choosing the state of life for which God had destined her."[7]

Fr. Frémin also gave her a few special rules of life which he did not give the others, in particular to stay home during the summer instead of following the others to the shore to see the Ottawas arrive. He also forbade her to go to Montreal.

This period of calm and great enrichment for Kateri did not last long. Her adopted sister, who was the mistress of her own hearth in Anastasia's longhouse, thought that being her elder, she was entitled to direct her in all things, even more so since her husband was the one providing for all the needs of the longhouse. Of course, Kateri was never reluctant to work and contributed enough in terms of food, but clothing was more difficult to come by. Therefore she had to get married,[8] and since everyone held her in esteem because of her well-known wisdom and piety, there would be too many suitors to choose from. A good hunter would provide abundantly for all the family's needs.

Kateri's sister anticipated some difficulty, for the young woman's resistance to marriage was well known; those around her knew how she had been assailed in the past, in her homeland, because of this, and how forceful her opposition had been. She thought long and hard about the motives which were most likely to exert power over her sister's mind and heart, and hoped to obtain her consent by dint of serious reasons, which she prepared like arrows in a quiver. One day she addressed her with many signs of affectation and spoke to her with the common sense and eloquence proper to Native Indians, especially when their interests were at stake.

"Kateri, my dear sister, you must agree that you are greatly obligated to Our Lord for taking you, as well as ourselves, out of our miserable country and for bringing you to the Sault, where you can work out your salvation in peace of mind, without anything to trouble you in your devotions. If you are happy to be here, so am I to have you near me, and you make me even happier by the wisdom of your conduct, which earns you the approval and esteem of the whole village. There is one more thing for you to do, which will make me perfectly content, and you, perfectly happy: you must think seriously of settling down in a good and solid marriage. This is what every girl does among us; you are old enough and you need to do this, like the others, to avoid the occasions of sin and to provide for the necessities of life. Your brother-in-law and myself have been happy, up until now, to provide for you; but you know he is not getting any younger and we have a large family. If, through some misfortune, we ever came to fail you, where would you turn? Believe me, my sister, save yourself from the misfortunes which result from poverty for both the soul and the body, and think seriously about preventing them while it is so easy and advantageous for you to do so, both for yourself and for your whole family, which desires it."

A dark silence hovered between the two women. Kateri did not expect such a proposal, and her attachment to her elder sister made her hide her sadness. She thanked her for her wise advice, and since this was a decision of consequence, she promised to think about it. This gave her sister the impression the victory was half won.

All to the contrary, Kateri's first reaction was to go and knock on Fr. Cholenec's door to complain about these annoying pleas. The priest received her with kindness and answered:

"Kateri, this matter is under your control; it is solely up to you to decide; but think about it, it is worth it."

"Oh! Father," she said immediately and without hesitation, "I cannot give in to this; I dislike men and I have the utmost aversion to marriage; this is not possible."

The missionary saw clearly that there was more to this rebuff than a merely natural reluctance, and wanted to probe further the convictions of the one under his guidance. He, therefore, insisted on the excellent reasons put forward by Kateri's adopted sister, to which the young Mohawk virgin declared to him straight out: "I am not afraid of the poverty with which they threaten me; it takes so little to provide for the needs of this miserable life that my work will be enough to take care of it, and I will surely find a few lousy rags to clothe myself."[9] After these words, the priest then sent her away, with the advice to think about it seriously.

Kateri had not yet totally revealed her thoughts to her director, who later realized that her decision was already made. She was living in a perfect way in her current state, but she was not satisfied. Deep in her heart, her fiery desire always to seek what would make her more pleasing to God, told her that there was something better than the common life in the village.

No sooner had she returned home, when her adopted sister, unaware of the latest events, pestered her for an answer. She figured Kateri had had enough time to make a decision. To end the matter once and for all, the younger sister declared to her outright that she renounced marriage, that she would not run short of clothing for yet a long time, and that she would work in order not to be a burden to her, to her husband, or to anyone.

"What! my sister," said the other, all upset by such a discourse, "where does such a strange resolve come from? Did you give enough thought to what you are saying? Have you ever seen any such thing or heard of such an example among Iroquois girls? Where did you get the idea of this new fantasy? Don't you see that you will expose yourself to the mockery of men and to the temptations of the devil? Will you be the first to do what no girl has yet been able to do among us? Abandon these thoughts, my dear sister; don't be overly confident in your strength and walk in the ordinary way with all the other girls."

Kateri was unmoved. She replied that she had no fear of the mockery of men, that she would do no wrong intentionally and that she trusted in the grace of God to resist the temptations of hell. She concluded by begging her sister not to bring up this matter again. The elder sister did not dare approach her about marriage any more, but she confided her concern to Anastasia Tegonhatsiongo, whom they both considered as their mother. She immediately won the mistress of the longhouse to her cause. Kateri's resolve was quite unusual, although there had been is the past a few Iroquois women who had lived like the Roman vestals.

Anastasia who was a wise and prudent woman, tried her best to get her protégée to change her mind. She feared Kateri might have made such a decision too hastily and may regret it later. She, therefore, insisted for her to accept getting married. Contrary to her custom, Kateri replied wryly that "if she had such a regard for marriage, let her get married; as for herself, it would give her great pleasure if they never mentioned it to her again. No man in the world would ever be of any use to her. She then went back to Fr. Cholenec's house to tell him how "her mother and sister" were after her to get married. This is when she declared openly to him her intent to vow her virginity.

Greatly moved, the priest invited her to take three days to think about this decision, three days of prayer for enlightenment from above. He, himself, would join in her quest and discernment. After this triduum, if she persisted in her resolve, her spiritual father promised to put an end to the importunities of her relatives.

Kateri listened attentively to the advice of the priest and accepted his instructions willingly, but less than a quarter of an hour later, she was already back. This was plenty of time, she thought, to deliberate on a choice she had already made long ago. She told the missionary "that this was it: she could no longer go on with these uncertainties". She declared to him "plainly that she renounced marriage in order to have no other spouse but Jesus Christ and that she would count herself fortunate to live in poverty and misery for His love."

Fr. Cholenec no longer raised any opposition to her intent, which seemed to be inspired by the Holy Spirit. He then added that neither he "nor the other missionaries who would be at the Sault" would ever abandon her, nor would they allow her to lack anything. "With these few words," said the missionary, "I freed the soul of Kateri from a strange purgatory and, on the contrary, placed her in a kind of paradise; from that moment on, she truly entered into the joy of the Lord and began to experience such great peace, rest and contentment in the depth of her soul that even her outward appearance was completely changed. What is most remarkable is that this peace, rest and contentment lasted till her last breath without anything being able to alter it from then on."

"She thanked me in most affectionate words, and then went away the happiest person in the world. I remained in awe at such a heroic resolve, filled with veneration for the one who had the courage to carry it out and with tremendous joy at the sight of the goodness of God, who had provided the Mission with such a wonderful model of holiness."

Kateri had barely left when Anastasia came hurriedly to him, her face all tensed up. Her protégée no longer listened to anyone and only did as she pleased. The priest interrupted her and reproached her for her attitude towards the one who deserved the highest praise. Was not God doing her a great honour by choosing a young woman of her longhouse to be consecrated to Him?

At these words, the elderly Indian woman, whose faith was well known to all, recovered her senses, as though she woke up from a deep sleep. She blamed herself for not understanding sooner the generosity of Kateri. From this day on, she treated her with all her affection and admiration, and was always the first to support her in this new way of life. She succeeded in inspiring the same sentiments to Kateri's adopted sister.

During this peculiar struggle, Kateri had had the support of her faithful companion, Mary Theresa, who was more than ever her attentive confidante. The Oneida woman, stimulated by Kateri's fervour, also manifested an unusual courage in trying to follow her. Thus the two of them communicated support, courage and fervour to each other, which led them to walk steadily in the path of faith.

Notes 15

1. PO, Doc. XII, p. 272.

2. VCT, p. 38.

3. VBCT, p. 80-1.

4. JR, vol. 58, p. 154-8; JR, vol. 60, p. 90-2.

5. VBCT, p. 80-2.

6. Prise de possession de L'JSle au heron par les filles de la congregation de Montréal, le 2 mars 1674. Archives judiciaires de Montréal, No 1003.

7. VBCT, p. 82-4.

8. VCT, p. 35-43.

9. PO, Doc. XII, p. 267-8.

16

No More Red Shawl

At the end of August 1678, a few villagers went to see Fr. Frémin to tell him they had had a good crop[1] on an island of the river. Three times before, they had sown corn in this place, and every year the worms had devoured everything before the first green sprouts had had a chance to grow. The thought of abandoning those fields had occurred to them, buy they had not been able to make up their minds. They had asked the priest, one day, to bless this miserable land. The missionary had gone to the place, and moved by the faith of these poor people kneeling around him, had recited the prayers of the Church for a good crop. Now, a plentiful harvest was ready to be picked; there were more ears of corn in this field than in any other. This looked promising for the winter; it would enable them to feed the many immigrants and adventurers from the cantons. They remembered the shortage of food caused by the influx of visitors the previous year.

For the last few years, indeed, Hot Ashes, the Great Mohawk and Stephen had been going to preach in Iroquois land, bringing back to the Sault a good number of converts. Fr. Frémin who had previously baptized about seventeen people a year, was now baptizing up to sixty.

Obviously, the resulting loss of population in the Iroquois cantons infuriated their chiefs more than ever. Therefore, they had purposely provoked a famine at the Mission, the previous year. They had come with their men, four hundred strong. After hunting in the vicinity of Saint Francis Xavier, they had stopped in the village before setting out for the south. According to the laws of Indian hospitality, they were generously fed; moreover, the villagers filled their bags with all sorts of food. It was almost a disaster: there was not enough food left for those who didn't go to the winter hunt, and what is worse, when springtime came, there were not enough seeds to sow. This state of deprivation had the exact opposite result of what had been expected in the Iroquois land: "their fervour in time of famine won over and attracted here several people among their relatives."

That year, however, before going to preach the Good News elsewhere, it was necessary to get things in order at home, for there were four or five Frenchmen who had undertaken to run a cabaret in La Prairie, which was one and a quarter leagues from the Mission. This was a real headache for the missionaries and the fervent Indians. They had always made a rule to ban alcohol from the Mission.[2] This time, however, the merchants had the support of Governor de Frontenac.

Some fifty parishioners of the French settlement presented a petition against the cabaret owners. Fr. Chauchetière reported that "the petition having been ill received by Mr. de Frontenac, the claimants were condemned to pay a fine. They appealed to Mr. de Frontenac himself, since he had issued an ordinance four years before prohibiting cabarets and alcohol..." Finally, the Governor forbade the sale of alcohol to the natives, but permitted the operation of these bars in secret.

In spite of a few inevitable defections, the chiefs of the Mission always held their ground against the sale of alcohol. They exerted great ingenuity in countering this curse. Hot Ashes, in particular, distinguished himself by some remarkable clowning exploits. One day, a Frenchman of the island of Montreal received several Oneidas at his house. Since Hot Ashes had been their chief in the Iroquois cantons, he also was invited, and all of them began drinking to his health, purportedly to honour him. This irresponsible Frenchman had no other concern than to quench their thirst. He placed a bucket of liquor in their midst and kept filling it again as quickly as they emptied it. The Indians smoked and talked, while drinking from this inexhaustible fountain of youth.

Hot Ashes was urged to drink in order to show some enthusiasm, but he was satisfied with one or two sips. A refusal would surely have offended his hosts, who were his elders. Among the Iroquois, one must always show great regard for the elders. After having satisfied the requirements of Indian etiquette, our neophyte stopped short. Moreover, not wishing to offend God in any way, he imagined a clever trick to extricate himself from this wasp's nest. He stood up, began to dance, and pretending to be drunk, purposely stumbled and hit the bucket with his foot, spilling all the liquor on the floor. Everyone guffawed at the chief's blunder, and as they were already far into the night, they thought of nothing else but going to sleep - rather unusual behaviour for people who had started drinking.

Hot Ashes had attracted many of his people from Oneida and Cataracoui to the Mission of Saint Francis Xavier. A good number of them were converted. Seeing how much zeal and talent he had, they decided to choose him to be the fourth chief of the village.[3]

They proceeded with an election, according to custom, and then with the induction, for which there was a complex protocol. When all were assembled, the newly elected chief was invited to present himself. A fire was lit in his honour; then he was offered the calumet and given a few presents. Unfortunately, they forgot to present him with the traditional mat. After the ceremony, the new chief immediately went to complain to Fr. Frémin. They had made fun of him and treated him like a child; he was a captain without a mat and would have to hold his councils outdoors! The elders had to be convened once again to establish the new chief in proper form. After having received the insignia of his office, he conducted himself as a true chief and became the one who governed the whole village.

119

That year also, another smallpox epidemic struck the village at the beginning of autumn. Kateri who had already suffered from this disease as a child, was spared. Fortunately, to everyone's amazement, few people at the Mission died, while in the Iroquois cantons, they died in hundreds. The new converts realized once and for all what well trained Christians already knew: from then on, they no longer believed in this nonsense about faith and Baptism causing people to die.

Once the epidemic was over, they got ready to set out for the great winter hunt. The previous year, because of her first communion which was to take place at Christmas, Kateri had delayed her departure for the hunt until January. Now, however, in spite of the invitation of the hunters and their wives and in spite of the fact that life in the woods was considerably more pleasant and the food more varied and plentiful, Kateri firmly refused to follow them.[4]

Fr. Cholenec knew the real reasons for this decision; he knew why Kateri would not go to the woods. First of all because she would be deprived of spiritual support, especially the presence of Jesus in the Eucharist, and besides, she had not forgotten the mess in which she had been embroiled the previous winter because of her devotedness. Her marked inclination for the contemplative life contrasted with the tendency to austerity of the most fervent Christian women of the Mission, who performed so many extravagant acts of penance to atone for the faults of their past lives. These women preferred to go away to the hunt, far from the eyes of the missionaries who forbade them those kinds of excessive penance. "In the woods at least," they said, "I am the mistress of my own body!"

Convinced, however, that a change of air and food would do wonders for the health of his spiritual daughter, the missionary weighed the pros and cons. He called her in and advised her to follow her people to the hunt. Upon which she burst out laughing. Then, after a moment of silence, she answered: "Oh! Father, it is true that there is plenty of food for the body in the woods, but the soul languishes and starves to death there; while in the village, if the body suffers a little because it is not so well fed, the soul is fully satisfied, being closer to Our Lord. Therefore I abandon this miserable body to hunger and to all that may happen as a result, as long as my soul is content and has its usual food."

In view of the young woman's determination, the Jesuit stopped insisting. Kateri remained in the village and prepared for the feast of Saint Francis Xavier, on December 3rd. Bishop de Laval had given this holy patron to New France in 1667. On this occasion, Kateri intensified her life of prayer and, Fr. Chauchetière wrote, entered "into renewed fervour."[5]

Christmas was drawing near. Snow had already fallen on the roofs of the longhouses and of the little church, and there were heaps of it in the road and paths of the village. Kateri already had her presents for the New-Born Child: the poverty which she had tried to practice all through the year; her interior sufferings when she had been falsely accused; the efforts she had exerted in her struggle against her sister and old Anastasia who wanted her to marry; the sacrifice she had made by renouncing the joy of starting a family, in which she might have lived in security, protected against hunger and need.

To these presents which she already had in store, she added new ones. She gave up glossing her hair with grease, wearing wampum ornaments, so highly valued by young women her age, lovely blouses, well trimmed leggings and neat moccasins. She would have liked to cut her hair, but stopped short of doing so for fear of what people would say. She also deprived herself of the red "blanket" usually worn by her companions and adopted a blue one, which was new and quite simple, and with which she also covered her head to protect her eyes, contrary to other women who wore it on their shoulders.

These offerings of the heart formed a soft cradle to receive the Divine Infant. The young Indian woman was, therefore, especially showered with heavenly blessings on that feast of the Nativity of 1678. She was so "filled with God and savoured such sweetness in His possession that her whole exterior appearance was transfigured by it; in these moments; a fiery glow radiated from her eyes, her gestures and her words, and one needed not be with her for long before being moved and warmed by this divine fire."[6]

Thus provided with all the richness and strength from above, she was to encounter fully what she implicitly sought since her conversion, "crosses for the flesh and all the sweetness of heaven for the spirit."[7]

Notes 16

1. JR, vol. 63, p. 194-206.

2. Ibid. Ch. 10, p. 116.

3. OCI, p. 115-25.

4. VCT, p. 44-7

5. VBCT, p. 83-4.

6. VCT, p. 54.

7. VCT, p. 45.

17

The Devotion of a Whole Village

If a few people, such as Kateri, Mary Theresa and Marie Skarichions succeeded in hiding their individual acts of penance out of discretion, it was hardly possible for a whole village to do so.

In those days, indeed, the spiritual atmosphere of the Mission was one of fervour and mortification.[1] The Indians had feelings of self-hatred for the sins of their past lives, which had caused the sufferings of Christ. They manifested their indignation by inflicting upon themselves all sorts of heroic acts of penance to "avenge upon their bodies the insults which God received from sinners."[2] The men scourged themselves mercilessly several times a week till blood came; some of them wore an iron chain around their bodies while they felled trees or cut wood all day. One of the chiefs, the Great Mohawk, girded himself in this way every Friday and one the eve of holy days of obligation. The Huron, Paul Honoguenhag, first dogique of the village, did the same. Stephen, whom the Fathers called "the good Israelite", was of such austere virtue that his mere presence evoked the presence of God.

The women would not let themselves be surpassed by the men. Several of them wore penitential belts, after the example of the sisters of Montreal and Quebec. To the practices of their husbands and sons, they added some terrible acts of mortification. One would roll in the snow; another, strip to the waist and expose herself to the rigors of winter on the bank of the great river for the time it took to recite a Rosary in Iroquois. "Others went even further; after breaking the ice with an axe, they would plunge into the waters of ponds and rivers up to the neck in the worst cold of winter." For Stephen's wife, Anne, it was not enough to immerse herself in the icy water of the river, she also plunged her three year old daughter Marie in it. Fr. Cholenec reprimanded her severely for this, and when he asked her why she had done it, she answered naïvely that she feared that when her daughter grew up, she would become lax and fall into sin. This is why she had her do penance in advance!

Even though external penance is not a sure sign of holiness, we can believe it was in the case of these Christians, said Fr. Cholenec, for their lives corresponded to this ideal. "They lived in great innocence, union and charity, especially towards the poor and the sick. Not only did they strive for their personal salvation, they also had zeal for the salvation of their compatriots who came to the Sault, either to visit them or to live among them; they could be seen instructing them all day and late into the night."

She renounces wearing all these porcelain ornaments so well cherished by girls of her age.

The members of the Confraternity of the Holy Family were especially careful to protect the good morals of the Mission against the assaults of unbelievers.

It was now one year since Marie from Onondaga* had been converted. She still practised the most extravagant acts of penance. Shortly after becoming a Christian, she had spent most of the night "cutting up her flesh with a knife, with blood flowing from every part of her body, without her being affected at all by it. As a result, she was in great discomfort for several days, unable to sit or lie down."[3]

This young woman, who was intelligent and attractive, and only twenty-four years old, belonged to one of the most prominent families of her country. She was obsessed by the sins of her past and by the pictures representing the four last things - death, judgment, hell and heaven. In his catechetical instructions, Fr. Cholenec used pictures illustrating the power of Satan over sinners, similar to the ones seen, then, at the Seminary of Quebec. In no way was Marie going to let the devil get the upper hand of her. She chastised her body with intense scourging for having offended God. "My body," she would say in these moments, "you took pleasure in committing sin. Accept, now, being chastised. I deserved hell for obeying you, and I would have been there long ago if it were not for the mercy of God. Therefore, obey me now, that I may bring you with me, one day, to paradise."[4]

Having stayed in the village, like Kateri, during the hunting season, Marie confessed her sins regularly every eight days, and wept continuously at the tribunal of Penance, as well as before the Blessed Sacrament and in the privacy of her longhouse.

She often stayed in her longhouse, with her three adorable little ones, whom she loved with all her heart. Her children were the "most well-mannered of the village". Moreover, she was pregnant with a fourth child; for this reason, the Fathers forbade her to wear the "belt" which she was insistently asking permission to wear, for she was not satisfied with the many scourgings she inflicted upon herself.

She too sometimes escaped the vigilance of the missionaries. One day, undoubtedly out of spite, she buried herself "naked in the snow for three consecutive nights in the most severe Canadian cold, taking pleasure in rolling in it, though she was pregnant, in order to make her body bear the punishment of the disorders of her past."[6] By dint of tears and moaning, her interior and exterior acts of penance gradually ruined her health.

Kateri progressed by leaps and bounds, like a deer, in this exceptional atmosphere. She adopted the motto: "Who will teach me what is most agreeable to God that I may do it?" She, therefore, complained frequently to Mary Theresa that the Father was keeping things from her which he made others practise.[7] Her "keen and lively mind" soon made her discover part of it and she must have guessed the rest, for her spiritual father admitted that, "to satisfy her," he had to give her a scourge[8] and a small iron belt with long points "which she used to satisfy her extreme thirst for suffering. If I had left her on her own in this matter," said the priest, "she would soon have surpassed all the others; but as her strength did not equal her courage, it was necessary to curb the latter in order not to exhaust the former. Even with all the precautions I took, she nevertheless, at times, escaped my vigilance, as it happened that same winter, on the feast of the Purification."[9]

On that day, also called Candlemas, Kateri wanted to imitate in her own way the procession which took place at the church in honour of Our Lady. She could thus give the blessed Mother of her Saviour a token of her love. She walked around the perimeter of her field, which was quite large, reciting her Rosary several times and sinking in snow up to her waist. Fr. Cholenec, her director, who recounted this imprudent action of Kateri, said that she did this quite naturally, without even thinking that she should have discussed it with him beforehand.

Kateri's devotion to the Virgin Mother grew more and more intense.[10] She realized more perfectly each day the ideal proposed to the members of the Confraternity of the Holy Family and of the Slavery of the Blessed Virgin.[11] This was truly a slavery of love like that which carried Saint Paul to the third heaven. She recited her beads several times a day, savouring the mysteries. In addition to her Rosary, she used the rosary of the Holy Family. On Sundays, she took part in the meetings of the Confraternity, at which the members examined whether the rules were properly observed and whether there was any good they might do and any evil they might prevent. At three o'clock, she joined the rest of the faithful who recited or chanted the Rosary in two choirs. The young woman carried her rosary everywhere she went. She never forgot to recite the Angelus, whether she was in the fields or in the woods. At nightfall, after the evening prayer in her longhouse, she recited the Litany of the Blessed Virgin by heart. From her lips fell the melodious Iroquois words: "Takwentenr, Sewenniio: Lord, have mercy... Wari saiatatokenti, takwaterennaienhas: Holy Mary, pray for us!"

Warihne, Mary's day, that is Saturday, she allowed herself some severe acts of mortification to prepare for her confessions. After receiving absolution, she attended the blessing of Mary, a ceremony comprised of Marian prayers and hymns, and culminated by the blessing of the faithful with a small statue of Our Lady.

No visions or exceptional revelations threw Kateri in the arms of Mary. She never enjoyed any apparitions of the Blessed Virgin, like Jérôme Le Royer la Dauversière, founder of Montreal, like Jeanne Ouendite*, the young Huron woman of Ancienne Lorette, on April 14th, 1688, or like Martin Skandegonrhaksen, the young Mohawk of the Mission who died in December 1675. Her love of Mary sprang from her exquisite purity. Fr. Cholenec made no mistake about it: "From this source came her tender love of Our Lady, the Queen of virgins and the Mother of purity."[12]

Purity certainly was Kateri's most characteristic virtue, "that which most greatly enhances her merit", said Fr. Cholenec.

This virtue may be understood in its primary sense, which is the simple absence of sin, or else in its secondary sense, which is the shunning of the sin of impurity itself. We can admire it in Kateri in both senses of the word.

We tend to place more emphasis on the second sense of the word, but it seems that bodily purity was not a real problem for the Mohawk virgin, for "she had never fallen into this sin,"[13] even in the Mohawk country, said Fr. Chauchetière. Concerning the period of her life at the Sault, here is a no less convincing testimony of Fr. Cholenec : "I say this and I repeat it untiringly, it is a miracle of grace which cannot be understood in Kateri, that she spent more than twenty years of her life amid the corruption of her country and two years and a half at the Sault, a virgin in body and soul, without ever experiencing, in all this time, the least feeling contrary to this virtue, neither in her body nor in her soul. This, I say, seems unbelievable, and yet it is very true."[14]

On the other hand, what Kateri always fought for, all through her short life, was purity of heart. She always considered herself a sinner before God who is thrice holy, even though she was of "angelic innocence." "I don't believe she ever offended God by mortal sin," said her spiritual father. "I will say even more, she abhorred sin to such an extent and was so vigilant in order to preserve herself from it that I am not aware, in the two and a half years she lived at the Sault, that she ever wilfully committed any fault of a serious nature. She was so careful to avoid the least fault. This is what we call being truly a saint and having perfect charity."

We might say that this purity of heart was so powerful in her that it shone even in her body. The practice of this virtue led the young Mohawk virgin even further.

Notes 17

1. VCT, p. 45-7.

2. F. Martin, S.J., Une Vierge iroquoise ou Vie de Catherine Tegakoüita, ronéo, p. 70.

3. Extraict d'une lettre du Père Cholenec contenant le Récit de la Ste Vie et pénitences extraordinaire de quelques femmes sauvagesses, escrittes de St-François-Xavier du Sault proche le Montréal au mois de febrerier 1680, Séminaire de Québec, p. 31.

4. EPC, p. 37.

5. EPC, p. 39.

6. EPC, p. 31.

7. VBCT, p. 76.

8. Vx, Whip used as instrument of penance, Petit Larousse in colors Paris, 1988.

9. VCT, p. 49.

10. P., Dox. XII, p. 253-4; VBCT, p. 99-100.

11. JR, vo. 58, p. 86-8.

12. VCT, p. 60.

13. VBCT, p. 39.

14. VCT, p. 59.

18

Kateri's Vow

Jesus Christ Himself initiated the world to virginity. At the time of Abraham, marriage did not even exclude polygamy. With Moses, monogamy came to be observed. God, who is in no hurry, saved the ideal of voluntary virginity until the fullness of time, when the Son of the Virgin appeared on earth.

In his annual Chronicle of the Mission of Saint Francis Xavier, Fr. Chauchetière noted that, in 1674, there already were "young women living alone like angels, who paved the way of perpetual virginity for many.[1] There were others who had died virgins at the age of thirteen, fourteen, fifteen or twenty. Several had refused good suitors, dedicating themselves to God, body and soul, in great poverty, living on alms.[2] Another Catherine (of whom we know nothing more) had died "at the age of thirteen, having lived as innocent as an angel and died a victim for her virginity."[3] But no one had ever yet seen "what faith accomplished in Kateri; purity was depicted on her face and chastity seemed to have been born with her."[4]

One of the early biographers of Kateri wrote that she was "the first in this new world to have vowed, by the inspiration of the Holy Spirit, her virginity to Our Lord."[5] But Pope John Paul II, in his address for the beatification of Kateri, put a slight nuance to this statement by adding: "inasmuch as we know." Since then, our investigations led us to find out that, in fact, in 1679, there were already at least three Native religious sisters.

A young Huron woman, 15 years old, Sister Genevieve Agnes Skanudharoua* made her religious vows among the Augustine Sisters of the Mercy of Jesus in Quebec in 1657.[6] Some twenty years later, in Montreal, Mother Bourgeoys accepted in her Congregation the first two Indian religious of Montreal:[7] the Onondaga, Barbe Atontinon and Mary Theresa Gannensagouas*, who was born of a captive Huron father in the Seneca village.

It can be noted here, to her honour of the French, that they were the first ones to receive Natives into their ranks as religious men and women. Such was not the case everywhere else.

Kateri was now completely self-reliant and completely free of family ties. She had even been able to relax to some extent the bonds which united her so strongly with her old spiritual mother, Anastasia, and her adopted sister, after having settled, with the help of Fr. Cholenec, the last conflict over a proposal to marry. The villagers had noticed her particular conduct and sensed that her holiness was anything but common.

Ever since her trip to Montreal where she had admired the Religious Hospitallers who were consecrated to God by the vow of virginity, she had not ceased to pester Fr. Cholenec that he might allow her to "make the same sacrifice of herself."[8] Finally, after explaining the conduct of his spiritual daughter for several weeks and noting how profusely the divine Master communicated Himself to His handmaid, the missionary acquiesced to her desire to make her vow.

He wrote: "It would be difficult to express the joy this gave her and the fervour with which she disposed herself for this great act. But when the day came, this day which she so ardently desired, the happiest and most beautiful day of her life, she made an ultimate effort to offer her sacrifice to the Lord with all the piety, devotion and ardour of which she was capable."[9] As a token of her filial love of the Virgin Mary, Kateri chose the feast of the Annunciation for this great event.

There was also her friend, Marie of Onondaga,[10] who aspired to complete detachment of herself. In this holy season of Lent, "she doubled her practices of penance" and was "the very first" to make a vow to Our Lord "to acknowledge as much as she could the great mercy He had shown her by taking her away from the miserable state in which she had been." On the day of Our Lady, March 25th, "she devoted and consecrated herself totally to Our Lord." And since "she may still have had some attachment for her husband and children," she also made, on that day, the sacrifice of her husband. She promised that, if she ever became a widow, she would "never have any other husband for her body than the One to whom she had consecrated her soul." She made this vow in spite of all the opposition she anticipated on this point, on the part of her family, clan and tribe, "especially since she was still in her prime" - she was only twenty four years of age.

Marie's oblation engaged her future, but it was mainly an offering of the heart since she was still married, and therefore, had a husband to provide for her needs. Kateri's case was different. Virginal chastity is such a great gift that some have compared it to the state of the angels of heaven.

When the moment came, one can imagine how this chaste young woman must have withdrawn into her interior fortress. From then on, she had reached her goal. From her early youth, she had freed herself from the suitors others had tried to impose on her; today, she freely and solemnly chose Jesus Christ to be her only and eternal Spouse. She felt deeply that her vow would unite her ever more intimately to the One her heart loved, and that she would lose herself in Him.

During the last Mass, at eight o'clock, "a few moments after Jesus Christ had given Himself to her in Communion," she renounced forever all human love and all the advantages which a traditional Mohawk marriage represented, to promise God perpetual virginity and abandon herself totally to the care of His Providence for a future vowed to His service. She gave her soul to Jesus in the Eucharist and her body to Jesus crucified.[11] In the fire of her love, she prayed Iesos to become her Spouse and to accept her as His bride. Then she turned to Our Lady and prayed that she might present her to her divine Son; after which she consecrated herself to Mary, earnestly begging her to be her Mother and to take her as her daughter. She made this vow in private.

These moments of fervour "undoubtededly gave great joy to all in heaven," said Fr. Cholenec. Kateri was "overjoyed: her greatest desires had been fulfilled."

It is said of Marie of Onondaga that, since the offering of herself to Our Lord, her soul "was in almost continuous union with the divine Spouse in the Blessed Sacrament, and her body, incessantly attached to the Cross" through her continual practices of penance. Concerning Kateri, Fr. Cholenec added that "after her heroic sacrifice, she was in a euphoric state and her whole conversation was in heaven," that she "spent many hours before the altar, her spirit being totally absorbed in prayer and in perfect union with God" and that from then on, she was more ingenious than ever "in imagining new ways each day to afflict and crucify her flesh."[12]

Notes 18

1. Jr, Vol. 63, p. 186.

2. Ibid., p. 202.

3. VBCT, p. 34.

4. VBCT, p. 107.

5. VCT, p. 49.

6. AMHD-Q, LETTRES CIRCULAIRES ET NOTICES BIOGRAPHIQUES, 1641-1755, Vol. 1, Archives du monastère, Hôtel-Dieu de Québec; K, No. 116, Printemps 1989, p. 16-28.

7. Histoire de la Congrégation Notre-Dame de Montréal, t.I,C.N.D., Montréal, 1910, p. 361; t.II (1693-1700), Montréal, 1913, p. 134-44; K, ibid.

8. PO, Doc, XII, p. 272.

9. VCT, p. 51.

10. EPC, p. 35, 38, 39.

11. PO, Doc. XII, p. 274.

12. Ibid.

19

The Summer of Penance

In the summer of 1679, the last of Kateri's life, the voluntary sufferings of the young Indian woman reached their peak. As the small circle of her friends grew wider and wider and emulation encourages greater excellence, the little village was the scene of the bloodiest offerings and acts of mortification ever heard of in this new world. Although everyone always meant to act in the greatest secrecy, the truth managed to come to light.

Two newcomers at the Mission, Francis Tsonnatouan,[1] a valiant warrior called by the French "la Grosse Bûche" (the Big Log), and his wife Marguerite, intrigued by what was said quietly about the behaviour of "good Kateri," sought to contact her. They wanted to get their information from a reliable source, for the young couple in their twenties wished to live according to all the requirements of their faith. No watered down Christianity for them. Knowing how shy the young woman was and how her humility would prevent her from talking, they sent for Mary Theresa at the same time as they invited Kateri to meet with them in their longhouse. The young Iroquois woman seldom went out any more, except to go to church or to work in the field, for her health was beginning to fail.

As soon as all four of them were gathered. Marguerite pulled the bear hide down in front of the entrance. The two visitors understood from this that the conversation was going to be confidential. Francis spoke "to both of them, Kateri and Theresa, saying that he knew what they were doing and the penance they had embraced." He said this in order to make them talk. Surprised by these statements, Kateri remained silent and asked Mary Theresa to answer for her. Both of them were astonished that people thus knew about their conduct. When she had first come to the Sault, Kateri had been able to penetrate the wall of silence surrounding the Christian practices of her new compatriots. Now, her own secret was uncovered - she who preferred not to mortify herself rather than appear mortified.[2] In a short time, the conversation of these proselytes moved on to the subject of what might be the most pleasing to God. Kateri and Mary Theresa not wishing to play the spiritual director, advised the couple to consult one of the Black Robes.

In fact, Francis, who was newly married, was thinking of living with his wife as brother and sister. He hoped to expiate in this way the immorality of his conduct before his Baptism. "His aversion to the sins of the flesh came from the fact that he had been overcome in the past, being an unbaptized infidel." Impressed by this visit of the Mohawk virgin, Francis, from then on, modelled himself on her, and Marguerite who was very devout, also drank to this source of living water.

Another Marguerite was beginning to draw a little too much attention to herself in the village. A member of the Confraternity of the Holy Family, Marguerite Gagouithon,[3] who was only twenty years old and very beautiful, was the wife of the oldest captain of the Mission, and her first cousin (considered in Iroquois land as her brother) was the second chief; the Fathers called him "the pillar of the Mission". Considering the twofold privilege of her noble birth and of her reputation as a Christian, the bad conduct of Marguerite, seen and known by all, was a cause of surprise, sadness and scandal in the peaceful village.

Married to an old man born during the wrong moon and who looked like an old bird of prey, and deprived of any respect or consideration on his part, she was sensitive to the compliments and advances of her compatriots. As the many good-looking young men of Saint Francis Xavier frequently turned their eyes to her, she succumbed to the provocations of one of them. The whole Confraternity of the Holy Family was very saddened at the sight of their fellow-member indulging in sin and they poured out their prayers and acts of penance for her conversion. Many holy women intensified their fervour.

Mary the Penitent,[4] who had given birth to a little Ignatius, "a child of tears and weeping, since she had carried him and given birth to him during her most fervent period of penance", came back to ask for the penance belt which had been refused to her during her pregnancy and which she used on Mondays and Fridays from early in the morning until twilight, in addition to her many scourgings. This young mother of a family also adopted an attitude which is difficult for us to understand. She prayed and offered acts of penance to ask the Lord to take her four children away from her. To Fr. Cholenec first who was astonished by this attitude, she gave "three admirable reasons. The first one, she said, is to prove to Our Lord the extent of my love by making for Him the greatest sacrifice I possibly can in this world, which is that of my children, who are what I hold dearest. The second one is that I shall then have the assurance that my children will never offend God, which is the only thing I fear for them. (...) The third one is that, having no more children and no more impediment in this respect, I shall be able more than ever to give my soul entirely to Our Lord, being detached of all my natural affections, and to plunge my body all the more into penance, not being obliged to preserve it for others."

Although Marie the Onondaga was most sincere in her prayers and we cannot doubt that her penance was genuine since she had such a great love of Our Lord, her prayer was not answered it seems; undoubtedly, God prefers to try His faithful ones in the manner of His own free choice.

Fr. Cholenec, who was the appointed spiritual guide of the Mission, had admired the conduct of the Onondaga woman ever since her conversion. On the strength of this example, he set out to approach Marguerite Gagouithon*, giving her the example of Marie, without mentioning her name. He had several conversations with her. He reminded her, as he had reminded Marie the previous year, of the four last things and gave her a tour of all the tribunals of the next world by means of pictures illustrating the tyranny of Satan against sinners. The result of these encounters was to open the eyes of Marguerite, and since she had "a keen and enlightened mind for her age," she immediately realized her sinfulness and was converted at once. She made a general confession to Fr. Frémin, her ordinary confessor, and a few days later, Fr. Cholenec, with his superior's permission, gave her holy communion secretly to avoid gossip.

Marguerite "devoted herself entirely to Our Lord at this first communion," and as the priest was about to leave after assisting her with her thanksgiving, she pulled him by his robe and, holding the little copper crucifix he had given her (as he had given Kateri and Marie), she confided to him that she had made four great promises which engaged her future. She had given up jewels, games, dancing and night amusements. We can judge what major resolutions these were when we know the "passion she had for these four things, which is not surprising for she was young and attractive, and a woman of the highest quality among the (Natives)." Marguerite did not make these resolutions lightly, and she always remained faithful to them.

Without consulting each other, Frs. Frémin and Cholenec deemed it appropriate to ask her to make a fifth resolution, which would be "a sacrifice infinitely more agreeable to God than the other four put together, i.e., whatever ill treatment she would receive from her husband, she would never tell him anything and would not come out of her longhouse."

Marguerite fulfilled this resolution willingly and was seen, in fact, going back to her longhouse in spite of the ill treatment, insults and threats of her ill-tempered husband. She became so firm and peaceful in these dreadful circumstances that it seemed that God had granted her the gift of patience in return for the sincerity and generosity with which she had devoted herself to Him.

Finally, the young convert, "becoming more and more inflamed with the love of Our Lord and the hatred of herself and her sinfulness," begged her spiritual guide instantly for instruments of penance, and the missionary deemed it appropriate to grant her this permission. These were his reasons why:

"Firstly, because she is robust, has never had any children and will apparently never have any. Secondly, because I considered these kinds of austere practices which holy penitents have exercised against their bodies as a very effective way for her to become completely detached of herself and everything else, and because this spirit of mortification would maintain her in the interior compunction and humility in which I saw her. Thirdly, because I had no doubt that Our Lord would bless this fervour and subsequently strengthen her youth with the extraordinary interior support which a twenty year old woman surely needs in order to persevere in the way of life she is leading."

Marguerite used these instruments, not with the Ignatian moderation which had been recommended to her, but with the fury of a true Iroquois. "She uses two kinds of instruments," said Fr. Cholenec, "a belt made with serrated wheels and a scourge. She wears the belt on her bare flesh every Tuesday, Thursday and Saturday (while Marie uses it on Mondays and Fridays). She puts it on at dawn and takes it off only at night. She is no less fervent and no less admirable in her scourging," which she practices regularly four times a week. The frequency of these scourgings increased from one month to the next.

Kateri and Mary Theresa, for their part, innovated by experimenting with fire.

One day, the wise Anastasia told Kateri that "the fire of hell scared her more than everything God uses to punish sins"[5] and that "the constancy of the martyrs who had suffered this torture to defend their faith must have been of great merit before the Lord." We also know from Mary Theresa that, when the two friends chastised each other, Kateri confessed her sins; she reproached herself, among other things, with not having endured martyrdom for her faith.

That night, Kateri withdrew to her longhouse, her mind filled with these thoughts. Penetrated with sorrow for her sins, she stretched out on her mat, and when everyone else had gone to sleep, she decided to inflict upon herself the penance she thought she deserved. She spent quite some time burning herself with a brand, beginning with the tip of her toes and continuing up to her knees. Then, in the silence of the night, she ran to the church, on her sore legs, to present herself, purified, to her divine Master. She remained thus plunged in adoration until the first light of dawn.

Another time, her companion Mary Theresa told her that she intended to "burn herself like a slave and to place a burning coal between her toes" for the length on an Ave Maria in Iroquois. The devout Oneida woman wanted to initiate the torture often inflicted on the captives. Not only would she thus atone for her faults, but she would also make herself a slave of the Lord. Kateri who - contrary to her companions[6] - was perfectly innocent and of incomparable purity of heart, nevertheless wanted to expiate her least imperfections. The two of them followed through with their plan. Mary Theresa, who was healthy and robust, admitted later that her heart had almost failed because of the intensity of the pain. When she saw her friend, the following day, she found her with a large hole in her foot, which must have caused her atrocious pain.

No such examples of mortification had ever been seen before in the history of the Church. They simply demonstrate that these young Native women of a burgeoning Church were determined to go as far as they could in the gift of themselves to Jesus Christ, like the Christians of the early Church. Here, there was no lions' den, but they imitated the Christians of the first century according to their own mentality and culture.

The excessive mortification of Kateri - excessive in intensity, but not in intent - coupled by her constant effort to be united with God in spirit, wore out her strength, so that she fell dangerously ill. She had great difficulty recuperating and never got rid of the after-effects of her illness: stomach pains, frequent vomiting and a slow fever which reduced her to a state of languor of which she could not recover.[7]

Notes 19

1. OCI, p. 145-9.

2. VCT, p. 55.

3. EPC, p. 42-5; OCI, p. 191-8.

4. EPC, p. 31-42; OCI, p. 181-9.

5. VBCT, p. 90-2; VCT, p. 55-6.

6. EPC, p. 51.

7. VCT, p. 51.

20

"Kateri's Band"

In early fall, as the bobolink flew south, the village of the Sault prepared for the great departure of Fr. Frémin for France.

The day of his farewell, during the Mass which was attended by almost every villager, Fr. Frémin invited his little flock to pray for the success of his trip. At the same time, a prayer of thanksgiving rose from his heart at the sight of the tremendous progress which had been achieved at the Mission since its beginnings. It was now three years since these Indian people had their own village and their own church. The bark chapel was no longer but a memory. In the past, when they were in La Prairie, they would go to Vespers, but they would not sing with the white people, for they knew neither French nor Latin. Since 1677, the praying Indians had gradually come to participate in the liturgy and to sing in their own language. The superior was delighted that the leaders of the village preached admirably well in Iroquois. There were lay people attending to the services and teaching the young boys to serve Mass, Vespers and Benediction of the Blessed Sacrament, perfectly dressed as little clergymen. Native catechists taught the children and newcomers the elements of the faith.

The superior of the Mission had decided to return to France in order to watch over the interests of his flock. Among other things he wished to settle the issue which opposed him to Governor de Frontenac.[1] Going against the orders of the Great Onontio, he had taken the Indian converts, who lived among the French in La Prairie, out of this environment to establish them on the lands of Sault Saint-Louis granted by Intendant Duchesneau. The Governor, who was quite autocratic in his ways, had retained the title of this concession and was trying to persuade the king to approve of his arbitrary methods. The missionary was not put out by the malevolence of Frontenac. He decided to appeal to His Majesty during his trip to France. He was so successful that, while he was there, the Governor received a letter from King Louis XIV, on April 19th, 1680, conceding to the Jesuits the lands which they had requested.

After the departure of Fr. Frémin, new difficulties arose at the Mission. A rumor went around concerning a store which was going to be built on the west side of the village.[2] It was to serve for the fur trade and for the transport of equipment, vehicles, arms and weapons needed by the soldiers of Fort Cataracoui. It was said that the plan had been approved in France. Such a post in the proximity of the Mission would mean a flood of alcohol! There were also insinuations that the first Chief of the village might be imprisoned in Montreal, having allegedly complicated the situation between White Skins and Red Skins, and being even responsible for the hostility of the Iroquois of the cantons toward the French. The accusation was pure nonsense. In addition, a French gunsmith who was helpful to the Indians, was planning to establish himself permanently among them to supply them with all the liquor they wanted.

Worse still, a Christian Iroquois was accused of killing the chief of the Wolves in the vicinity of Fort Chambly*. What was not mentioned was that, in the same year, another Indian of the Mission named Jaque had saved from the stake a Wolf captured by non Christian Iroquois. This Wolf was a leader of his nation and Jaque had risked his life to save that of this man. He had untied the prisoner and led him into a longhouse. Then, standing in front of the entrance, Jaque had declared himself ready to die rather than allow these men to kill the Wolf. He was actually ready to give his life for the defense of peace between the French and the Iroquois, which the death of the Wolf would have jeopardized.

The Great Mohawk was away hunting when he heard about Jaque's predicament. He immediately returned to the village to sort out truth from falsehood and settle the case of whoever was guilty. He even invited the French of La Prairie to pray for this intention during the High Mass. He then went over to the scene of the tragedy, demonstrated the innocence of the accused and restored peace, not only in his village, but also in the entire country.

This quandary was soon followed by another. The Frenchman who had often visited the Christian Indians during the summer and repaired their guns, had succeeded in winning their trust. He was welcomed in their longhouses. He was already setting up a small bar in the center of the village, where he envisioned making a fortune. Frs. Cholenec and Chauchetière were greatly concerned about this undesirable presence. The intruder planned to spend the winter in the village, but the two Jesuits finally appealed to Intendant Duchesneau, who expelled him from the Mission, where he was not to be seen again. Moreover, contrary to what the Fathers had feared, the trading post was not built. As usual, the captains of the place fought alongside the missionaries for this new victory.

New groups of proselytes were recruiting many members at the Mission. In addition to the dogiques and the members of the Holy Family, people now talked about "Kateri's band". The selection of this little group of thirteen occurred by symbiosis. The holiness of Kateri attracted the most fervent women like a magnet; the Mohawk virgin, for her part, laid down a few requirements. Thus, it is said that, one day, she parted gently with a companion because she noticed a great deal of pride in her. We must certainly count among these intimate few, - in addition to Mary Theresa and Marie Skarichions, - Marie of Onondaga, Marguerite Gagouithon, the Virago, another young Mohawk woman whose name is not known, Anne, the dogique's wife, and maybe Jeanne Gouastraha.

138

Kateri and her "sisters" gathered regularly to progress in virtue. Everyone in turn exhorted the group.

Kateri and her "sisters," as they were called, aimed at "the highest perfection." "The kind of monastery which they form here has its rules," said Fr. Chauchetière.[4] They met regularly in order to progress in virtue. Each one in turn would exhort the little group; they would also frequently reprimand each other for their faults.

These Kiken Konnonkwe (excellent women) devoted themselves to the care of the poor and the sick. Discreetly at night, they would bring wood to them, unknown to everyone else, and then go away quickly for fear of being seen, thus adding humility to all their good deeds. They worked towards their personal sanctification through "mortification and by shunning the pleasures of the flesh, which they abhorred as the devil's lure". They promised God never again to wear fineries and to renounce the stylishness of wampum ornaments, facial colouring, earrings and bracelets. They were never seen idle, but always busy carrying faggots, helping each other in the fields, sowing and harvesting, grinding, sewing, or else making necklaces, bags or other handicrafts. One of them was later to be accepted among the Religious Hospitallers in Montreal.

Two or three years after Kateri's death, her adopted sister said that she felt a mixture of respect and joy at the sight of the logs and of the two wooden boxes made by her, which had been placed in the chapel of the Sault, until its fall.[5]

It is also said that, some time before her last illness, Kateri, along with other women, was digging a grave in the cemetery to bury one of her little nephews who had died. As the conversation went on to the topic of this general rendezvous where everyone had his place, Kateri was asked jokingly where her place was. "It is there," she said, pointing to a certain place with her finger."[6] This incident was remembered after her death, for she was buried at the very spot she had indicated, without the knowledge of Fr. Cholenec, who attended to the digging of her grave.

There were about ten of these devout women who wore a penance belt, and Marie went as far as wearing it even when carrying wood, which caused her racking pain. Fr. Cholenec having been informed of this, ordered her to "quit wearing the belt from then on;" but shortly after, the Onondaga woman asked permission to wear it once again, saying "that she no longer had any concern about her body."[7]

Kateri always did as much without letting any of it show. One day, as she was bent under a heavy load of wood with this penance belt around her loins, she slipped on the ice and tumbled down a hill from her field to the village. The iron spikes penetrated deep into her flesh. She laughed heartily and would not unload her faggot as Mary Theresa was begging her to do. Having returned to her home, she hid her pain so well that no one noticed.[8]

Marguerite did even more in this area and attained a count of three thousand lashes on her shoulders.[9] Perplexed by such unparalleled and merciless penance, her spiritual guide finally asked her for some explanation. He questioned her as to what she thought about while chastising herself in this way, so ruthlessly and for such long periods of time; he also inquired whether her body felt any reluctance in the course of all this mortification. "Gatatichwahens," she answered, "I hate myself, I want to hurt myself, I am angry with myself and my body for having offended Our Lord so much." Finally, she admitted that her body felt reluctance only in the severe cold of winter because the pain is more acute then and because being naked added even more to the torment. The priest concluded that he could not comprehend how such a young woman could demonstrate such endurance to suffering.

The missionary did not hesitate to express his admiration for these tremendous acts of penance. No one was more simple or more ingenuous than Marie and Marguerite, he said, and he called the former "illa mirabile prorsus femina,"[10] a totally admirable woman, and he praised the merits of the latter with these verses from Virgil, which he paraphrased in his own way: "O quantum mutata ab illa peccatrice quondam, nunc autem vere pretiosa Marguarita! O! from a sinner that she was, behold, Marguerite has now become a true pearl!"[11]

The Mohawk virgin, for her part, was becoming increasingly sick. Yet she would not resign herself to remain in bed idle. Whenever she could, even if the freezing cold, like the bite of a wolf, pierced her through, she would go quickly to the church where she would spend part of the day on her knees, sometimes leaning over a pew. Seeing how cold she was, Fr. Cholenec sometimes sent her back home, or, more often, he would take her into the Fathers' house to warm herself near the fire. A few moments later, with a faint smile, she would tell him she was no longer cold and return to the place where she had left her heart.[12]

Most of the time, however, she was seen inside the longhouse preparing soup or sewing like the French women; if she was unable to get up, she was found in meditation or reciting her Rosary, a true Native sunflower who, from the depth of her weaknesss, lifted her eyes toward the divine Sun.

Mary Theresa saw Kateri regularly and noticed how her face was getting more and more withdrawn by illness. She had often seen her friend grind corn and even new wheat from France into powder on a flat stone like she herself did. Now Kateri herself was being ground like fine wheat by the divine Miller.

Besieged by the frantic images raised in her mind by remorse, Mary Theresa asked herself some questions.[13] Was Kateri going to die? Had she not encouraged Kateri for more than one year to indulge in bloody practices of penance before each weekly confession? Was she not the one who had suggested to her to place hot brands between her toes, as their unbelieving compatriots did to the slaves? Could she let her dear companion die without telling the Father about their practices of penance? She confided her concern to Kateri, who consented to these revelations,

When she was able to she rushed to the church where she would spend part of the day kneeling in prayer.

all the more willingly since she felt no guilt whatsoever, having simply tried to imitate the saints of God about whom her director so frequently talked.

Mary Theresa went sheepishly to Fr. Cholenec, interim superior of the Mission. She told him in one breath about the sorts of penance she and Kateri had inflicted upon themselves and asked him if she was responsible for the condition of the dying woman. A long silence followed. The almost arctic sun of January shed some light into the room without providing any heat. Deep within himself, the priest was in awe at these two Christian women who, in a prodigious forward leap, had passed from a heathen land to the heart of Christianity. He could not, however, tolerate such excesses. He frowned and reproached Mary Theresa for her lack of measure and for drawing along with her a woman in ill health. He then lowered his voice, and the Oneida woman contritely listened to him as he urged her to practice Ignatian moderation in the use of penitential discipline. In the semi-darkness of her longhouse, Kateri, in turn, heard the same reprimand.

Notes 20

1. C. de Rochemontaix, S.J., Les Jésuites et la Nouvelle-France au XVIIe siècle, t. III, p. 146, note 1; E.J. Devine, S.J., Historic Caughnawaga, Montreal, Messenger Press, 1922, p. 51. Indicated hereafter by the abbreviation HC.

2. JR, vol. 63, p. 206-14.

3. Ibid., 202-204.

4. JR, vol. 62, p. 178.

5. VBCT, p. 87-8.

6. VCT, p. 66.

7. EPC, p. 36.

8. VBCT, p. 89-90.

9. EPC, p. 48-9.

10. Ibid., p. 41.

11. Ibid., p. 49.

12. VCT, p. 54.

13. VBCT, p. 95.

21

Father Pretends to be Angry

Even if Fr. Cholenec displayed great firmness toward his spiritual daughters, the tacit approval of Heaven for this life of penance still left him perplexed. He wrote concerning Kateri that, though she had a limp and was always sick, "she would knock her body senseless if she were left to her own".[1] Yet such a marvellous thing happened to her that the priest could hardly refuse her anything she requested.

One day, while she was scourging herself with admirable fervour, as she was accustomed to do, in a very dark place, "she suddenly found herself surrounded with a bright light, like that which shines at noon".[2] And the priest added: "We have no reason to believe there is any illusion here, for this woman has no such tendencies and is very humble. On the contrary, after carefully examining the case, we have every reason to believe that this is a grace which Our Lord granted His faithful servant, who is totally dedicated to Him and serves Him with such innocence and fervour as to enrapture the angels."

Kateri recovered somewhat from her illness. She resumed her daily treks on the snowy road to the kind missionary's house. She pestered him relentlessly until he finally gave her his consent to "do something to prevent her body from taking over."[3] The priest allowed her to do a few acts of penance, but hardly any; he also regulated as much as he could the necessary pains of the Indian life which was hers.

When Lent began, on March 6th, the "band" resumed the practice of penance with renewed fervour. "They renewed their mortification to such an extent," said Fr. Cholenec, "that it seemed as if they had done nothing up until then."[4] Marguerite had left for the hunt with a little notebook to record all her religious practices. This is how we came to be so well documented. When she returned, from being rather plump, Marguerite Gagouithon had become a featherweight. Marie was no longer recognizable, to the point where "Fr. Chauchetière confused her twice with another woman"; she was disfigured and had not stopped weeping for her sins since the previous year.

A new companion joined Kateri's group. Fr. Cholenec, in his correspondence, called her the "virago."[5] This Mohawk woman, who had an imposing stature, the shoulders of a warrior and the gait of a mighty feline, had a thirst for God. She scourged herself with the same energy as the other members of the group.

In the coldest spell of the winter, Mary Theresa and a few other Indian women set their minds on going to La Prairie[6] to bring a parcel, perhaps buckskin jackets or mocassins. They set out on the icy path and Kateri went with them despite the intense cold. The total distance of a round trip journey was eight leagues. Unfortunately it was too great an effort for Kateri and her health began to deteriorate once again.

Fr. Chauchetière went every day to visit her in her longhouse. Sometimes he would bring the little children under his care.[7] Their silvery voices brightened the sick woman's home and their friendly faces delighted her. Despite her great weakness, Kateri took advantage of the catechism lessons given by the priest and tried to sit up in order to see the pictures he drew to explain Bible stories to his young pupils. Fr. Claude found her admirable. She was amazingly cheerful amid her sufferings and her laughing face expressed "the tranquillity of her soul and the pleasure she felt in her pain. This is not surprising. This holy maiden having lived on the Cross with her Saviour and Spouse, was happy to die also on the Cross after His example,"[8] said Fr. Cholenec.

Kateri hoped that he would never go away. The way she thanked him and insisted that he return as soon as possible moved the missionary. She continued insisting in this way until the week of her death.

One day, Fr. Claude found her so sick that he had the vivid impression that the Lord would soon call her to Himself. He even had a premonition that it would be exactly on Wednesday of Holy Week.[9] This holy maiden would receive her reward that year. After having had such a devotion to the Eucharist and to the Cross in this world, she would soon go and celebrate these two mysteries in Heaven. The missionary communicated his impression to his interim superior, Fr. Pierre Cholenec.

As she felt her strength declining, Kateri figured that the time had come for her to undertake her purgatory. She went out one day to collect firewood and rested a few moments near a thorn bush. She undoubtedly recalled Our Lord's crowning with thorns. Shaken in the very depths of her being, she walked in spirit with Jesus during His terrible way of the Cross. What could she offer Him in return? Overcome with fervour, she gathered her load of wood and hid in it a large bunch of long, sharp thorns. Had not Saint Louis de Gonzague used these to do penance? Fr. Cholenec himself had spoken of him with praise. She was forbidden bloody scourgings, but not thorns...

Upon returning to her longhouse, Kateri hid the thorns under a piece of bark, and that evening before going to bed, strewed them on her mat.[10] She then lay down on them under a light blanket. One hundred chains made of toothed wheels would not have caused her more pain. The following evening, after another day of exhausting work, she spent another painful night, followed by another even worse. This is when her strength failed her.

Mary Theresa sensed the cause of these new sufferings and questioned Kateri, who admitted to her penance, even adding that she was determined to continue till she died.

"Oh! really?" replied her companion. "Do you know that it is an offense to God to perform these excesses without permission from your confessor?"

Kateri needed no more to drag herself immediately to the house of her spiritual father, for she was frightened by the very shadow of sin.

"Oh! Father, I committed a sin!" And she described to him the nights she had spent on her thorn strewn mat.

Filled with emotion, the priest realized full well in what state the young woman was. Death is written all over her face, he thought. Fr. Cholenec could not approve of such conduct, even if it was inspired by the best intention in the world: "I showed great displeasure and blamed her for her imprudence, and to prevent her from going back for more, I commanded her to go and throw these thorns into the fire, which she did at once with great submission."

This is how the missionary put an end to the penance of the thorns. It was too late, however, for the fever which Kateri had been suffering for more than one year, her persistent stomach pains and frequent vomiting[11] recurred more virulent than ever, forcing her to remain in bed. From the month of March and thereafter she suffered terribly. She had to remain in the same position day and night; the least movement caused her shooting pain. Even then she did not complain, happy as she was to suffer with Our Lord.

Kateri was now alone in her longhouse, for the mothers and wives who had not left the village while the men had gone hunting, worked from morning to night in the neighbouring woods. They left their sick and infirm alone all day with a dish of sagamity and a little water close at hand. The whole day long, nothing disturbed the silence of her longhouse but the barking of dogs in the distance.

The deep solitude of which Thomas Merton sang so beautifully, a solitude in which the soul finds itself, and in finding itself, finds God, came to alleviate Kateri's painful illness. Every time her strength permitted, she observed her long-time custom of conversing with the Love of her heart. She went in spirit before the tabernacle and fell in adoration. She generously united the sacrifice of her own self to the perpetual sacrifice of Jesus throughout the world in the Mass. "She used this solitude to attach herself more fully to Him and to become more and more inflamed with His love. She thus found and tasted within herself an abundance of joy and of the purest spiritual delight,"[12] all the purer since she was empty of everything else.

"As the Father has loved me, so I have loved you," Jesus said to His disciples. "All this I tell you that my joy may be yours and your joy may be complete." Jn 14, 9. 11.

Notes 21

1. Po, Doc. III, p. 13.

2. EPC, p. 51-2.

3. VBCT, p. 95-6.

4. HI, p. 191.

5. HI, p. 192-4.

6. VBCT, p. 97.

7. VBCT, p. 111-2.

8. VCT, p. 62.

9. VCT, p. 64.

10. VBCT, p. 96; VCT, p. 56-7.

11. VBCT, p. 114; VCT, p. 61.

12. VCT, p. 62.

22

"Iesos! Wari!"

On April 7th, Passion Sunday, Fr. Cholenec felt that Kateri's great departure for the heavenly dwelling was imminent.

In the morning of Holy Tuesday, Mary Theresa Tegaiaguenta found her companion's condition worsening and refused to leave her side. Fr. Cholenec came to visit Kateri, and in spite of the continuous pain torturing her, she asked her director to allow her to do some kind of penance, for instance to abstain from food and drink for one day. He knew well that what she desired was not the suffering in itself. He also knew that perfect identification with Jesus Christ, which she desired, is obtained through submission of one's will to that of the heavenly Father, and he flatly refused her request. He told her that God would be pleased to accept her obedience instead of the sacrifice she wanted to perform, and he added very gently that, being satisfied with her love, the Lord might even come soon and show her His. He then announced to her that Holy Communion would be brought to her in her longhouse.

The dying woman was overjoyed by such unexpected and most unusual news, for this was an unprecedented privilege. Indeed, it was not customary to bring holy communion to the sick in their homes; instead, they were carried to the church on a bark stretcher. Fr. Chauchetière noted that "they had great qualms about letting her die without giving her this Sacrament" and everyone was delighted that the Lord was brought to her at home.

Gathering the little strength she had left, Kateri turned to Mary Theresa and told her of her desire to be well dressed in order to receive the Lord Jesus appropriately. Her poverty was such that she didn't own any suitable clothes. Shortly after, the missionary arrived with the holy Viaticum. This extraordinary ceremony attracted the whole village on this chilly morning of early spring. No one found fault with this special favour, so great was the esteem everyone had for the dying maiden. The priest reverently carried the Blessed Sacrament, accompanied by a cross bearer and two acolytes. All these good people entered the longhouse to see a "saint" die.

They began by reciting the Confiteor in Iroquois, in which Kateri also joined. Within herself she renewed all the gifts she had made two years before, to God and His Mother. She renounced once again all the works and seduction of the evil one, as on the beautiful day of her Baptism. In a surge of gratitude, she went over all the graces she had received in her life, especially that which enabled her, with the help of her good Master, to keep the integrity of her soul and body, which she now surrendered to Him pure and intact.

The priest raised the sacred Host and uttered the ritual words: "My sister, receive the Viaticum of the Body of Our Lord Jesus Christ; may He keep you from the evil spirit and lead you to eternal life." Kateri received her good Master "with angelic love and devotion, like a true spouse of Our Lord," said Fr. Cholenec. Everyone present was charmed by such edifying piety.

The crowd left slowly until the longhouse was empty, except for the priest who remained alone with Kateri. At this moment, it must be said that Fr. Cholenec failed in tactfulness, for he wished one more time to confirm what was the miracle of Kateri's life: her indefectible purity. "I questioned her again on this point on the eve of her death," he said, "after having given her the Viaticum, and though she had difficulty speaking, she made an effort to answer with a firm voice: "No, no", with a gesture which expressed her sadness at being questioned even on her death bed concerning a sin she had loathed so much all her life."[2]

At the same time, alarmed by Kateri's great weakness, the priest leaned over and asked her if she wished to receive the Sacrament of Extreme-Unction. She answered that there was no hurry; so he postponed the rite till the following day.

After this, there was a continuous coming and going of people near her mat. They wanted to see her, and especially to commend themselves to her prayers. Marguerite Gagouithon and Marie of Onondaga received some precious advice from her.[3] She exhorted them to continue their life of penance, saying that it was most agreeable to Our Lord. She took special care of the virago, making sure she became a member of the group. Kateri requested the other members, as a grace to herself, that they include her permanently into their holy alliance, appointing Marguerite Gagouithon as her sponsor. At the same time, she urged the new adherent to conduct herself the best she could, to be descreet, and especially to take care not to spoil the harmony which existed among them all. Kateri finally asked "good Marie" to "make a novena of scourging for her after her death".

A number of her compatriots who needed encouragement came to visit her. Experience had shown that the sick, and especially the dying, could act as apostles with the healthy. Their exhortations had, in the past, drawn many Natives closer to Christ, people who hesitated to be baptized or did not find the courage to go to confession. The priest took advantage of the occasion and invited Kateri to use her influence on her people. An expression of distress could be read in her dark eyes. She who was so unworthy, was to give lessons to others! She accepted, however, and talked privately with some and openly with others. The results of these conversations exceeded everything that had been seen up until then.

There was a commendable custom among members of the Holy Family to keep watch over the dying. The night of Tuesday to Wednesday, all the women of the Association wanted to stay up with Kateri. Fr. Cholenec chose two of them, the virago and the youngest Holy Family member, Marguerite Gagouithon. At nightfall, the latter hastened to the priest's house to ask permission "to go to the edge of the woods to perform a few acts of penance to obtain a happy death for the one she was going to watch, whom she loved and who loved her too". The priest granted her request. She went over imediately and inflicted upon herself a painful scourging of a quarter of an hour.

When she returned home, the virago came to her and said: "Kateri is asking for you; she wishes to speak to you right now!" Marguerite rejoined Kateri at once. The sick woman whispered in her ear to let her companion go to sleep because she had a secret to tell her. As soon as the virago had fallen asleep, Kateri said softly to Marguerite: "Come here, my sister, I have something to tell you!" Holding her arm she said to her: "Courage, my dear sister. Oh! how happy I am with the life you are leading; how agreeable it is to all those in Heaven."[4] Marguerite would not let her continue, but began accusing herself: she was but a sinner! What good did she do? Did Kateri know her as well as she thought she did? Indeed, she knew nothing about her!

"My sister, I know very well what I am saying," Kateri added. "I even know where you came from just now, and I can assure you that all you do is well done and most agreeable to Our Lord. Take courage and continue to persevere; pray for me after I die that I may come out of purgatory as soon as possible. I shall repay you in paradise, I promise!"[5]

Kateri never dared to think she had reached the apex of holiness. This is why she didn't believe she would be exempt of purgatory. The greatest saints and mystics had the same belief. Saint Catherine of Genoa in her Treatise on Purgatory which became a classic, Saint Bernard, Saint John of the Cross, Saint Teresa of Avila and Saint Theresa of the Child Jesus, and many others, have taught that we cannot attain perfect union of love with God in Heaven until our soul is completely stripped of all that is contrary to His infinite purity and holiness. If this purification does not take place here below, it will have to be achieved in the beyond.

Kateri spent the long hours of her last night on earth in sweet and frequent conversation with Our Lord, Our Lady and her crucifix.

The following day, which was Wednesday of Holy Week, she seemed to her companions to be extremely low. Her breathing had diminished since nine o'clock. Mary Theresa who felt she was nearing death, would not leave her side, but since these devout women had to go and cut wood and take it in before the Holy Days, what were they to do? They decided to consult Kateri herself about this problem, which they did through the intermediary of Fr. Cholenec. He returned with the answer. Kateri had already sent Mary Theresa to the field with the promise to send for her when the time came. The others could also go without worry: they would return on time for the moment of her death. With this assurance, they left her.

At around ten o'clock, Kateri's breathing became imperceptible, and she sent for her faithful friend. Mary Theresa arrived at the longhouse a little before the last Sacraments were to be administered, just in time to receive Kateri's last dying words. Just then, Fr. Cholenec who thought he had already delayed too much giving Extreme Unction to the dying woman - though Kateri felt that this could still wait - came in with the last Sacraments, which she received devoutly.

After this moving ceremony, Kateri whose voice had grown very faint, spoke to Mary Theresa who stood by her in tears. "I'm leaving you," she said. "I'm going to die. Always remember what we have done together ever since we knew each other. If you change, I will accuse you before God's tribunal. Take courage. Disregard the words of those who have no faith. When they want to persuade you to get married, listen only to the Fathers. If you cannot serve God here, go away to the Mission of Lorette. Never abandon penance. I shall love you in heaven, I shall pray for you and help you."

Around three o'clock in the afternoon, Fr. Cholenec had the church bell rung to call Kateri's companions from their tasks and the other villagers wishing to be present for her death. The two Jesuits and all the Indians who could find a place in the longhouse knelt around the dying woman to commend her soul to God. Fr. Cholenec who watched her constantly, encouraged her the best he could. Kateri's eyes were lifted up to heaven. Her friend surrounded her with one hand while holding her cheek with the other, listening, in case she might speak once more. Kateri uttered very softly the holy names of Iesos, Wari, Jesus, Mary, after which she fell completely silent. At this moment, her "sisters" came into the longhouse. "She waited until they were all inside," wrote Fr. Cholenec. "The marvellous thing I saw with my own eyes is that no sooner was the last one inside and all of them were around her on their knees, than she went into agony." "An agony which was the sweetest in all the world."

Fr. Cholenec recited the prayer for the dying: "Go, Christian soul, leave this world in the name of Jesus Christ, Son of the living God who suffered for you; in the name of the Holy Spirit who poured all His gifts into you; in the name of the glorious and holy Mother of God, the Virgin Mary; in the name of blessed Joseph..."

Apart from a few brief moments at the end, Kateri's hearing was very good and she was completely conscious. One could see that she tried to join, at least in her heart, the prayers suggested to her. When prayers of faith or hope were said, she seemed to regain new strength, but when the prayers were acts of love of God, her face changed, so to speak, from that of a woman nearing death to that of one deeply absorbed in contemplation.

At almost four in the afternoon, Fr. Chauchetière who knelt at her right, noticed a slight shrinking of the nerves on that side of her mouth. Everyone thought she was asleep, and for a rather long time, no one realized that she had died. She had slipped away silently, as though fading in the light of God, on this 17th of April, in her twenty-fourth year.

As a young child, before suffering from smallpox, Kateri had had a beautiful face,[6] said Fr. Chauchetière. Now, with sickness and excessive penance adding to the scars, she was completely disfigured. But suddenly, less than a quarter of an hour after hear death, Fr. Cholenec who had remained in prayer by her side, let out a loud cry. The features of the deceased woman were restored and her face had become marvellously beautiful.

Fr. Cholenec sent at once for Fr. Chauchetière who was working at the repository for Holy Thursday. He came quickly with the people around him, and until the time of burial, everyone was able to admire this prodigy. "Her face looked more beautiful than it had been while she was alive; it gave joy to everyone and strengthened them in the faith they had embraced; it was a new argument of credibility, which God gave the (Indians) that they may have a taste of the faith." Fr. Cholenec's first impression, by his own admission, was that the Lord had already received Kateri in heaven and that He was allowing a small ray of the glory she now possessed to shine on her virginal body.

In the longhouse which was again filled with people, the priest praised the merits of the Iroquois virgin and encouraged everyone to imitate her. His words joined to the spectacle everyone could behold, encouraged Kateri's people to consider her body as a precious relic. Furthermore, they kissed her hands and took away as mementoes items that had belonged to her. But they didn't yet know her deeply, for she had kept interior life very much to herself. It was only during the night prayers at the church that Fr. Cholenec revealed to all the treasure they had possessed and had just lost.

The next day, which was Holy Thursday, two Frenchmen from La Prairie de la Madeleine came to the village to attend the Holy Thursday service. At the sight of Kateri lying on her mat, with her face so fresh and sweet, they said to each other: "There is a young woman who sleeps very peacefully!" A few moments later, they found out that she was dead. They immediately went back, "not to pray to God for her," noted Fr. Cholenec, "but to commend themselves to her prayers."

In this Christian village, it was no longer the custom to make elaborate preparations for funerals. They would grease the hair of the deceased and sometimes dress them up and put new shoes on their feet; other times they would simply cover their bodies. They had started making coffins for them like the French. The two visitors, obviously moved by the sight of this face which had been touched by the kiss of God, wanted to give Kateri a public sign of veneration; one of them made a coffin for her. They placed the body in it according to custom, but "were unable to cover her face as everyone found such delight in looking at it and read on this body what had been said of her, that she was a picture of chastity and virginity. They understood more on that occasion than was ever written in catechisms; therefore they left her face uncovered until she was lowered in the grave." Paradoxically, she who had hidden her face all her life out of necessity and humility, was already compensated and rewarded here on earth.

The population celebrated her funeral with universal joy and such tender piety that they all felt the Mohawk virgin exerting her influence deep in their hearts. From then on, said Fr. Cholenec, she would be considered as "the support, the bulwark and the guardian angel of this Mission."

Fr. Chauchetière tried to persuade his superior to bury Kateri in the church, but to avoid any peculiarity, her body was interred in the cemetery at about three in the afternoon. Without realizing it just then, they placed it in the exact spot where she had predicted she would be buried while digging her "little nephew's" grave the previous fall.

The salutary effects of this holy death were felt the next day, Good Friday. After the sermon on the Passion of Jesus, Fr. Cholenec removed the purple veil covering the Cross and offered to the veneration of the faithful the crucifix which Kateri had loved so much. The whole congregation burst into tears and the sobbing was such that for a long while, the priest could not continue. Again after intoning the Vexilla Regis - The King's Standards - he was unable to sing any further than the second verse because of the cries of sorrow rising from all sides. People everywhere talked of nothing but penance, self-denial and conversion. They flocked into Fr. Cholenec's house to confide these "good and holy resolutions" to him. Marie came to ask permission to perform the novena of scourging which Kateri had asked of her; her director was very reluctant to allow this after all that she had inflicted on herself during Lent; she fulfilled her promise faithfully.

In the evening of Holy Thursday and in the morning of Good Friday, Marguerite, Marie and two other Mohawk women, "all four scourged themselves together, as the religious do."[7] One woman "spent the entire night of Good Friday rolling herself in a thorn bush, as Kateri had done; another did the same for 4 or 5 nights in succession."

For eight days after Holy Saturday, there were acts of penance done in the village which were so great that, as Fr. Cholenec wrote two years later, "it would be

"It was not possible to cover her face, as they all took pleasure in gazing at it.

difficult for any greater ones to be performed by the most austere penitents in the world." This quality of devotion spread to the whole population. Many, after Kateri's example, wanted to leave all their possessions to give themselves to God. "A number of married people separated to live in continence; widows abandoned the thought of a second marriage; others, being younger, promised not to remarry if their husbands died before them. These women later kept this holy resolution and persevered in it despite their youth and despite the other very strong reasons which seemingly obliged them, for their own benefit and that of their children, to marry again, which they could easily have done since they were sought by very advantageous suitors. Such were the great fruits which the life and death of Kateri produced at the Mission of the Sault and which her memory, so dearly kept here, continues to produce every day..."

Notes 22

1. VBCT, p. 112-119; VCT, p. 63-7; PO, Doc. XII, p. 277-8.

2. VCT, p. 59-60.

3. HI, p. 191-4.

4. Narration of Fr. Cholenec in LCC, p. 11.

5. HI, p. 193-4.

6. VBCT, p. 11.

7. HI, p. 192.

8. Narration of Fr. Cholenec in LCC, p. 11.

PART THREE

23

Apparitions
First Miraculous Cures

On the day of Kateri's burial, before sunset, Fr. Chauchetière who considered her a saint, went to her grave.[1] The clumps of freshly turned soil were frozen hard. As he stood alone, his head lowered in prayer, he felt his heart warming up despite the cold air of Canadian spring. On Holy Saturday and Easter Sunday, he went back to the cemetery to pray to her. She soon manifested her gratitude to him.

On Easter Monday,[2] six days after Kateri's death, as Fr. Chauchetière was beginning his ordinary meditation in his frigid room at four in the morning, the deceased woman appeared to him as bright as the rising sun. He heard a voice which was not hers saying: "Adhuc veni in dies: I appear every day". Kateri stood before him with a majestic bearing, her face radiant with light and her eyes raised to heaven, as if she were in ecstasy. This vision lasted two full hours.

The apparition did not speak to him, but the priest saw very clearly several prophetic symbols on each side of Kateri. On her left he saw a church toppled over, and on her right, an Indian tied to a post amid the flames. The first prophetic sign was to be realized three years later, on August 19th, 1683.[3] Concerning the second prophecy, the Indian burnt alive, Fr. Chauchetière would find out his name seven years later:[4] Stephen Tegan234okoa, the first martyr, followed by two heroic imitators, Frances Gannonhatenha and Marguerite Garongouas.

Kateri also manifested herself to her good old instructor to console her. On April 24th, 1680, two days after her first apparition to the priest, she was seen by Anastasia Tegonhatsiongo.[5] That evening, as soon as the people of her longhouse had gone to bed, she remained alone in prayer. She suddenly became very sleepy - not having slept since Kateri's death because she was overwhelmed with grief - and fell sound asleep on her mat. The elderly woman herself told the story of what happened to her:

"...I had barely gone to sleep when I was awakened by a voice calling me and saying: "My mother, get up and look." I recognized Kateri's voice; I sat up at once, and turning to the direction from which the voice came, I saw her standing beside me. Her body was surrounded by such a bright light that I could only see her face, which was of extraordinary beauty. "My mother," she added, "look carefully at this cross which I am wearing. See how beautiful it is; Oh! how I loved it on earth, Oh! how I still love it in paradise! How I wish that all those of our longhouse loved it and valued it as I did!"

"This is what she told me, and then she disappeared, leaving me filled with such joy and such sweet consolation that they have lasted ever since, up until now (around March 1682). Moreover, the cross she held was so beautiful and radiated so much light and brightness that I have never seen anything so delightful and charming."

Fr. Cholenec interpreted this thoughtful gesture of Kateri as a proof of her gratitude to her instructor. The good Lord had many crosses in store for the wise Anastasia. Three of her sons, the eldest of whom was one of the village captains, were to die at war. To prepare her to bear these sorrows valiantly, Kateri, whom she called "her daughter", showed her the cross, so beautiful and ravishing and the source of all joy.

Around that time, Kateri's companion, Mary Theresa[6] reported an apparition which she had. One morning, before daybreak, someone came and knocked on the outside of her longhouse near the place where she was lying. This person asked: "Are you asleep?" She answered: "No." The voice said: "Good bye, I come to say good bye, I'm going to heaven." She recognized Kateri's voice and went out at once to see her. She was not there, but Mary Theresa heard the voice far in front of her saying: "Good bye", although she saw nothing. The voice added: "Go and tell Father that I'm going to heaven."

Another day, Mary Theresa got angry with her sister. The following night, someone came and sat near her. She saw a person wrapped in a blanket as Kateri was in her lifetime, and heard her say in a stern voice: "You don't remember the good resolutions you made". The person added many other things until one of the people sleeping next to her woke up, and then she stopped talking. Mary Theresa heard someone walking out as though it were a living person and she immediately repented of her fault.

*　　*　　*

Since the first apparition of Kateri, Fr. Chauchetière was torn between two alternatives: to publicize the virtues of the Mohawk virgin, or to remain silent.

That year, 1680, he wrote in a little notebook an exact account of what went on concerning Kateri and sent it to his superior in Quebec "in order to discover what was of God in these events, and what was perhaps not on Him." The Superior manifested some difficulty in believing all these things, - as did many Frenchmen at that time, and as did the Fathers on the Mission themselves in the beginning of all these events - and failed to give Fr. Chauchetière the support and enlightenment he desired.[7]

Fr. Claude therefore opted for a middle-of-the road solution to his problems: he wrote other short works, such as the "Narration annuelle de la Mission du Sault",[8] in two booklets, and another on "the perseverance of the Indians who fought against the Iroquois and gave their lives for the faith in fire and under the head of an axe."

At the end of October 1680, Fr. Frémin returned from France, quite satisfied with his intervention with the King.[9] The title of the new territory of the Mission, which Frontenac had refused to grant the Jesuits, were restored to them. The missionary had also interested numerous benefactors in his Indians, and brought back with him several gifts, one of which was the vermeil "sun" to be used for expositions of the Blessed Sacrament, still preserved at the Saint Francis Xavier Mission. He found out very soon about Kateri's death and heard the verdict of the Iroquois: "She died as she had lived, that is, as a saint."[10]

In December, the appearance of a "comet with a tail" created much unrest in the minds of the people.[11] The French as well as the Indians saw in it a bad omen, which was confirmed by the continual rumours of war which kept all of Canada on edge.

Five days after the appearance of the comet, a sick man who had lost hope of recovering, invoked Kateri of the Sault. The following day, he was cured.[12] But this wonder on earth didn't seem to set a balance against the one in the sky, for everyone lived in uncertainty and began to invoke all the saints of the land to draw their protection upon themselves, and now they added Kateri to the list!

In January 1681, Fr. Chauchetière was still hesitant. He was afraid to give in to illusion,[13] to some extent because of the gossip which had been spread concerning Kateri during her short life. He sometimes disapproved of the honours rendered to the deceased one, and again, sometimes, he himself went to her grave and, convinced of the holiness of the one he had known so well, did as much as the others, and even more.

This is when someone came for him, asking him to assist one of his friends, Claude Caron,[14] who was on the point of death. The sick man lived approximately one league away from the Mission, at La Fourche, one of the concession roads of La Prairie de la Madeleine, of which Fr. Chauchetière was the serving priest. A short time earlier, a surgeon from Montreal, undoubtedly Antoine Barrois, had come to Caron's house and promised to bring him medicine, but without any hope to cure him.

Upon hearing this, Fr. Chauchetière went to the cemetery. Kneeling on Kateri's grave, he prayed the good Master to dispel his doubts and asked Him "in all confidence to make known to him, through the cure of the sick man, if what was being said of Kateri was true and if what he had been feeling was from a good spirit." He then went to Caron's house with great confidence in Our Lord.

160

The priest found the sick man very near death. "If this night is as bad as the last," Caron confided, "I don't expect to see the morning!" A third spell of violent suffocation did not prevent him from going to confession. Fr. Chauchetière gave him Holy Communion and invited him to have confidence in God. In addition, he urged him to recite one Our Father, one Hail Mary and three Glory Be's and asked him to have three masses celebrated in thanksgiving to the Lord for the graces granted to Kateri - not naming her, however, - after which he left.

The priest was unable to go back to Claude Caron's house before three or four days. When he saw him again, to his great surprise, he found in perfect health the friend he had left in the grip of death. Caron told him at once how he had been cured.

As soon as the Jesuit had left, members of the household wanted to get the sick man up to make his bed. He fell flat on the floor, unconscious. They lifted him at once in their arms and laid him on the bed, convinced this time that the end had come. On the contrary, he was peacefully asleep. Half an hour later, he felt as if a large rock had rolled off his chest. When he woke up, he was cured. He ate heartily, went back to bed and slept all night like a healthy child. The next day, the surgeon having returned with his medicines was astounded to find his patient sitting near the fire, completely revitalized. Never, he said as he took leave, never had he seen a man be so sick and not die.

"Everyone was amazed by this cure, which completely enlightened me; yet I remained silent,"[15] said Fr. Chauchetière, and he adds in confidence that the sick man was also delivered of certain temptations and that he only came one year later to thank him "for teaching him such a good remedy, i.e. dust from Kateri's grave, which cured a man from sickness and temptations."[16]

One month had not gone by before the Iroquois virgin looked after the wife of François Roaner[17], aged sixty, of La Prairie de la Madeleine. The story of this new intervention is straight from the golden legend of Jacques de Voragine.

Having fallen seriously ill, the poor woman was soon dying. Fr. Chauchetière decided to administer the last Sacraments to her. Confident in Kateri, who had helped Claude Caron to regain his health, he placed in her hands the crucifix which had been used in the first cure. He bent over the dying woman and exhorted her to invoke the Mohawk virgin with confidence. The good old woman listened to the priest and someone hung the precious crucifix around her neck. She came alive again, there and then, and was cured. Her children who witnessed the scene could not believe their eyes.

Before leaving the family members to the joy of their reunion, the priest wanted to take back the crucifix. The cured woman would not let him, until the missionary gave her in exchange a sachet containing earth from Kateri's grave, which she accepted against the crucifix. "What a marvellous event! and how powerful Kateri is in the sight of God!" the Jesuit thought as he fastened his snowshoes before setting out on the snow-covered road to the Mission.

A few days later, the cured woman, now in perfect health, took the sachet of earth off her neck. Instantly she fell ill again, so violently ill that she thought she would die. The others hastened to put the miraculous sachet back around her neck: healing came instantly, as quickly as the illness had recurred.

The following year, Mrs. Roaner still wore the precious sachet on herself out of devotion, and also, perhaps, "out of fear of falling ill a third time if she took it off". But now, her husband Francis suffered an acute attack of lumbago coupled with rheumatism.[18] Deeply worried, she spontaneously tied the sachet of earth around his neck. He was cured at once.

By a strange return of things, however, his illness came on her. She screamed and yelled: "My husband is killing me!" The sachet of earth, therefore, had to be taken off Francis's neck and returned to his dear better half. She sat up double-quick, feeling fine and rejuvenated like a brand new coin!

What are we to think of this crisscrossing of sickness and healing? No doubt Kateri manifested a great deal of humour here. Fr. Cholenec explained it as follows: "All this is certainly so marvellous and seems so unbelievable that one would think it is all but a fable and a fancy tale if it had not happened just as I have said, in full view of the whole population of La Prairie de la Madeleine."

*   *   *

On September 21st, 1681, Fr. Chauchetière was favoured with a second apparition.[19]

This time the Servant of God appeared to him "like the sun at noontime" saying these words: "Inspice et fac secundum exemplar", which means "Look and do according to the model." God made him "understand through this message that He wished pictures of Kateri to be painted, which we had resisted to do for a long time." Fr. Claude went to work, therefore, to do what seemed to him to be "an invitation of Kateri herself": he began to paint.[20]

He first made a few paintings to instruct the Indians, and used them to exhort those whom Kateri "wanted to bring to heaven after her.(...) So I got down to work with incredible difficulty," he said, "sometimes annoyed to the point of quitting; and having abandoned everything, I had strange feelings of guilt and could enjoy no rest or peace except in obeying what Catherine was asking of me. The first work I undertook was a painting of the pains of hell as drawn by a German and sent to me by Mr. de Belmont. This work greatly pleased the Indians; even the missionaries requested a copy. The fact that this painting seemed acceptable to people gave me the courage to do the portrait of Kateri, which was the only painting I wished to do in order to accomplish what I had been so strongly inspired for my own consolation and that of others. I undertook it one year after her death, seeing that there was no one else to whom I could turn but myself. I made the pictures on the leaflets which many people have."

Some of these pictures were to be placed on the heads of the sick and to perform miraculous cures.

You will say that this is quite a number of people who have received great graces. There are still, even today, many people fervently devoted to Kateri, who claim to have benefited, one day, by a remarkable favour from the Mohawk virgin.

Notes 23

1. VBCT, p. 119.

2. VCT, p. 68.

3. VCT, p. 68-9; JR, vol. 63, p. 228.

4. See further on, p. 160.

5. VCT, p. 70; LCC, p. 12.

6. VCT, p. 71; Catherine Tegagouita. Recueil de ce qui s'est passé depuis le décès de Catherine Archives ASJCF, Saint-Jérôme, NO. 343, p. 1-2. Indicated hereafter by the abbreviation RDDC.

7. VBCT, p. 1-7.

8. JR, vol. 63, p. 139-245.

9. HC, p. 51-4; JR, vol. 63, p. 220.

10. HI, p. 190.

11. JR, vol. 63, p. 222; this comet was the first in history to be discovered with the help of a telescope, by the German astronomer, Gottfried Kirch, on Nov. 14, 1680. It was visible with the naked eye as it attained magnitude 2, on Dec. 4. The tail of the comet became longer and longer till the end of December, then it retracted progressively and was observed for the last time by telescope on Feb. 18. Extract from Comets by Gary W. Kronk., A descriptive catalog, Enslow, Hillside, N.J. 1984, p. 12. Documentation supplied by Mr. Chastenay, scientific advisor at the Montreal Planetarium.

12. JR. vol. 63, p. 222.

13. VCT, p. 72.

14. VCT, p. 72-3; RDDC, p. 2; Narration of Fr. Cholenec in LCC, p. 12-3.

15. NA, p. 4.

16. DDC, p. 3.

17. VCT, p. 73-4.

18. VCT, p. 74.

19. VCT, p. 69-70.

20. VBCT, p. 4-5.

24

A Seedbed of Stars

In spite of Kateri's apparitions, her memory could have been lost in the brushwood of time. This is all the more true since the Black Robes deemed it inappropriate, at the time, to actively promote her devotion. The Mohawk virgin, however, soon scattered her favours all across the skies of New France like a seedbed of stars.

Another spectacular cure took place among the Indians.[1] Up until then, Fr. Chauchetière had kept silent, not daring to talk to anyone about these miracles; but he decided to have recourse to Kateri once more, in March 1682, for the cure of a warrior of the Mission. The sick man did not have such a good name; yet he had received the Sacraments in the best possible dispositions and had only to wait for his last hour. The priest made him drink a cup of water, with a small amount of earth from Kateri's grave, and the man was cured.

The missionary felt he had to tell Fr. Frémin and Fr. Cholenec about his latest initiative. The two Fathers disapproved, but they had to realize afterwards that the man who had been at the point of death no longer went astray, after having struggled with his fault for five years. Of course, the priests were happy to see that Kateri's favours were beginning to spread among the Indians and among the French as well, but there were plenty of other sick people in the village who were good Christians, they thought. Fr. Cholenec added: "This is why I said to Father: 'Why don't you make this effort for this person instead?' and I named a young woman who was completely paralysed and had suffered attacks every year in the spring with medication not doing her any good."

This crippled woman[2] named Catherine, the sister of Mary Theresa, was also a friend of Kateri in her lifetime and lived in the same longhouse.

Fr. Chauchetière went to visit her one day, and was deeply affected by the sight of her hands and feet wrapped in bandages, while a child suckled at her breast and her husband kissed her. The priest told her about the cure of the Indian warrior and lent her the miraculous crucifix for her to wear respectfully. He then urged her to make a novena to her deceased friend: one Our Father, one Hail Mary and three Glory Be's. She agreed to do so, and this was the first of a myriad of novenas which were to be made up to our day. Moreover, the poor woman whose main fault was her passion for gambling, promised never to gamble again. On the eve of the last day of the novena, this young woman walked in the village as though she had never been sick. "People asked her if she felt any pain. She said she felt a slight pain in the small toe of her right foot. They said: 'Catherine left you this as a warning. You had better keep your promise." Fourteen years later, Fr. Cholenec was able to write that she had never again deviated from the right path and was still in good health.

In April of that year, in the same longhouse, Catherine's husband,[3] who was the eldest son of Anastasia, was also struck by the same illness as his wife. He immediately thought of calling upon Kateri for help. His sister-in-law, Mary Theresa, also prayed to her: "Kateri", she said, "you know that I have no other support but my brother-in-law, and you know that I will never get married. Who will provide me with clothes if you don't cure my brother-in-law?" The next day, the husband was well again. But Kateri went further. "She delivered him from a fit of despair which could have thrown him in hell." A few days later, during an argument with his mother, the young man "who had a hot temper" went out of the longhouse in a rage. Furious and as quick as one of those "snow snakes" with which Indian children have so much fun playing, he ran toward the river to drown himself. The path he took happened to pass near Kateri's grave. When he reached that place, "his feet stopped short and became motionless." He remained frozen to the spot until he recognized his mistake. He went to confession at once, and then went from one longhouse to another telling everyone about the wonders of Kateri.

Another Christian Iroquois commended himself to the Mohawk virgin, this time following the advice of all the Fathers. He took earth from the grave and was instantly saved. He was left, however, with an acute pain in his side. He prayed once again to his benefactress, and after applying the precious earth from the grave to the painful spot, he felt some improvement. The next day he woke up completely cured.[4]

Finally, one man[5] had been in depression for more than ten months. He looked like a living corpse and people said it would take a miracle to cure him, for nothing was known about this illness. One evening, using a little earth from Kateri's grave, someone rubbed the spot where he felt such great pain that it could not be touched even with the tip of a finger. Being cured the next day, the sick man said to the person who had taught him this remedy and who touched the painful spot to check out the cure: "I am cured. Don't be afraid to press hard. I feel no more pain." From then on, they called him "the resurrected one".

Hot Ashes, the Oneida who had helped Kateri to escape from her country, also felt the power of the dear deceased woman in the case of his beloved wife. Marie Garhio[6] gave birth while working in the field and had to be carried home, for she was dying. Her companions did their best to alleviate her suffering, with the help of a French midwife. It was all to no avail.

In desperation they urged Garhio to pray to Kateri. Mary Theresa Tegaiaguenta lent her the blue blanket of the Mohawk virgin. At that moment, the church bell rang, calling the faithful for the Mass. Everyone went and prayed for her. The sick woman wrapped the azure blanket around herself, begging Kateri to have pity on her, and was relieved at once.

*   *   *

Fr. Frémin stayed only a short time in Kahnawake. Having become infirm, he was transferred to Quebec in 1682 along with Fr. Cholenec. They were replaced by Frs. Jacques Bruyas and Vincent Bigot.[7] It was obvious on this occasion that the Indians had difficulty adjusting to new pastors. Moreover, that same year there was a change of governor and intendant[8] - Le Febvre de La Barre* replaced Count de Frontenac, and de Meulles* succeeded Duchesneau - which contributed in unsettling their spirits.

In June, the first bell of the Mission donated by the members of the Holy Family was given a solemn blessing. This bell named Marie weighed eighty-one pounds. It was bought "for public convenience because the one they had was too small and the fields were too far from the village" for people to hear it.[9] The Indians also asked that a small monument be erected for Kateri. Before becoming Christians, the Natives had often erected tombstones for their dead, painting on these monuments various mythic animals and birds which they called "genies or masters of life". In 1673, upon the death of his wife Catherine Gadeaktenha, the founder of the Mission, Francis Xavier Tonsahoten, had ordered, as captain of the village, to stop this custom. Since then, the Indians had noticed that the French set up small crosses on the graves of their departed ones. They wished to do the same for the Mohawk virgin. With the agreement of the Fathers, they erected a modest memorial to her in 1683.[10]

Despite all these good intentions, the people of the Mission could not manage to live in peace. Drunkenness and loose morals kept prowling about due to certain Frenchmen and to the Iroquois of the South. A band from the cantons had even come that year, "with presents supplied by the Dutch to lead many of them astray and persuade them to return to their country."[11]

There was such disorder at this time that, on the 1st of July, La Barre officially forbade the French, not only to run a bar in La Prairie, but also to receive transients who brought along with them trouble and debauchery.[12] The Indians of the Sault, for their part, offered 150 men to the Governor to help him fight the enemies of the French colony.[13]

"Finally, all the monsters of hell being outdone, made a last effort in August. Mingling their forces with a windblast at midnight, they overthrew the sixty-foot chapel"[14] with such violence that it was completely demolished. The sacred furnishings remained undamaged, with the exception of five crosses which were broken. The statue of the Blessed Virgin fell from a height of eleven feet without any damage.

That night, three priests were sleeping in the area below the stairs of the church. Fr. Chauchetière was awakened by the storm and rang the bell to warn the village of the danger. As he did so, he felt the rope being pulled from his hands and he himself was lifted away from the place where he stood. Fortunately for him, the falling beams drove a large hole through the wooden floor at the spot where he had been standing. Realizing that he was unhurt, he gratefully kissed the relics of the servant of God which he wore. The other two Fathers jumped off while holding on to the falling rafters, which formed a protective cage around one of them, but cast the other among the ruins, out of which he came with one shoulder out of joint, which was healed soon afterwards.

Filled with joy at having survived the disaster, the three priests went to the cemetery to give thanks to Kateri for her protection.

"I offered the Mass in honour of Kateri today," said one of them.

"I went to her grave this morning," said the other, "to commend myself especially to her."

"For my part," added Fr. Chauchetière, "I have thought very much in the last year that some kind of misfortune was going to happen to the Mission. Therefore, I have gone every day since then, and again today, to pray to Kateri at her grave that she may deliver us from it, and I have not ceased all this time urging the Superior of the Mission to have Kateri's remains taken into our church, without knowing why I was doing it."

This is how the first prophetic sign accompanied Kateri when she first appeared to Fr. Chauchetière on Easter Monday, 1680, came to pass.

The poor Indians were very saddened by the loss of their chapel, "one of the loveliest buildings around Montreal."[15] They lamented "that God had chased them from His Church because they didn't deserve to enter it." They were inconsolable at the sight of "their Fathers who were hurt and sick and said that these Fathers were suffering for the sins of their children who would not listen to them and live as good Christians."

They immediately decided to rebuild the chapel. An experienced architect happened to be in the area and agreed to look after the construction. Meanwhile, the Great Mohawk who had just built himself a beautiful longhouse only two weeks before, "moved out of his home to give shelter to Our Lord." There was his house transformed into a church in which Kateri continued to intercede for her people and where crowds of pilgrims came to make novenas. It no longer had the advantages of the lovely chapel destroyed by the wind, but people prayed fervently there, despite the inconvenience of the building, the rigors of winter, the rains of spring and the heat of summer, which would normally have kept the faithful away.

In early fall, everyone eagerly helped to rebuild the chapel, either through gifts, or prayers, or by giving a hand in the work. "There was no one who would not work with all his strength. The women and children carried their load of materials, and many went at it with such fervour that they hurt themselves and were ill for a long time". The men "carried pieces sixty feet long and proportionately wide, and thus assembled all the pieces needed to erect the building."

Finally, Kateri poured a little comfort on her dear Mission and, on October 8th, healed Fr. Jean Morin,[16] the one whose shoulder had been dislocated during the collapse of the chapel. This missionary suffered from a paralysed leg and had come to Quebec to get medication. He stayed for a while at the Sault where he had spells of intense shivering due to fever, an illness which he had caught in Tsonnontouan. He had devoted himself to the missions for many years. Kateri now came to him affectionately to allow him a few more years of apostolate among her people. He celebrated a Mass and invoked her, and was healed of all his ailments. He remained at the Sault for the next four years, after which he went to Quebec and died, barely 48 years of age.

Another priest was healed in France, in the province of Guyenne or Aquitaine. Having returned to France from the Caribbean Islands completely paralysed, he didn't know which saint to pray for his cure. One day, he heard about Kateri Tekakwitha and implored her to take pity on him; he vowed to return to the Islands to work if she granted his request. She did put him back on his feet and he boarded the first ship bound for the New World. He worked there with great zeal, noted Fr. Cholenec, "and it was from there that he wrote to us about this wonderful event, asking us to thank Kateri for him at the Sault."[17]

Notes 24

1. VCT, p. 75.

2. Ibid.

3. Ibid.

4. Narration of Fr. Cholenec in LCC, p. 13.

5. RDDC, p. 3-4.

6. PO, Doc X, p. 228.

7. JR, vol. 63, p. 222.

8. JR, vol. 63, p. 232.

9. JR, vol. 63, p. 226.

10. JR, vol. 63, p. 240.

11. JR, vol. 62, p. 246.

12. P.-G. Roy, Archives de la province de Québec, Ordonnances, Commissions etc, etc, des gouverneurs et intendants de la Nouvelle-France, 1639-1706, vol. II, Beauceville, "L'Eclaireur" Ltée, 1924, p. 40-1.

13. JR, vol. 62, p. 254.

14. VCT, p. 68-9; Jr. vol. 63, p. 228.

15. JR, vol. 62, p. 252.

16. VCT, p. 78; RDDC, p. 6,8; JR, vol. 62, p. 228.

17. VCT, p. 78.

25

The Genevieve of Canada

So many Natives and so many white people were cured through Kateri's intercession those last three years that Fr. Chauchetière felt the time was right, in 1684, to ask Fr. Jacques Bruyas, his new Superior, for permission to carry the remains of the Mohawk virgin into the new church. The transfer was made by night in the presence of the most devout villagers.[1]

In the same year, the devotion to Kateri was to spread to the island of Montreal thanks to René Cuillerier,[2] first warden of Holy Angels Parish in La Chine. This man visited the Mission of Saint Francis Xavier to attend the Holy Sacrifice out of devotion, and then went to greet Fr. Bruyas. Now just before celebrating the Mass, the Jesuit had made an interesting discovery. While looking through the Lives of the Saints for some captivating detail which he might use in his exhortation of the faithful, he happened to find a collection of narratives of the most outstanding and edifying actions of the life of Kateri Tekakwitha. Fr. Chauchetière had written these pages and left them at the Sault before going away to his new parish in La Prairie.

Fr. Bruyas read these pages to his guest and "both of them admired the Spirit of God who had led Kateri during her life. They blessed the divine Kindness for making them aware of such a great wonder." Cuillerier* hastened to make the young Mohawk woman known in his area.

His two year old son Lambert[3] was afflicted with tuberculosis. Unable to eat anything at all, the little one was nothing but skin and bones. His parents who believed him to be dying, took him to the church of the Sault and placed him on Kateri's tomb; they had a Mass offered and made a novena to obtain the cure of the little boy. At the end of the novena, he began feeling better, and some twelve years later, still enjoyed perfect health.

Shortly after this event, Mrs. Marie Cuillerier[4] "went into labour and suffered extreme pain without being able to give birth to her child". She commended herself to Kateri Tekakwitha, who had cured her little Lambert, and promised to go and give thanks on her tomb if she granted her the grace of a happy childbirth. Her husband did the same without telling her. After this, Marie drifted into a gentle sleep during which she gave birth to her child, who woke her up by his cries. She first said to her husband: "I owe Kateri a pilgrimage to her tomb." - "So do I," he replied, and a few days later, they crossed the Saint Lawrence River to go and thank the one who had heard their prayers.

After the Cuilleriers in 1684, Catherine Godin,[5] surnamed La Grandeur, wife of Louis Fortin, was the second one to promote devotion to Kateri Tekakwitha after having received favours from her. At twenty-seven years of age, she had been afflicted with haemorrhages for three months and was hospitalized at the Hôtel-Dieu of Montreal. The numerous remedies given to her for two months had done her no good. She was pronounced incurable and went back home in La Chine where she met a Jesuit of the Saint Francis Xavier Mission, which was close to her home. She told him about her affliction, and the priest encouraged her by telling her about Kateri Tekakwitha, who had died a saint and helped many sick people regain their health. The missionary suggested that she "have a novena made" by a woman of the Mission. Catherine asked him to please take this errand upon himself. "At the end of the novena, this woman who had been haemorrhaging for three months, was completely cured."

Another parishioner of Holy Angels received favours from Kateri. Madeleine Bourgery,[6] a thirty-two year old woman also afflicted by a bleeding condition for several months, could not find any relief. Her neighbour Michelle Perrin advised her to have recourse to "the good Indian woman of the Sault". Madeleine promised at once to have a Mass celebrated in the little church where Kateri's remains were kept. From that moment she felt relieved, and soon afterwards was completely cured of her bleeding.

At the Saint Francis Xavier Mission, there were adults who were cured, but no children. The earth from Kateri's grave and the objects she had used had saved elderly people, but seemed instead to draw children to heaven. Her grave soon became surrounded by smaller ones containing the bodies of little children, as if this Iroquois virgin, "whom we believe to be in glory, took pleasure in having her chaste body surrounded by all these innocent children, as so many lilies."[7] One day, one of the Fathers, most probably Fr. Chauchetière wanted to obtain the cure of a little girl through Kateri's intercession.[8] Despite his prayers, she continued to languish. The one who looked after her and implored Kateri each day to come to her help suddenly felt guilty about it. He feared to displease the Lily of the Mohawks and withdrew his plea, leaving it up to the servant of God to decide herself. The little girl died instantly.

Yet the time came when Kateri began to intervene in favour of a stream of little children at Saint Francis, Pointe-aux-Trembles and La Chine. In January 1684, one mother implored Kateri to save her little one from a fish scale which was choking him; her prayer was answered. Another child who was very sick was cured when they placed on his head a picture of Kateri drawn by Fr. Chauchetière. This picture was passed around in the whole countryside and was never found again! A third mother laughed at Kateri when advised to have recourse to her for one of her little ones who was very sick. The illness was getting worse by the minute. In her anguish, she acknowledged her fault and invoked the one she had made fun of; her son recovered at once. Many such cures were witnessed "in Montreal, Pointe-aux-Trembles, Boucherville, La Prairie, Saint Lambert, and again in La Prairie de la Magdeleine and in other places."[9]

*   *   *

Despite all these blessings, 1684 was a particularly perilous year for the Mission. The chiefs of the Five-Cantons came back to threaten the Iroquois of the Sault of the most brutal treatment if they did not return at once to the cantons. They would then no longer be considered as relatives, but as mortal enemies like the white people among whom they lived.

As soon as Governor de La Barre heard that the cantons were actively preparing for war, he decided to take the hostilities right into their villages. To this end he called upon all the allies, especially some of the native tribes who were as interested as the French in attacking them, since they "seemed to have a mind to dominate all of this great continent and to become the sole masters of trade."[10]

Meanwhile at the Mission, people wondered how they should respond to the animosity of their compatriots from the south. Finally, the captains proposed three solutions to the population. If they wished, they could return to the Iroquois land, or else, if they remained in Kahnawake, they could barricade themselves in the village; as a third alternative, they were free to go and fight the war alongside the True-Axe-Makers.

The first solution did not please them at all, for they thought that separating themselves from the French also meant losing Christianity which they had brought. The second alternative was not much better, for the French would distrust them. They decided therefore to accept the third solution because they felt that people of the same faith must take risks together. "Who would have said that faith and religion had united them so closely to the French that they would take arms against the Iroquois and their own nation? Yet they did so...and we are much obliged to the captains who presented the matter so well that men and women preferred to perish rather than lose the faith."[11]

In the month of August, before going to war, the Great Mohawk[12] offered an eight branch bronze candlestick to decorate the church. He had bought it from the Dutch Protestants of his native country for fourteen beavers, which was the equivalent of 240 pounds in Orange currency. The women donated stripped taffeta dresses which they had bought at La Chine and an antependium or frontpiece for the altar. On a beam overhanging the altar, near the exhortative necklace* sent to the Saint Francis Xavier Mission in 1677 by the Hurons of Lorette, they added more necklaces, head bands, bracelets and shields made of white or dark purple wampum. The most beautiful decoration of the little church, however, was undoubtedly the remains of the "good Kateri", who held the first place in everyone's heart.

Fr. Chauchetière had already painted many pictures of the young Mohawk maiden, but they were too small to be seen from a distance. He therefore made a large painting of the servant of God, which he exhibited in the church of the Sault[13] in order to make the life and virtues of Kateri known to all the Natives. Moreover, to facilitate the explanation of this large painting, the priest wrote a booklet in which he described all the actions of the Mohawk maiden and all the cures she had obtained for the sick, as well as the prayers ordinarily used at her tomb.

In September 1684, Governor de La Barre wanted to compel the Natives to trade with the great French merchants instead of trading with the British who offered more for their furs. He figured a good little war would do the trick! In order to get the Christian Indians to fight, he assured them that the Iroquois had attacked Fort Saint-Louis on the Illinois River. But on the battle field, La Barre gave way before the Onondagas at Famine Bay and returned empty-handed to Montreal. The people of the colony were displeased, the Court even more so, and the Governor was replaced by Jacques-René de Brisay de Denonville*.

The Marquis de Denonville, the Marquise and the Bishop-elect, Monseigneur de la Croix de Chevrière de Saint-Vallier*, left La Rochelle, France, together in June 1685, bound for New France. A short while later, all three of them were at Sault Saint-Louis: the future bishop on a pastoral visit of all the missions of the colony, and the new Governor, a man of zeal and good works, had wished to take the people of the Sault by surprise in order to avoid any ceremony. As for Madame la Marquise, she may have found in this blessed place the inspiration which was to nourish her all during her stay in Canada. Indeed, Her Ladyship "headed every good work in the colony."[14]

On this occasion, the Bishop-elect spoke in praise of the servant of God and graced her with the title "The Genevieve of Canada".[15] This new name given to the humble Mohawk maiden created an amazing stir and drew lyric flights from mystics and writers.[16]

This was quite a comparison. Saint Genevieve, a young maiden of angelic purity, had consecrated herself to God forever through the solemn vow of virginity which she made before Saint Germain at the age of fifteen. She is believed to be the first saint of France, or at least the first one to be recognized as such. She persuaded the Parisians not to flee before Attila the invader, and a little later, saved them from famine. The saint performed many miracles, was the object of widespread devotion for centuries and was invoked as the patron saint of Paris.[17]

Kateri, whose innocence was innate, caused great amazement in her nation by refusing marriage by instinct even before being a Christian. As a young convert, she consecrated herself to God forever by the vow of virginity as soon as she came to know about this state of life. After her death, she performed many miracles. The people of that time had a great devotion to her, went to her tomb in increasing numbers and sought her protection against the dangers which threatened the new colony.

On the feast of Saint Peter 1686, the Marquis returned to the Mission for an official visit and was received with full honours. The French and the Indian soldiers first escorted him to the church, and then to a longhouse decked in leafy boughs and woven blankets. The Governor spoke to them like a father. "My children, I have wished for a long time to do what I am doing today," he said, "and to come to your fort and enjoy with you the happiness which is yours of being perfect Christians. I had heard even in France that you had grown considerably in the highest and most solid piety and that to live in innocence and good works, to spend many hours in prayer before the Blessed Sacrament, to hear two or three Masses in succession on work days, to take clothes off your own backs to clothe the poor, to take, so to speak, food out of your own mouths to feed them, to receive the sacraments with fervour and to constantly perform the most heroic acts of mortification and charity, was nothing to you but the common and ordinary life of a Christian. I am now in awe as I see with my own eyes that all the things that were said of you are beneath what really is. You cannot overestimate or acknowledge too highly the grace God has given you and I shall most willingly do everything in my power that you may enjoy in this place the peace and freedom which your zeal for the faith has led you to seek in our midst."[18]

He then assured them of his paternal protection for as long as they would demonstrate their "affection and filial obedience" to him. After this, he warned them vigorously against the malicious plans of the Senecas and of the other Iroquois infidels, and added in conclusion: "I rely on your vigilance and on your sincerity, and I regard you as the guardians and defenders of the French colony."

Charmed by his words, the captains responded in the same vein. The time of combat was at hand.

In June 1687, the Marquis de Denonville left Montreal at the head of an imposing army to go and pillage the Senecas. Fr. Bruyas and 100 warriors of Kahnawake joined 200 other Natives, plus 832 of the King's soldiers and about 1000 Canadians.[19]

When the army reached the vicinity of the Seneca villages, it was attacked by 800 warriors. The French army won the victory, but six combatants were killed, among them Hot Ashes, and twenty were wounded including Fr. Jean Enjalran*, S.J. The warriors of the Mission had distinguished themselves under the leadership of the Great Mohawk. "Our Christian Indians," wrote Denonville, "outdid everyone

175

else and performed acts of valour, especially our Iroquois, about whom we had not dared to be sure since they were fighting against their own people."[20]

The French rested for some time after their victory, planning their next invasion of the cantons. While preparing, negotiating and receiving messages of intimidation from Colonel Dongan who proclaimed the Iroquois British subjects, they wondered what was really going on in the Mohawk canton. The Great Mohawk offered to go and promised to bring back news. On his way, he met a party of 60 Mohawks sent by Dongan to capture prisoners. "He addressed them fearlessly, assuring them that Onontio did not wish to make war, and spoke to them with such conviction that they were persuaded to return home. He even told them about Jesus Christ in a way which moved them greatly and brought four of them back with him to Sault Saint-Louis". He then sent his nephew with the same message to the cantons of Oneida and Onondaga, where he got the support of Garakontie "who stopped all the violent intents of his Canton."[21]

In November, the enemy counter-attacked. A large company of British soldiers, Mohawk and Mahican warriors invaded Fort Chambly.[22] The French had the upper hand and the enemy tribes learned once more that they had to respect the True-Axe-Makers.

These aggressions kept the settlers away from their usual occupations. Nevertheless Kateri Tekakwitha continued to work in people's hearts. Several parishes around the Saint Francis Xavier Mission kept coming in large numbers or having the Mass of the Trinity sung in honour of the Mohawk maiden. Yet the pastor of La Chine, Fr. Remy, who had recently come from France, was opposed to this custom although his predecessors had always agreed to it. Most of his parishioners could not "help saying that he would soon be punished for his refusal, and indeed, that same day he fell dangerously ill."[23]

The pastor suddenly became deaf[24] in his right ear, which prevented him from hearing confessions. He tried many remedies for three months, even holy water on the advice of his confessor. Meanwhile one of his parishioners, Jeanne Merein, requested that he offer the Holy Sacrifice in thanksgiving for a cure she had obtained through the intercession of Kateri. A short time before, the pastor had thought that he also should pray to the "good Kateri" for the healing of his deaf ear. He made a vow to celebrate three Masses, one in honour of Saint Ouin who cures ear ailments, a second one in honour of Saint Aurel, who had been recommended to him by a devout soldier, and the third one in honour of Kateri Tekakwitha. Immediately after communion that day, he felt much better and his deafness passed completely after the reading of the final Gospel of the Mass. The pastor fulfilled his triple vows and his confidence in the Lily of the Mohawks was unshakable thereafter.

In the spring of 1688, Denonville sent a considerable convoy to Cataracoui. On its way back, some thirty Iroquois unexpectedly attacked one of the canoes and beheaded two of the men. The Marquis understood that the enemy would not hear any talk of peace, and wrote a letter to Fr. de Lamberville, who was then in Cataracoui. The missionary persuaded one Iroquois of the cantons to go and harangue his compatriots in favour of the French. This envoy founds all the cantons assembled in Onondaga and a formation of one thousand warriors ready to pounce on Canada. He nevertheless succeeded in persuading them to negotiate with Onontio.[25]

The Iroquois sent to Fort Cataracoui a delegation escorted by 500 warriors. They demanded a French lieutenant to lead them to the Governor's house.

When they had reached Lake Saint-François, the warriors camped with a large number of Iroquois already bivouacking on the banks of the lake. They let the delegation continue on its own to Montreal. It was already known in Denonville's entourage that "from the river of Sorel down to La Prairie de la Madeleine, people could not go out of their homes without exposing themselves to fall into some enemy band." Added to this, the unsettling news that 1,200 Iroquois were two days away from Ville-Marie threw "the entire population into deep consternation."

The delegates spoke arrogantly to Onontio to impress their superiority upon him. Yet the Governor had to comply with their demands. Finally, a truce was concluded and the Iroquois left five of their people as hostages.

At the beginning of summer, Denonville decided, out of prudence, to have the whole village of Kahnawake moved to Montreal. The French soldiers took six weeks to transport the corn of the Christian Indians from the bay of La Prairie to Montreal. The move was completed just on time.[26]

Notes 25

1. JR, vol. 63, p. 242.

2. VBCT, p. 5-6.

3. Rémy, p. 9.

4. VCT, p. 76-7.

5. Rémy, p. 12.

6. Ibid, p. 13.

7. Narration of Fr. Cholenec in LCC, p. 13.

8. RDDC, p. 4.

9. VCT, p. 78-9.

10. HDNF, vol. I, p. 487.

11. JR, vol. 63, p. 240.

12. JR, vol. 63, p. 242..

13. VBCT, p. 4-5.

14. Mgr J.-B. de Saint-Vallier, Estat présent de l'Église et de la colonie française dans la Nouvelle-France, Québec, Augustin Coté & Cie, 1856, p. 88.

15. VCT, p. 87.

16. VBCT, p. 57; HDNF, vol.I, p. 586; F.R.De Chateaubriand, Oeuvres romanesques et voyages, Texte établi, présenté et annoté par Maurice Regard, Collection la Pléïade, Paris, Gallimard, 1969, vol. 1, Les Natchez, livre IV, p. 216-17.

17. Sainte Geneviève et son temps, Tours, Maison Alfred Mame et fils, s.d.

18. EP, p. 65.

19. HDNF, vol. 1, p. 514.

20. HC, p. 83; National Archives of Canada, MGI CIIA, vol. 9, folio 65, Reel F-9.

21. HDNF, vol. 1, p. 519.

22. Ibid, p. 523.

23. Ibid, p. 586.

24. Certificate of Mr. Remy Pastor of la Chine, of the miracles made in his Parish by the intercession of B. Cath. Tegakwith (1696) p. 1-3. Indicated hereafter by the abbreviation REMY.

25. HDNF,vol. 1, p. 527.

26. HC, p. 89; DDNF, vol. II, p. 98.

26

The Martyrs

While the French colony lived in this precarious peace, England declared war against France on May 17th, 1689.[1] The Iroquois cantons heard this important news from the authorities in New York before it was known in Canada. It took no more than this for the Iroquois to abandon the idea of peace with the great Onontio, happy as they were to be able to take their revenge for Denonville's acts of war against them. There was no more negotiating for the British and the Dutch; they had only one thought in mind: to become masters of territory and trade.

The war plan of this Anglo-Iroquois coalition was to hit Montreal and Quebec at the same time, by land and water. The Indians would attack Montreal first, and then be joined by British and Mahicans. This troop would then go on to Trois-Rivières and along the river to the "narrowing of the water" (Quebec), where the British fleet was to attack in front of the capital. They flattered themselves in advance that at the end of this campaign "there would be no French left in Canada."[2]

In the execution of this plan, the night of August 4th to 5th, 1689, in a blinding hail and rain storm, 1,500 Iroquois sailed along the village of the Sault, crossed Lake Saint-Louis and went on shore near La Chine. They massacred several inhabitants, women and children, and took many prisoners, some of whom were never seen again. They burned and pillaged everything except the forts. The French troops went in small detachments to chase the Iroquois, but soon had to return to the forts. The Iroquois, on the other hand "invaded the whole island of Montreal and left a bloody path in their wake."[3] This situation lasted through most of the fall.

Count de Frontenac and Governor de Callières* having returned to Canada, arrived in Montreal to survey the disaster. They realized once more that in order to implement the war plan that had been prepared in Europe to chase the British out of New France, they would also have to subdue the Iroquois.

In order to repay the British in kind and to restore the prestige of the French government in the eyes of the Natives, Frontenac directed an attack against a British settlement in New York. At the same time, war parties left Quebec and Trois-Rivières for New England and ransacked the area.

After these expeditions the people of the Sault resettled in the La Prairie bay area, a few miles above the old location. The new village was named Kahnawakon*, which means "In the Rapids."

On August 29th, 1690, British detachments joined by their native allies reached the outskirts of Chambly. Governor General de Frontenac immediately gave the order to assemble the troops, the militia and the Indian allies at La Prairie de la Madeleine, where he reviewed his army of 1,200 men.[4] Louis Ateriata, son of the king and one of the most influential chiefs of the Sault, spoke eloquently in the name of the Christian Indians. He invited all the chiefs to open their hearts to their father Onontio and to refuse him nothing. These words fell like seed in good earth. Frontenac ended the meeting by promising them that, once the enemy was driven away, they could all return to their homes.

The next day, the scouts returned from reconnoitring the area and said they had seen nothing, nor had they noticed any suspicious tracks, after which the army was disbanded until further orders. The people returned to their harvest, which they had feared not to be able to complete.

*   *   *

Many of the Indians had set out for the autumn hunt. Stephen Tegananokoa,[5] a Huron turned Iroquois, accompanied by his Mohawk wife Suzanne and a companion, fell into the trap of 14 Cajugas who chained them and brought them to Onondaga (today Butternut Creek, N.Y.), capital of the Iroquois Confederation.

This was not a pleasant trip for our three Christians. By day they went down rivers and across lakes tied by the neck and arms to one of the bars of the canoe. When travelling on land, they were held by a Cajuga on a leash like dogs. At night, they were stretched naked on the ground, so that their bodies were exposed to the fiery sting of mosquito bites. Ropes tied to hooks planted in the ground held their legs, arms and neck so tight that they were unable to move. Other longer ropes held their hands and feet in such a way that they couldn't move without alerting their captors.

When they arrived within one or two leagues from Onondaga, the leader of the band sent a runner to announce their prize capture. Custom required that the people wait for the captives at the edge of the village, but this time, because the Onondagas were so pleased to have compatriots from the Sault in their hands, they ventured further out to see them. Like on a day of festival, they were dressed in their finest attires. Stephen saw them coming towards him armed with knives, tomahawks and sticks, their faces filled with hatred.

"My brother," one of them said, "you are dead; it is not we who are killing you, you are killing yourself because you left us to go and live among those dogs, the Christians at the Sault."

-"It is true that I am a Christian," the captive replied calmly, "but it is no less true that I am proud of it. You can do with me as you please, I have no fear of your insults or torments. I will gladly shed my blood for God, who has shed His blood for me."

They then attacked him from all sides; first they cut off several of his fingers, and then, with razor sharp knives, they hacked at his arms, thighs, legs and at all his body, which was soon bathed in blood.

"Pray to God!" yelled one of the fiends.

"Yes I will," replied Stephen, and lifting his tied hands, he did the best he could to make the sign of the Cross. They chopped off half of the fingers that were left on this hand and then cried to him again: "Pray to God now!" Once again Stephen made the sign of the Cross on himself and now, they cut off the rest of his fingers down to the palm of his hand. For a third time, they challenged him to pray to God, hurling at him every possible insult. Without hesitation Stephen made the sign of the Cross with the stump that was left of his hand, after which they cut the rest of it off completely. Not content with this horrible treatment, they carved holes in his forehead, chest and shoulders where he had touched himself to make the sign of the Cross to remove the holy marks he had imprinted in these places.

After this bloody prelude, they brought him close to a large fire from which they took red hot irons and placed them between his legs violently pressing his legs together. He then heard enraged voices ordering him to sing the traditional "death chant" of the Iroquois, which goes like this:

"I am brave and unfearing.
I do not fear death or any kind of torture.
Those who fear are effeminate men,
they are less than women.
To a courageous man, life is of no account.
Let my enemies be strangled by despair and rage!
How I would love to feast on their flesh
and to dring their blood to the last drop!"

Stephen ignored the score. Instead he repeated his daily prayers in a loud voice, at which point one of his tormentors took a branding iron and thrust it deep into his throat. They then tied him to the death stake loosely enough for him to turn around it at will. To everyone's astonishment, the martyr cried out: "Courage, my brothers, burn me well and enjoy seeing me roast; do not spare me. My sins deserve more than any pain you can inflict on me, and the more you torment me, the more I will be rewarded in the next life!"

These words infuriated his torturers, who slowly burned his body in its entirety without his letting out the slightest gasp. When he felt he was about to collapse, Stephen pleaded with the Lord to have pity on him, to pardon his murderers and to bestow on his people the grace of conversion. "He appeared at peace, his eyes lifted to heaven to which his soul clung in continuous prayer." Shortly after, he gave up his soul to the One who had created it for His glory.

The heroic death of Stephen affected a good number of his compatriots, who fled their cantons to go and replace him at the Saint Francis Xavier Mission. Later, his hunting companion who had been spared, having come to Montreal with a war party, stealthily took his leave and returned to the Christian village. As for Suzanne, Stephen watched over her from heaven. One of her sons having gone down from Canada one day, freed her and brought her back home.

*   *   *

On October 16th, 1690, a fleet of thirty-four British sail ships dropped anchor in front of Quebec and Admiral William Phips summoned the French government to surrender.[6] The cleverness of Frontenac and his army combined with the valiance of the local people won against the enemy, but the colony came out of this disaster considerably weakened and, what is worse, a prey to famine because the people had not been able to plant in the spring due to the Iroquois incursions.

In the middle of winter, 140 Mohawks and Dutchmen surprised a group of people from the Sault in Chambly. Many were killed and ten or so were captured. But it turned out that three deputies from the Mohawk canton returned these prisoners to the Sault and stated their desire to make peace with their father Onontio; however, they first wished to know if the Governor would accept to give them a piece of land in the vicinity of the Sault that they might settle there, close to their brothers. To show their sincerity, they let it be known that this very moment, 800 Iroquois warriors were preparing to take over the area between Montreal and Trois-Rivières. The Governor suspected some underhanded manœuver by British and Iroquois forces, and to play for time, convinced the Chevalier de Callières to drag on the negotiations by calling for the mediation of the people of the Sault.

As had been announced, the enemy showed up in Montreal. At the beginning of May, a first detachment of 120 men attacked Pointe-aux-Trembles (a district of the island of Montreal), where they exacted the usual ransacking and massacre. A second contingent of 200 warriors slipped in between Chambly and La prairie de la Madeleine, where they surprised 12 Indian men and women of the Sault. The next day, they repeated the manœuver, returning these prisoners to their homes at the Sault and asking for peace. Once again, the facts belied these proposals. Another party showed up and took away 35 women and children from among the Christian

182

Iroquois of the Mountain. Many other bands invaded the areas stretching from Repentigny to the islands of the Richelieu and wreaked havoc everywhere.

This time, the Onondaga canton sent two women prisoners from the Mountain with two necklaces to be presented secretly, one to the chief of the Mountain village, and the other to Louis Ateriata, chief of the Sault. By these gifts, the two men were summoned to return to their country of origin with their relatives and friends, otherwise they would perish along with the French. The two chiefs, after receiving the necklaces, proudly brought them to the Governor of Montreal and swore their total allegiance to him.[7]

Callières, having learned from the two women that the enemy was approaching, had 7 or 800 men bivouac in the vicinity of La Prairie de la Madeleine.[8] He also sent reinforcements to Chambly, 200 troops led by the Sieur de Varennes.

The night of August 10th to 11th, the combatants of LaPrairie, drenched with rain, retired into the fort where Mr. de Callières was suffering from a high fever. A sentinel stationed at the left of the fort fired a single shot to warn that the enemy was sliding along the walls of the fort. This party made up of British troops and Mohawk warriors under the command of Major Peter Schuyler, seized the area of the militia on the left side of the fort and set up camp there.

At the sound of the sentinel, Mr. de Saint-Cirque set out with his troops who had been posted at the right of the fort, and as he arrived within sight of the militia, he cautiously hesitated. The British fired at once a violent discharge of musketry which killed three officers, among others. A second battalion led by Mr. de Chassaigne rushed to their aid and forced the enemy back. The defeated attackers retreated, yelling and waving the scalps of many Frenchmen like banners in the wind. They had reached the edge of the forest when two detachments caught up with them, one after the other. They beat back the first one, but Mr. de Varennes, gallant commander of the second detachment, succeeded in putting the British army completely to rout.

At the beginning of November, there was a new alert. Two Indian women captives escaped from the cantons warned the Chevalier de Callières that two war parties of 350 men each were marching to Sault Saint-Louis in a surprise attack. The Governor of Montreal immediately dispatched his troops there as well as to the other forts of the area. The first contingent was made up of Onondagas, Cajugas and Senecas, who came through Lake Ontario. When they approached the edge of the woods, there were several skirmishes with about equal losses on each side. After this, the enemy who had counted on a surprise attack to win the battle, was forced to break camp. The second contingent of Mohawks, Mahicans and Oneidas came from Lake Champlain, but were alerted on time and did not attack. Nevertheless some of the inhabitants who had ventured too far away from the French settlements, were captured.[9]

At the end of the month, 34 Mohawks surprised a group of hunters from the Sault near the mountain of Chambly. They killed 4 and took 8 prisoners, some of whom escaped and alerted the village of what had happened. Fifty villagers set out in pursuit of the aggressors and caught up with them near Lake Champlain. Sixteen Mohawks were killed, 15 captured and their prisoners rescued.

The following year, at the beginning of February, Callières received orders from Frontenac to assemble a party to oust the Iroquois from the peninsula located at the junction of the Saint Lawrence and Outaouais Rivers. A troop of 300 French and Indian men was formed. Led by Captain de Beaumont, they attacked a roving band of Senecas at Tonihata, a short day's march from Cataracoui, and pursued them right into their camp where they killed 24, captured 16 and rescued one officer.

They learned from the prisoners that a hundred or so Senecas were hunting in an area along the great Outaouais River called Sault à la Chaudière and that they were awaiting the arrival of Black Bucket*, one of the most renowned chiefs of the Onondagas, expected to bring 200 men along with him. They planned to spend the whole summer there to stop any Frenchman who would travel to or from Michilimakinac to deal in the fur trade. The Sieur de Saint-Michel tried twice in vain to reach this trading post. During a third attempt, 30 or so men were killed, wounded or captured including Saint-Michel himself.

In July, Black Bucket appeared in La Chesnaie and abducted 3 Indian children who were fishing and 14 settlers who were drying hay. A short time later, a French captain and his lieutenant were ambushed at Richelieu. And finally, a band of Onondagas, Cajugas and Senecas captured the woman who was to become the second martyr of the Saint Francis Xavier Mission.

*   *   *

The Onondaga woman, Frances Gononnhatenha,[10] lived at Chasteau-Guay, three leagues upstream from the village. Her husband was out fishing when the warning came of the approach of the enemy. She immediately set out in her canoe, along with two of her friends, to alert her husband of the danger. They paddled vigorously, their hearts pounding with anxiety. Every turn in the river, every island, every hill could harbour the ferocious aggressors. They succeeded in finding her husband and he joined them in the canoe. They thought they were saved.

Unfortunately, less than a third of a league from the Sault, they found themselves surrounded by a hoard of Iroquois. As soon as everyone was on shore, they decapitated the husband and led the women captives to the enemy encampment.

184

The first night, the ravishers amused themselves by tearing out these women's fingernails and, according to tradition, "smoking their bloodied fingers in their peace pipes."

As was customary in these circumstances, runners brought the news of their capture to Onondaga. When the women arrived, they were immediately beaten with sticks. The warriors turned one of them over to the Oneidas, another to the Senecas, and Frances was given to her own people. They led her to her sister, who was greatly considered in Onondaga, but she offered no food to the unfortunate woman, which meant that she did not take her under her protection, thereby condemning her to be burned alive.

The condemned woman was made to go up a scaffold erected in the centre of the public square. In front of everyone gathered around, she declared in a loud voice that she was a Christian from the Sault Mission and that she considered herself fortunate "to die in her homeland at the hands of her closest family, in the same way that Jesus Christ was crucified by those of his own nation."

These words infuriated one of her relatives who had made the journey to Canada, five years earlier, to persuade Frances to return to her native land and avoid a worse fate. He jumped on the scaffold, ripped off the crucifix from her neck and, with a knife, made two incisions on her chest in the form of a cross.

-    "There now," he said, "there is the Cross which you hold so dear and which stopped you from returning with me when I took the trouble to go and get you at the Sault."

-    "I thank you, my brother," replied Frances. "I could lose the cross you took from me, but you gave me one which I will not lose except with my life."

She spoke then of the mysteries of the faith with extraordinary vehemence and unction, "even beyond her capacity and talent :"

"No matter how terrible are the torments which I am destined to endure at your hands," she said, "don't think that my fate is to be pitied. It is your fate which deserves tears and moaning. The fire which you have set to torture me will only last a few hours; but the fire prepared for you in hell will last forever. Yet it is still in your power to avoid it: follow my example, become Christians and live according to the holy rules and you will save yourselves from the eternal flames. In any case, I assure you that I wish no harm on those I see all prepared to take my life away from me. I not only forgive them for my death, but I also pray that the sovereign Judge of life and death will open their eyes to the truth, touch their hearts and give them the grace to be converted and to die as Christians like me."

These words did not break down the wall of hate confronting Frances. For three nights they paraded her from longhouse to longhouse to make her the plaything of everyone. On the fourth day they tied her to the stake, signalling the moment of great torture.

The torturers applied flaming firebrands and red hot gun barrels to her entire body. This torture lasted several hours and the victim never let out one cry: her thoughts and eyes were fixed on heaven.

After this macabre entertainment, the most furious of the band untied her, scalped her and threw hot cinders on her exposed skull, and they chased her around the compound hurling insults at her. Suddenly a hail of stones fell upon her.

The Sieur François de Saint-Michel, also a captive of the Onondagas, was a witness to this gruesome spectacle and condemned as well to the same torment. He admitted shivering in horror and breaking down in tears "when he saw this virtuous neophyte fall to her knees, her eyes lifted to heaven, offering to God in sacrifice the last breath on her life." "She died as she had lived, repeating her prayers and in union with Our Lord," wrote Fr. Cholenec.

*   *   *

That same autumn, the French had to battle the British near Plaisance (Newfoundland) and at Pemkuit.[11] Because of this, the troops were somewhat depleted when they heard that 800 Iroquois were marching to attack Montreal. One band was coming by way of Lake Champlain and the other, by Lake Saint-François. Their plan was to meet near Sault Saint-Louis, to entrench themselves there and, through fake negotiations, to attract as many people of the Sault as possible and to massacre them once they had them in hand.

It was impossible to go and meet these two armies because of the lack of troops. But everyone kept a close watch everywhere and the Governor of Montreal sent reinforcements and ammunition to the Marquis de Crisafy, who was the commander of the Sault at that time. The people of the Sault promised to outdo the Iroquois and their wily traps. The forts of Chambly and Sorel were also reinforced and the inhabitants forbidden to leave their homes. All officers received orders to remain at their posts.

The war party coming from Lake Saint-François arrived first at the Sault. When they discovered that they were expected and that the village was quite ready for them, while they counted on a surprise attack, they beat a hasty retreat. The other party did the same.

Count de Frontenac wanted to exact as much punishment on the Mohawks as they deserved for all the evil they had planned to do, for it was this canton that had formed the latest war party and he was concerned about their connections with the Indians of the Sault. He ordered the Chevalier de Callières to form an army corps made up of Canadians and Indians. Six hundred men were assembled.

This army arrived in Mohawk land on February 16th, 1693 and pillaged the first two villages to which it came. In the third village, which was much larger, they killed 20 warriors and a few women and captured 250 prisoners. But in this place, it was too much to ask of the Iroquois of the Sault to fight their own people and particularly some of their own families. They became somewhat unsubmissive and because of them, the expedition failed in part. They spared some of the men instead of refusing them quarter - as the orders were - and they forced the army to encamp in an improvised and uncomfortable place where they lacked food. A great number of prisoners escaped and they returned to Montreal with only 64. They learned from the captives that 3,000 British soldiers were planning to descend on Montreal in the spring, while an equally large fleet would lay siege to Quebec. La Plaque, a Mohawk lieutenant of the French army, and d'Iberville confirmed these news. They once again fortified the forts of Chambly and Sorel.

In the summer of 1693, the Sieur François de Saint-Michel reappeared in Quebec. He has escaped from the hands of the Iroquois only one hour before he was to be burned at the stake. His return had an enormous impact on the people who surrounded him to hear about what had happened to him and to Frances the martyr. Everyone was moved to tears.

He was also the bearer of other news of the war. The Onondagas had built a fort in their main village with eight bastions and three palisades to protect themselves should the French come to attack them as they had done in the Mohawk canton. He added that 800 Iroquois were about to set out in a campaign to stop the inhabitants from taking in their harvest. In fact these aggressors were already at the rapids, at the end of Lake Saint-Louis.

Frontenac dispatched five companies of the king's troops and 500 soldiers who had just arrived from France, to meet them. The Chevalier de Callières joined them with 7 or 800 men. On hearing this, the enemy appeared to break camp. Not so completely, however, as not to be able to capture the woman who would be the third martyr of the Mission of the Sault.

* * *

One fine day, Marguerite Garongouas,[12] a twenty-four year old Onondaga, her child in her arms, went to her plot of land about a quarter of a league from her house. She was captured by two Onondagas, probably relatives of hers who flattered themselves at the triumph they would receive in the canton when they arrived with this lovely capture: a woman in her prime with a child at her breast.

The Iroquois believed that a woman was worth two men because when a woman died, the elders saw the loss of a long line of descendants.

As soon as the news of their arrival began to spread in the headquarters of the war, some 400 inhabitants of Onondaga climbed on a high place to watch them come. When they saw them, they broke out in a formidable clamour and many hands grasped at the captive woman as she passed by. Someone grabbed her son, others tore off her clothes, and instead of the usual beating with sticks inflicted on captives, they all pounced on her in a jumble. With knives bought from the Dutch glittering in the sun, they stabbed her repeatedly and soon she was but one large wound.

A French prisoner who was witness to this horrible scene, attributed it to a sort of miracle that she had not died on the spot. Marguerite recognized him and, in a clear voice, called him by his name and said to him in his language:

"Well, you see my fate; I have little time left to live. Thank God! I am not afraid of death, no matter how cruel is the one they are preparing for me. My sins deserve even more. Please pray to the Lord that He may forgive me and give me the strength to bear the suffering."

They brought her into the longhouse of a French woman from Montreal who was also a captive. This brave woman showed no revulsion at the sight of the unfortunate one all covered with blood. She comforted her and encouraged her "to suffer this passing torture with determination in view of the eternal reward that would follow."

Marguerite thanked her and stated once again that she had no fear of martyrdom and was quite willing to die. She even revealed that, ever since her Baptism, she had asked God for the grace to suffer for Him. God had answered her prayer and she would die content. Like Frances Gononnhatenha and Stephen Taganakoa before her, Marguerite harboured no rancour against her family and compatriots and prayed to God to forgive them and to give them the grace of conversion.

The two women, Red-Skin and White-Skin, were still sharing on the joys of heaven when a handful of Onondagas irrupted into the longhouse. They had come for Marguerite to put her to death. They had no consideration for her youth, her origins or the advantage she had of being the daughter of Todaho, the hereditary chief of the Iroquois Confederation, which "would undoubtedly have saved the life of any other but a Christian from the Sault."

They tied Marguerite to the stake and her murderers methodically burned her whole body. She endured this long and rigorous torture as a typical Iroquois, without showing the least sign of pain. She invoked the holy names of Jesus, Mary and Joseph, begging them to help her to sustain this terrible battle to the very end. From time to time, she exhorted her compatriots to embrace the Christian faith. At times also, she asked for a little water, but after reflection, told them to refuse it to her in spite of her asking:

"My Saviour was thirsty on the Cross for my sake", she said; "is it not fair that I should suffer the same discomfort?"

Marguerite bore these excruciating torments from noon until sundown. At dusk, they untied her from the stake, scalped her and covered her skull with hot cinders, after which they commanded her to run. Instead of obeying them, she knelt, lifted her eyes and hands to heaven and commended her soul to God. They hit her several times on the head to stop her from praying. It was all in vain.

"Will this Christian bitch never die?" shouted one of the fiends, who seized a brand new Dutch knife and thrust it into her abdomen. The blade, which had been thrust hard, broke and, to everyone's astonishment, fell in pieces at her feet. Another pulled up the torture stake and hit her with it over the head several times. As she was still alive, they set fire to a pile of dry wood and threw her into the flames.

Added to her endless tortures was the painful thought of her baby abandoned to the fury of unbelievers. Three days after Marguerite's death, at nightfall, a piercing scream rent the air. Everyone rushed out of the longhouses and all, including the French woman, ran to the place from which the screaming had come. The adoptive father standing near a fire was about to cast the baby into it when the little one stretched his arms with a smile and called "Mamma" three times, as if wanting to hug her. The Montreal woman felt that Marguerite had appeared to him. At this point, a chief who deeply hated the French, grabbed the infant by the feet and smashed its head against a rock. The Christian Indians had the feeling that the Christian mother had asked God to save her son from becoming an unbeliever by taking him with her.

Ten years after Kateri's apparition to Fr. Chauchetière, Stephen had sealed the prophecy of the Iroquois virgin.[13] It seems that Frances and Marguerite were not asked to sing the "death chant"; but this did not prevent them from overcoming fear and showing a courage which fully equalled that of the warriors. According to Fr. Cholenec, there is no doubt that Kateri obtained for these martyrs "the invincible constancy which they demonstrated in their torments."[14]

Notes 26

1. L. Groulx, ptre, Histoire du Canada Français depuis la découverte, Montréal, L'Action nationale, 1950, p. 171-6.

2. HDNF, vol. I, p. 550.

3. D, Girouard, Le vieux Lachine et le massacre du 5 aout 1689, Montréal, Gebhardt-Berthiaume, 1889, p. 38; VCT, p. 84.

4. HDNF, vol. II, p. 60-1.

5. Letter of Fr. Cholenec to Fr. Jacques Bigot, Paris 1691, in K, no. 37, June 1969, p. 12-5; OCI, p. 203ss; LEC, p. 62sss; HDNF, vol. I, p. 587ss.

6. HDNF, vol. II, p. 78-91.

7. Ibid, p. 99ss.

8. Ibid, p. 102-6; HC, p. 102.

9. HDNF, vol. II, p. 111ss.

10. HDNF, vol. I, p. 590-2; LEC (1819), p. 67-70; OCI, p. 213-7; K, Spring-Summer 1961, p. 26-8.

11. HDNF, vol. II, p. 125ss.

12. HDNF, vol. I, p. 592-5; LEC (1819), p. 70-4; OCI, p. 219-23; K, Autumn 1961, p. 30-2.

13. Ibid. p. 101.

14. VCT, p. 69.

27

The Guardian of Canada

To prepare for Christmas 1693, the people of the Sault, toughened by the war but wounded by so many trials and sorrows, "were moved by God to do something which deserves to be recorded; it was called "hotouongannandi," that is, public penance because it was done in the name of everyone.[1]

This practice started in the usual Iroquois manner, with a festive meal during which the men proclaimed in a loud voice their contempt for drunkenness so dominant in their midst. After a thorough examination of what they might do to atone for their sin in order to better prepare for Christmas, they resolved to each accuse himself in front of everyone,and if anyone was sick or had another reason to be absent, other relatives or friends could replace him. When the time came, each one spoke according to the spirit of penance that moved him, and in many cases, through the tears spilling from their eyes more than through their words interrupted by sighs.

The women proved to be as generous as the men. According to Fr. Chauchetière, the demons of the female sex were many: their names could be either gambling, or vanity or carnal desire. The women, especially young girls, set up their own associations to help one another to live as true Christians and to prepare themselves for the most heroic actions.

This public penance done with such sincerity and devotion, undoubtedly moved heaven, for after those years of trouble, the Mohawk virgin granted remarkable favours to Europeans and Canadians as well as to Sault villagers.

In the spring and summer of 1694, the island of Montreal endured all kinds of incursions on the part of Iroquois unbelievers. In addition, a drought which lasted two months destroyed all the grain that had been sown.[2] The people of Lachine feared a famine. The women and the girls decided to invoke Kateri Tekakwitha. They made three novenas in succession to obtain through her merits and intercession "rain and the protection of their families, of themselves, of their animals and of their crops". Each in turn went to confession and communion at the Mass celebrated at their request. On the second day of the novena, some rain fell, and on the ninth day, there was a downpour which lasted several days. The grain which had been drying up and dying regained its vigour. The crop was abundant and, better still, not one parishioner was captured or killed, nor was cattle or grain damaged by the enemy, contrary to what was happening in other parts of the island.

On October 28th, always in Lachine, Marguerite Picart,[3] thirty-three years old and seven months pregnant, had the stable door fall on her back. Fearing that she was going to give birth prematurely, Marguerite sent for midwife Anne Malteau, who confirmed that the baby had been displaced in the womb. Anne counselled her to pray to Kateri Tekakwitha. She readily agreed and, for nine days, drank water in which ashes of the clothing and tomb of the servant of God had steeped. Two days later, the baby returned to its original position and she gave birth normally two months later.

At Kanawakon, Kateri smiled upon an Onondaga woman, the sister of Marguerite Gagouithon. She had gone on the annual hunt with her husband. In the beginning of spring, she reached the full term of her pregnancy in the middle of the forest. The labour pains were terrible. In her despair she thought of asking Kateri for help. She said to her from the bottom of her heart: "O Kateri, have pity on me. Arrange it so that I may give birth quickly, and if it is a girl, I promise to give her your name." At that moment she fell asleep peacefully and was awakened by the cries of her child, a little girl. When she returned to the village, she took her at once to Fr. Cholenec to have her baptized and named Kateri.

The following year, 1695, proved to be "the great year" for the Mohawk maiden because of the favours she poured upon the two major cities of the country, Quebec and Montreal.[5] Her patronage was felt among the most prominent people of the colony. Jean Bochart de Champigny, Sieur of Noroy and Verneuil, Chevalier and Intendant of New France, was the first to benefit by her favour.

For two years, the Intendant had been suffering from a bad cold which kept getting worse to the point where he had difficulty talking. The Intendant's wife, née Marie-Madeleine de Chaspoux, Lady of Verneuil and Du Plessis-Savari, wrote to the Jesuits of the Mission to ask them to make a novena to Kateri. The Fathers spoke to "Kateri's band", who fortunately happened to be at the village then. During the novena, the Intendant was completely cured in Quebec.

The gratitude of the eminent couple soon became evident. Mrs. de Champigny quickly had pictures of Kateri made and distributed them in Canada and even in France, where she sent some to the leading members of the court. A dying woman was cured in Paris that same year.

On hearing the account of the favour granted to Mr. de Champigny, Canon Joseph Seré de la Colombière, brother of the future Saint Claude and Great Vicar of the Diocese of Quebec, who was also clerical advisor to the Superior Council of New France, prayed to the Iroquois virgin to cure him of the illness that afflicted him. He promised to go and thank her at her tomb. She answered his prayer.

A few days later, in the summer, the Great Vicar travelled from Quebec to Saint

Francis Xavier to thank his benefactress. In September of the same year, he came back to Sault Saint-Louis to reiterate his gratitude to Kateri. In addition to a considerable donation for the works of the Mission, he also left in the hands of Fr. Cholenec the following account of his healing.

Having been sick in Quebec last year from the month of January to the month of June with a slow fever against which all medication had been ineffective, and with a flux which even epikakuana* could not cure, I was advised to make a vow, if God were pleased to put an end to these two illnesses, to go to the Mission of Saint Francis Xavier and pray at the tomb of Catherine Tegahkoüita. The fever ceased that same day, and the flux having diminished considerably, I left a few days later to keep my promise. I had hardly made a third of the journey when I found that I was completely cured. My health being such a useless thing that I would not have dared to ask for healing if it had not been for the deference I owed the servants of God, I cannot help but believe that God, in granting me this healing, had nothing other in mind than to show in what esteem He holds this good woman. As for me, I fear that it would be an injustice to keep this truth to myself and to refuse to give this Canadian Mission the glory it is due if I were not to attest, as I am doing, that I owe my healing to this Iroquois virgin. This is why I am giving this testimony with all the feelings of gratitude of which I am capable, in order to increase, if possible, the confidence of the public in my benefactress, but even more to encourage the desire to imitate her virtues. Given in Villemarie, September 14th, 1695. J. de la Colombière, P.J., Canon of the Cathedral of Quebec."[6]

Mr. J. Daniel Greysolon du Luth, a squire, standard bearer and constable of the house of the King, explorer and founder of trade-posts in the West, also recorded the account of his healing at Fort Frontenac*.

Other women of Quebec were healed: Catherine Foucault, Miss de Martigny and little Genevieve de Granville, whose father, Officer de Carignan, spent the summer in Montreal and brought earth from Kateri's grave back to Quebec.

In Montreal - in the presence of Mr. Dollier de Casson, Seigneur of the Island of Montreal, of Mr. Michel Caille, the pastor, of Mr. de Fonty and of her entire family - Mrs. de Fonty being close to death, swallowed earth from the grave of the Indian virgin dissolved in water, and was healed instantly.

Again in Montreal, a Mrs. Potier was delivered of a stone; a Mr. Boisseau was cured of a chancre, this "malignant infection which eats the flesh to the bone wherever it lodges itself"; Marie-Madeleine Fortin and several others were relieved of their ailments. Add to this a woman from La Chine who obtained the healing of her cow and a man from Montreal whose bull was also healed![7]

All these people made novenas or asked the Fathers of the Mission to have

"Kateri's band" make one, and often they drank the earth from her tomb or ashes of her clothing dissolved in water.

Physical healings affect us greatly: we can see and feel them, so to speak. But even more to be estimated are the spiritual healings. Fr. Pierre Cholenec mentions about thirty people who found the right road with the help of Kateri. Among others, she delivered at least thirty from "obsessive temptations of the flesh and obtained for them the gift of chastity."[8] It is mostly this type of healing that the Mohawk virgin performed.

In 1696, when the pastor of La Chine heard that Fr. Cholenec was writing about the life of Kateri, he wrote to him to report the favours that had been obtained for himself and his parishioners through the intercession of this "saintly girl".[9] She is our guardian and advocate before God, he wrote, and the people of La Chine seek refuge under her protection.

Mr. Remy had himself been favoured with two healings and was filled with zeal for the Mohawk virgin. He also admitted having received another grace concerning the mind and the imagination. "It is for this type of help from heaven which I have frequently received, when in need and which I hope to receive for the rest of my life, that I am more obliged to this servant of God than for any other assistance I have received from God through her, be it for bodily or temporal matters, for myself or for several of my parishioners."[10]

When Mr. Remy suggested to his faithful that they turn to Kateri for healing, he almost always proceeded in the same fashion. He would ask that a novena be made consisting of nine Hail Marys and sometimes nine Our Fathers each day, or that they have one made by a devout Indian woman of the Mission, and that they promise to have a Mass said at the tomb of Kateri or to make the trip to the tomb in gratitude if the favour was received. He would offer the sick person ashes of Kateri's clothing or earth from her tomb mixed with water, or added to medication or to holy bread or to an ointment given by Bishop de Laval. He would also promise to commend them to the Lord every morning at Mass through the intercession of the Mohawk virgin.

We have in our possession this report[11] in which 35 healings are described in detail. Here are a few of them.

Barbe Brunet, daughter of Francis le Bourbonnais and Barbe Beauvais, was 13 years old in 1688. She had been sick for two months with "tertian* fever" which had degenerated into "double third fever"; she looked like a skeleton. She could take neither food nor medicine and the doctors, at a loss had abandoned her case. Someone then recommended that she pray to Kateri Tekakwitha. She promised to have a novena made at her tomb and to go and pray there herself. Two days later, the fever disappeared, after which she went to the tomb to fulfill her promise.

The same year, Marie Maupetit, eldest daughter or Madeleine Bourgery, lived in a house which was highly exposed to Iroquois attacks. Indeed the Iroquois had been ravaging the upper district of the Island of Montreal and burning the settlers' crops. Mrs. Bourgery promised to have a Mass celebrated in honour of Kateri if her daughter's and son-in-law's house and their pea patches were spared. With the exception of Marie Maupetit's house and another where Fr. Remy occasionally celebrated Mass, all the houses were burned. The pea crop to which the assailants had set fire were only burned superficially. This "was certified by Jacques Chasle, husband of Madeleine Bourgery, who helped to thresh the peas."

In 1689, a three year old child, François-Joseph Le Noir Rolland, was paralyzed in his hips and legs. His mother dedicated him to the "Iroquois saint", sailed across the river to take him to Kateri's tomb, had a Mass celebrated for him and asked one of the devout Indian women of the Mission to make a novena. Nine days later, the little boy was able to take his first steps!

In 1690, Joseph Cuillerier, 12 years old, brother of little Lambert who bad been cured in 1684, was suffering from a wasting fever which reduced him to the point of death. His father obtained some of Kateri's ashes from the Fathers of the Indian Mission. "He had his son take some of it and by this means, the boy was healed and has been well ever since," wrote Mr. Remy.

In 1691, a young woman of about twenty-two, Marie Beauvais, the wife of Master Jean-Baptiste Potier, Royal Notary of Montreal, was afflicted by kidney stones. The couple made a promise to have a Mass celebrated at the church of Saint Francis Xavier of Sault Saint-Louis, which houses the remains of Kateri. After this promise, the cure was obtained and the husband went to the Sault to have this Mass offered. "This is what she and her husband have told me," wrote Mr. Remy.

In 1693, André Merlot, nicknamed "Le Petit Laramée," fifty-three years old, was suffering from an eye ailment which made him unable to distinguish objects; he feared to lose his eyesight altogether. His pastor recommended devotion to Kateri with the usual practices. At the end of the novena, André Merlot regained his sight. "Quod vidi testor," "What I saw I attest," wrote Mr. Remy.

In 1694, Marie, daughter of Marie Matour and Pierre Cardinal, was only five years old and suffered from scrofula, a tubercular inflamation of the lymph glands in her neck. Her mother brought her to Montreal, where surgical treatment proved ineffective. Finally, the poor mother who had been cured herself by Kateri two years before, had recourse once again to the "Indian saint" and performed the usual devotions: she visited the Mission, had a Mass offered and made a novena. When all was done, Marie was cured of scrofula, which "is an incurable disease in this country."

In the month of August 1695, Louis Fortier, aged thirteen, afflicted by an incurable disease, was put in the hands of the doctors and Hospitallers of the Hôtel-Dieu of Montreal. Several days of treatment had no effect on his condition. His mother, with tears in her eyes, asked Mr. Remy to offer a Mass in order to obtain the healing of her son through the intercession of Kateri Tekakwitha. Soon after, the remedies took effect and he was able to return home in perfect health.

And finally, in the month of March 1696, on his way back from his mission, Mr.Remy passed by Fort Cuillerier* where Jacques Lanthier, a farmer, and his wife Angélique Matour told him that their three month old daughter Catherine was dying. The Lanthiers had already dedicated her to the Mohawk virgin and asked the priest to offer a Mass for her that she may be healed. The same day, little Catherine began improving, and the next day she was cured.

*   *   *

The pastor of La Prairie, Mr. Geoffrey, attested, for his part, having been "an eye witness to the marvels Kateri was working in his parish and being prepared to publicize this fact everywhere."[12]

"Finally, so many healings occurred in the years that followed,", wrote Fr. Cholenec, "that we have stopped recording them." Fifteen years after Kateri's death, all of Canada was beginning to witness the power of the Iroquois maiden with the heart of God. Mother Juchereau* de Saint-Ignace, superior of the Hôtel-Dieu of Quebec, wrote in her Annals a brief biography of Kateri, which she ended by saying that since Kateri's death in 1680, "people call upon her in all parts of Canada and God has performed many miraculous cures through her intercession."[13] This shows that the favours of the Mohawk virgin were known even in this medical environment, quite far from Montreal for the time.

Yet the greatest grace[14] of Kateri is unquestionably the "preservation of the Mission". Fr. Cholenec declared: "We can only attribute (this preservation) to her prayers and to her precious bones which we have." She is "a powerful guardian against all the enemies, visible and invisible," of this Mission and of the entire French colony.[15]

"Is it not a most amazing wonder, indeed, that a handful of people such as ours at the Sault, compared to the five Iroquois nations, were able to hold their own while such a large number of enemies driven by uninhibited fury against them, beat them, kill them and even go and capture them at the gate of their own village to make slaves of them. True, we have lost all our brave elders and the best of our warriors in this long war; but for one hundred men that we lost, we could count 700 of their bravest men killed either by our Indians alone or by our Indians battling together with the French against them."[16]

One day, the warriors of Kahnawakon accompanied a convoy to Fort Cataracoui. That season, there were only elderly people, women and children left and they were busy moving the village: pulling, carrying and dragging their belongings to the fourth location (Kanatakwende*) of the Mission on the Suzanne River, near the La Chine Rapids. The enemy was aware of the situation and it would have taken only twenty or so warriors to cut down the entire population. Yet nothing happened; only one band attacked the old village.

A group of warriors hiding near the grave site of Kateri Tekakwitha saw five or six canoes filled with thirty women, some of whom were among the best known and members of Kateri's band. They set up an ambush for them and, as the women came near the shore, fired a volley of bullets at their canoes. One of the oldest and bravest women began reciting the Litany of Our Lady in a loud voice. The women managed to retreat a distance without being hit, even though several of the enemy, fuming with rage, had jumped into the water to try and grab the canoes. The sight of Kateri's grave "blinded our enemies and inspired these poor women the confidence and presence of mind they needed to escape from their hands," said Fr. Cholenec.

Another group of Christian women met an army corps from the Mohawk canton in the woods. Several of these women had relatives among these men. The warriors seeing that they were discovered and fearing that an alarm would be given, wanted to turn back. They tried to bring the women back with them, but they resisted. These Christian women preferred to die rather than renounce "the prayer." Let the warriors kill them like slaves! The warriors amazed by this attitude and unwilling to take any revenge on them, decided to take them to the Sault and to agree on a truce with the chiefs of the Mission. Everyone felt that only the special care of the Mohawk maiden for her compatriots could explain the happy turn of events, thanks to these courageous Iroquois women.

Thus the Mohawk virgin had become the "Saint" of New France, the one on whom everyone could count, the one who attracted to her tomb people of all stations and races. "All the French of this new world," wrote Fr. Cholenec, "also hold our Kateri in special veneration. They talk about her everywhere with great praise and, like the Indians, see her as a powerful patroness whom God gave them in heaven to protect the country, and everywhere she is invoked as such."

The "Mission thus preserved" contributed, as we know, to the safety of the entire French colony because of its strategic position in New France, and because of its brave warriors devoted above all to defending and promoting the faith. Moreover, since the Christian converts were in unity with their French allies, they formed an important interior network; they frequently stopped before they had the chance to do any harm the worst plans of extermination made by the enemies of the colony, who were by the very fact the enemies of their faith. Some of them were faithful to the point of martyrdom.

The great historian F.X. de Charlevoix, - mandated by Louis XIV to record what had happened in New France up until that time, and who stayed in Kahnawake some time around 1721, - wrote in these terms the praise of "this saintly maiden so well known by the name of Catherine Tegahkoüita": "New France has had its apostles and martyrs and has given saints to the Church in every state of life; and I do not hesitate to say that each and every one of them would have been the honour of the first centuries of Christianity. I have made known several of them inasmuch as the sequence of this history permitted. The lives of some of them have been written for the public; but God, who was glorified during their lives by the great things He did through them; by the brightness which their holiness shed on this vast Continent; by the courage which He inspired them to establish through enormous efforts a new Christendom amidst the worst Barbarism and to seal it with their blood, has chosen none of them to unfold on their tombs all the richness of His power and mercy; He reserved this honour for a young Neophyte almost unknown in the country during her lifetime. She has been, for more than sixty years, universally regarded as the Guardian of Canada, and it has been impossible to oppose the kind of devotion which is publicly rendered to her."[17]

Notes 27

1. JR 64, p. 124.

2. REMY, p. 18-9.

3. Ibid, p. 11.

4. PO, Doc. X, p. 232-3, add. ms. LeBrun.

5. VCT, p. 79.

6. PO, Doc. XII, p. 279-80.

7. PO, Doc. X, p. 237-8, add. ms. Le Brun; VCT, p. 82-3; REMY, p. 13-20.

8. VCT, p. 83.

9. REMY, p. 5.

10. Ibid, p. 3.

11. Ibid, p. 1-22.

12. VBCT, p. 120.

13. Extract from the annals of Hôtel-Dieu in Quebec (1713-1723) p. 108.

14. VCT, p. 83.

15. VCT, p. 10.

16. VCT, p. 84.

17. HDNF, vol. I, p. 572-3.

GLOSSARY

AGARIATA: Mohawk chief who would have killed Mr. de Chazy, nephew of Lt. General de Tracy. He was executed in punishment of his crime in 1666.

AGNIÉ (Mohawk): one of the Five Iroquois Cantons, the one located further East.

AGNIER: people who live in the Mohawk Canton. English name: Mohawk.

AGNIERS (Mohawks): River of the Mohawks today, tributary of the Hudson River in the State of New York.

AILLEBOUST: Mrs. Louis d'; see Boullogne.

AKWESASNE: (where the partridge beats its wings) St.Francis Regis, Mohawk Reserve established in 1752, located close to Cornwall, where the territory overlaps Quebec, Ontario and the State of New York. (Old name = St.Regis).

ALGONQUINS: nomad Indians in the vicinity of the Ottawa River.

ANDAGARON: (or Andoraque or Ganafaro) Mohawk village inhabited by the Bear clan, located between Caughnawaga and Tionnontoguen.

ANDASTES: important tribe of the Huron-Iroquois family who lived by the Susquehanas River, whose members are also called "makers of wampums."

ANDIATAROCTE: (where-the-lake-is-enclosed) Lake of the Blessed Sacrament, named later Lake George by the English. A watercourse 32 miles long which flows into Lake Champlain.

ANNE: Wife of Etienne, the catechist.

ANENDASSE, Pierre: a Mohawk chief who died in 1675, one of the first converts amongst the elders of Tionnantoguen.

ATERIATA, Louis: an Onondaga baptized in France, god-child of King Louis XIV; one of the pioneers of the Mission of Laprairie established in 1669. He later became one of the main chiefs of the village.

ANONTINON, Marie-Barbe: Onondaga born in 1656, who entered the noviciate of Congregation of Notre-Dame in 1679 and died in 1691.

AURIES: a tributary South of the Mohawk River.

BEARS (ours): Mohawk clan who lived in the small town of Andaragon.

BLÉ D'INDE (corn): name given to maïs.

BONIFACE, François: a Jesuit born in Arras (France) in 1635; came to Canada in 1669; worked in the Missions of Caughnawaga and Andagaron (1670-1673) ; died in Quebec in 1674.

BOQUET, Charles: oblate (in French: donné), interpretor who worked with Fr. Bruyas at Oneida. Mother Marie de l'Incarnation describes him in a praising way as the courier between the missions, knowing all the roads, also known to Indians who esteemed him and and feared him.

BOULEVARD: old meaning of rempart, a protecting wall surrounding a village as a fortress.

BOULLONGNE, Marie-Barbe de: (1618-85) spouse of Governor Louis d'Ailleboust, co-foundress of the Confraternity of the Holy Family in Montreal, benefactress of the Hotel-Dieu of Quebec. According to the Relations of 1647, she took interest in the Indians, learnt their language, and the Algonquins would have named her Chaouerindam-aquetch, "the one who pities us in time of misery."

BOURGEOYS, Saint Marguerite: born in Troy in 1620, died in Montreal in 1647; founded in 1650, at Ville Marie, the Congregation of Notre Dame; canonized by John Paul II in 1982.

BRESOLLES, Judith: see Moreau.

BRISAY DE DENONVILLE, Jacques-René de; governor of New-France from 1689; he succeeded to Le Fevre de la Barre.

BRUYAS, Jacques: Jesuit born in Lyons; came to Canada in 1666; worked as a missionary amongst the Onondagas, Oneidas and Mohawks (1667-1692); Superior General of the Jesuits in Canada (1693-1698); died at Saint Louis in 1712.

BUADE, de Frontenac and of Palluau, Louis of: governor of New France (1672-1682) and from 1689 till his death, in Quebec, in 1698, at the age of 76.

CALLIERES, Louis Hector de: succeeded to Francis Marie Perrot as governor of Montreal in 1684; man of war, a prudent and wise commander, an able negotiator.

CAROUGE, red-winged black bird (agelaius phoeniceus): birds in abundance in the marshes and the fields, flock in enormous groups; a little red on the shoulder or the throat.

CATARACOUI: see Fort Cataracoui.

CENDRE CHAUDE: (or Ogenheratarihiens or Hot Powder) an Oneida chief who migrated to the Missions of the Sault where he converted himself and his whole family in 1676; he helped Kateri to escape in 1677; first chief of the village in 1683; died while fighting with the French against the Senecas in 1687. His wife, Garhio.

CHAMBLY: see Fort Chambly.

CHAMPLAIN, Lake: also called Big Sea or Lake of the Iroquois.

CHARLEVOIX, F.-X. de: (1682-1761) Jesuit mandated by King Louis XIV to make the trip to New France and to write what-so-ever happened there since the beginning of the colony. He sojourned in Kahanawake around 1721.

CHAUCHETIÈRE, Claude: Jesuit born at Saint-Porchaire-de-Poitiers (France) in 1645; arrived in Canada in 1677; was a missionary at the Sault Saint-Louis in Kateri's time; died in Quebec, April 17, 1709. First contemporary biographer of Kateri. For more details see Ch.XII.

CHEKATABUTT: (House on fire) Chief of the Mahicans.

CHAUMONOT, Pierre-Joseph-Marie: Jesuit born at Châtillon-sur-Seine (France) in 1611; came to Quebec in 1639; he served long as a missionary among the Hurons; died in Quebec in 1693.

CHAUDIERE NOIRE (Black Pot): a redoutable Onondaga Chief; enemy of the French who died in 1697.

CHOLENEC, Pierre: Jesuit born at Saint-Paul-de-Léa (France) in 1641; came to Canada in 1674, served as missionary in LaPrairie and at the Sault (1674-1682); spiritual director and contemporary biographer of Kateri; died in Quebec in 1723. For more details see Ch. XII.

CINQ-NATIONS (Five Nations): or Five Cantons i.e. the Five Nations which form the Iroquois Confederacy.

CONFEDERATION OF THE IROQUOIS: composed in the XVIIth by the Mohawks, the Oneidas, the Onondagas, the Cajugas and the Senecas.

CÔTÉ (side): same meaning as a row today; a road which passes in the back of series of land, very often, located alongside a course of water, whence "côté", side of the river.

COURCELLE : See Remy.

CUILLERIER, René: arrived in Canada in 1659 as a simple pioneer (explorer) hired by Mrs. de Bullion, in view of building the Hotel-Dieu of Montreal. Captured by the Oneidas in October 1661, he succeeded in escaping nineteen months later. On his return, he established himself as a settler in Montreal and took part in the founding of the parish in Lachine. His fortified home took the name of Fort Cuillerier in 1676.

DABLON, Claude: a Jesuit, born in Dieppe (France) in 1619, landed in Canada in 1655; Superior of the Jesuit Missions in New France (1671-1690) and (1686-1693); died in Quebec in 1697.

DALMA, Antoine: Jesuit who arrived in Canada in 1671, assassinated at Fort Saint Ann, Hudson's Bay, by Guillory, a French armourer.

DENONVILLE: see de Brisay de.

DAUVERSIÈRE, Jérôme le Royer de la: founder of the Congregation of the Hospitallers of Saint-Joseph and co-founder of the Society of Notre-Dame of Montreal in France. The said Society supplied la Dauversière with the "the moral and financial help" necessary to found Ville-Marie in 1642.

DEMEULLE, Jacques: intendant of New-France (1682-1686), successor of Duchesneau.

DOGIQUE (catechist): at the origin, name given to the companions of the Jesuit missionaries in Japan, i.e. one who presides the public prayers of the Mission and indoctrinates the people in absence of the missionaries.

DONNÉ (given): an elite of Frenchmen who offered their services free of charge to the missionaries.

DUCHESNEAU de la Doussinière and d'Ambault, Jacques: intendant of New France (1675-1682).

ENJALRAN, Jean: Jesuit who arrived in Canada in 1676; Chaplain at Fort Cataracoui.

EPIKARUANA: (ipecacuanha) a powder extracted from a South American shrub with emitic, diaphoretic and purgative qualities.

ERIE: Iroquian Confederation destroyed by the Iroquois in 1655.

EXERCICES SPIRITUELS (Spiritual exercises): a method of spirituality elaborated by Saint Ignatius of Loyola.

EXTREME UNCTION: ancient name for the Sacrament of the Sick.

FEDERATION OF THE HURONS: federation of nations who lived in Georgian Bay.

FORT ALBANY: not long ago Fort Orange or New-Orange; today Albany, N.Y.

FORT CATARACOUI (or Frontenac): founded by the Count of Frontenac in 1762 at the entry of Lake Ontario; important trading post; today Kingston, Ontario.

FORT CUILLERIER: fortified house of René Cuillerier in 1676. See Cuillerier.

FORT CHAMBLY: second fort built on the Richelieu in 1655; ancient name: Fort Saint-Louis; took the name of Chambly where Mr. Jacques de Chambly obtained its direction and its emplacement.

FORT FRONTENAC: see Fort Catacoui.

FORT LAMOTHE: erected on an island of Lake Champlain in 1666.

FORT ORANGE: founded in 1623 by the Dutch, will be called Fort Albany when the British conquer New Holland.

FORT SAINT ANN: built on an island at the Northern point of Lake Champlain in 1665.

FORT SAINT LOUIS: founded in 1648 on the Illinois River; also ancient name of Fort Chambly on the Richelieu River; a fort by the same name will be erected at the actual emplacement in Kahnawake in 1725.

FORT SAINT THÉRÈSE: third fort erected on the Richelieu River by Mr. de Sallières in 1665.

FRÉMIN, Jacques:

FRONTENAC: see Buade.

GAGOÜITHON, Marguerite: a married Onondaga, the most austere of the penitents, a friend of Kateri.

GANDOUAGUE: (Caughnawaga : by the rapids) small town of the Turtle, North of the River of the Mohawks, to-day Fonda, N.Y. Gandaouagué = Caughnawaga = Kahnawaké.

GANDEAKTENHA, Catherine: Erie, wife of Tonsahoten, died in 1673, foundress of the Saint Francis Xavier Mission at the Prairie-de-la-Madeleine. For more details see Chap. X.

GANENTAHA: Saint Marie Mission, established by the Jesuits in 1656, by the Lake Ganentaha. This attempt of a French establishment and Catholic Mission among the Iroquois failed after so many misfortunes.

GANNENSAGOUAS, Marie-Thérèse: grand-child of Thoroniongo, Huron brought as a slave to the Senecas and baptized by Fr. de Brébeuf. Freed after the death of his masters, the grandfather migrated to the Mission of the Mountain with his married son and his grand-child, who was adopted by Mr. de Courcelle. Trained by the Sisters of the Congregation, admitted to the novitiate in 1679, she was accepted, March 14, 1681. Mother Bourgeois sent this young mistress to teach to the little girls of her nation, at the Mission of the Mountain (Montreal), where she acquitted her task with perfection and practised the virtue of modesty, silence and mortification. She died in odour of sanctity at the Mountain, Nov. 25, 1695, at the age of 28.

GAOSEHA: a portable crib that the Indians carried on their back.

GARAKONTIÉ: Onondaga Chief who enjoyed a great influence in the midst of the Five Cantons, main negotiator with the French; baptized by Bishop de Laval in 1669 in honor of his godfather Daniel de Remy de Courcelle; his godmother, Miss Boutroue, daughter of the intendant.

GARHIO: baptized Marie in 1676, wife of Hot Ashes.

GARONGOÜAS, Marguerite: third martyr of the mission, see ch. XXVI.

GARONHIAGUÉ, Louis: (in heaven or celestial), Christian name of Hot Ashes.

GEORGE, Lake: see Andiataracte.

GONANNHATENHA, Françoise: second martyr of the Mission. See chap. XXVI.

GOYOGUINS (CAJUGAS) : one of the Five Iroquois Cantons located between Onondaga and Seneca.

GOUASTRAHA, Jeanne: Oneida, first companion of Kateri. Very little is known about her.

GOUPIL, Saint René: "donné" (given one), one of the seven North American Martyrs; the six others are:Jean de Brébeuf, Gabriel Lallemant, Isaac Jogues, Jean de la Lande (donné), Antoine Daniel and Charles Garnier.

GREAT MOHAWK: (or Togouiroui or Kryn for the Dutch or Ganeagwa) died in 1690, famous warrior, friend of the French. His wife: Saketon.

HONOGUENHAG, Paul: Huron catechist, died in 1691 in a battle against the English.

HOSPITALLERS of Saint Joseph: Congregation founded by Jérôme le Royer de la Dauversière at La Flèche, France. The Religious foundress of Hotel-Dieu of Montreal where Jeanne Mance was the first administratrix.

HURONIA: Georgian Bay.

HURONS: Indians of Iroquois extraction; sedentaries, French allies.

IESOS CHRISTOS: Iroquois word to designate Jesus Christ.

ISLAND OF THE HERON: small island in the Saint Lawerence, facing Verdun, by Sault Saint-Louis.

IROQUOIAN: linguistic family comprising the Hurons, the Iroquois, the Petuns, the Neutrals, the Eries and the Andastas.

IROQUOIS: The Iroquois group comprising five nations, allied with the French and Dutch. Inferior Iroquois: Mohawks and Oneidas i.e. the first that we met going down Canada by the Richelieu River and Lake Champlain.

IROQUOIS RIVER: the Richelieu River, southern tributary of the Saint Lawrence.

IROQUOISIA: the entirety of the towns of the Five Cantons.

JUCHEREAU de la Ferté, Jeanne-Françoise dite de Saint-Ignace: Superior of the Hospitallers of the Hotel-Dieu of Quebec; author of the "Annales de l'Hôtel-Dieu de Québec, 1636-1716." Born at Quebec in 1650, she is the first of Canadian origin to become superior of the community.

KAHNAWAKE: (by the rapids), last migration of the Saint Francis Xavier Mission of the Sault. Ancient name: Caughnawaga.

KANAWAKON: (in the rapids) third location of the Mission, 1690.

KENTAHE: see La Prairie.

KINNOUSKOUEN: Mohawk catechist.

LA BARREA: see Le Febvre.

LA CROIX DE CHEVRIÈRES DE SAINT-VALLIER. Jean-Baptiste de: Sulpician, second bishop of Quebec, successor of Bishop de Laval. Apostolic soul, but of an authoritative character, he was in dispute with the civil authorities as well as religious, particularly during the year 1693-1694. After a tumultous life and many returns to France, he came back to die in Quebec in 1727 at the age of 74 years old. He had guided the diocese of Quebec during 42 years.

LAMBERVILLE, Jacques de: Jesuit born at Rouen in 1641, came to Canada in 1674. First spiritual director of Kateri at Caughnawaga, he baptized her in 1676. Died in 1711 at the Sault Saint-Louis.

LALEMANT, Louis: Jesuit (1578-1635), one of the great masters of interior life during the XVIIth century.

LA PRAIRIE DE LA MADELEINE: (Kentake, in Mohawk) first location of the Saint Francis Xavier Mission of the Saint Lawrence River, in 1667.

LAVAL, François de Montmorency de: Bishop of Pétrée, Vicar Apostolic of New France (1659-1674); first Bishop of Quebec (1674-1688); founder of the Seminary of Quebec, declared Blessed by John Paul II at the same time as Kateri (June 1980). Named "The Founder of the Church of Canada."

LE FEBVRE DE LA BARRE, Joseph-Antoine: governor general of New France (1682-1685). At 60 years old, he arrived with the Intendant Demeulle in Quebec, city half destroyed by the great fire of 1682.

LE MERCIER, François-Joseph: Jesuit who arrived at Quebec in 1635, mission in Huronia and Superior General of the Missions of New France.

LE MOYNE, Simon: Jesuit born at Beauvais (France) in 1604; arrived in Canada in 1638; died at the Cap-de-la-Madeleine in 1655.

LORETTE: see Mission.

MAHICANS: called Wolves ("Loups") by the French. Indians who lived in the valley of the Hudson River.

MARIE D'ONONDAGA: (or Mary the penitent), mother of a family, friend of Kateri.

MARIE DE L'INCARNATION: (Marie Guyart) 1599-1672, born at Tours, France, mother and widowed; great mystic and business woman, foundress of the Ursulines in Canada. Great writer: her voluminous correspondence is a treasure of description for the Canadian history. She was affectionately interested in education, in catechism and instruction of young Indian girls, studied their languages, wrote dictionaries in Algonquin and Mohawk. Venerated as a saint as early as 1672, she was declared Blessed by John Paul II at the same time as Kateri (June 1980). Named the "Mother of the Church of Canada."

METABEROUTIN: (opened-to-all-winds), today the Saint Maurice River, Northern tributary of the Saint Lawrence.

MISSION DE LA MONTAGNE: (Mission of the Mountain) founded in 1676 by the Sulpicians.

MISSION NOTRE-DAME de la Lorette: Mission of the Hurons close to Quebec.

MISSION SAINT-FRANCOIS-XAVIER-DES-PRÉS: Name of the mission at its first location in 1667.

MISSION SAINT-FRANCOIS RÉGIS: Sister mission of Saint Francis-Xavier, See Akwesasne.

MISSION SAINT-FRANCOIS-XAVIER of the SAULT: name of the Mission where Kateri arrived in 1677; second location of the Mission in 1676.

MISSION SAINTE-MARIE of GANENTAA: see Ganentaha

MISSION SAINT-PIERRE: name of the mission Gandawaga

MITASSES: Indian shin pads.

MONTAGNAIS: Indians of Algonquin origin; nomad hunters North-West of the Saint Lawrence, allies of the French.

MONTAGNE: see Mission of the Mountain.

MOREAU de BRÉSOLES, Judith: foundress and first Superior of the Religious Hospitallers of Montreal; arrived with Jeanne Mance, she served the sick, French as well as Indians during 20 years.

NEUTRES (Neutrals): small Iroquois tribe named such because it remained at peace with the Hurons and the Iroquois who had agreed never to fight on their territory.

NOTRE-DAME: old street of Montreal, parallel to the River.

NOTRE-DAME-DU-BONSECOURS: chapel built by Marguerite Bourgeois.

NOTRE-DAME-DE-FOY: Statue of the Virgin, discovered in an enormous oak, measuring 8 feet in diameter, in 1609, close to Dinant in Belgium. A great devotion to Our Lady ensued. On this spot many miracles happened. It is in all likelihood a replica of this statue carved from the very oak tree, which was sent to the Jesuits in Canada. Nowadays, visitors are allowed at the sanctuary of Foy-Notre-Dame (Belgium) where the authentic statue is. Historical site as well as pilgrimage site. Hence the name of Sainte-Foy, near Quebec. Origin of name: "forge" Walloon name, from the latin "fagea" which signifies beechwood; name of the fief of the Baronny of Celles 1503). (Les Cahiers de Cap-Rouge vol. 9, no. 2, 1981).

NOTRE-DAME-DE-MONTAIGU: miraculous statuette to-day exposed at the chapel of Notre-Dame-de-Bonsecours in Montreal. Marguerite Bourgeois received this statue, 15 cm. high, through the intermediary of Baron the Fancamp, on April 30, 1672. Sculpted out of an oak in the woods of Montaigu, site of a famous pilgrim place in Belgium, it swayed fire more than once.

NOTRE-DAME-DE-LAURETTE: see Mission.

NOUVELLE-ANGLETERRE (New England): a part of the U.S.A. comprising Maine, New Hampshire, Vermont, Massachussetts, Rhode Island, Connecticut.

OGENHERATARIHIENS: see Hot Powder or Hot Ashes.

OIGUÉ: (by the river), Hudson River.

ONDESSONK: (bird of prey) name given by the Indians to Isaac Jogues, then to Fr. Simon Lemoyne.

ONNEIOUT: (Oneida) canton, neighboring that of the Mohawks.

ONONTAGUÉ: (Onondaga) one of the five Iroquois cantons, the one located in the center, chief town of the Iroquois Confederacy.

ONONTIO: (the lovely mountain). Iroquois name given for the first time to the Cavalier of Montmagny, successor of Champlain, and afterwards to all the representatives of the King, till the days of the conquest (1760). "Grande montagne" (grand mountain) is a free translation which means "Montmagny" (mons magnus).

ONSERONNI ONWE: (Real makers-of-axes) i.e. the French name given to the French by the Hurons.

ORANGE: see Fort Orange.

OSSERNENON: place of birth of Kateri; today Auriesville, N.Y. "According to the Relations of the Jesuits, Fr. Isaac Jogues describes the location of Ossernenon as equally distant between the Mohawk River and the Scholarie River." Ossernenon: center + nonwe: there. Thus "in the midst of the region." Then it is not an alteration of Caughnawaga, as it was alleged. (Dr. Solomon Cook of Saint Regis).

OUENDITÉ, Jeanne: Huron of Ancient Lorette, of a great purity, died as a saint around 1667, at age of 14; would have had the apparition of the Holy Virgin; before her death, she asked to pronounce the vow of chastety in the presence of Fr. Chaumonot.

OUTAOUAIS (Ottawa), River: tributary of the Saint Lawrence.

OYANDER: important woman of the nation because of her social rank.

PERROT, François-Marie: governor of Montreal (1669-1684). Succeeded to Maisonneuve.

PIERRON, Jean: Jesuit born at Dun-sur-Meuse (France) in 1631; arrived in Canada in 1667.

PIERSON, Philippe: Jesuit born in 1642 at the Ath (Belgium), arrived in Canada in 1667; ordained priest at Quebec in 1669; died at Lorette in 1668.

PORCELAINE: (English: wampum) The necklaces or branches of porcelaine came from marine shells (periwinkle, sea snails, concha venera, porcela) that the Indians broke in little pieces and rubbed them on stones to give them a cylinder shape, flattened and extended. Then they would pierce these to string them on leather laces. These necklaces often took the shape of belts. They were used for money or ornaments, for gifts or signs of dignity. They were of great importance in negotiations.

PROUVILLE DE TRACY, Alexandre de: military by career, advisor to the King named Lieutenant-General of the Americas in 1663; came to Canada in 1665, ordered the Forts Richelieu, Saint Louis and Sainte Thérèse to be built; in 1666, the Forts Saint-Jean, Sainte Anne and Lamothe. According to Bishop de Laval and Marie de l'Incarnation, Mr. de Tracy was a person of merit and piety who did many good works.

RASSADE: pearls of low value (imported from Europe) used in the past to make bracelets and necklaces; other name given by the French to the porcelain beads. See porcelaine.

RAFFEIX, Pierre: Jesuit born in Clermont (France); came to Canada in 1663; co-founder of the Saint François-Xavier-des-Prés Mission with Catherine Gandeaktenha and François Tonsahoten; died at Quebec in 1724. For more details see Ch. X.

RATSIHENSTATSI: Father, in Iroquois.

RAWENNIO: God, in Iroquois.

RELATIONS of the JESUITS: work comprising 73 volumes which contain the correspondance exchanged between the Jesuits of New France from 1610 to 1894, and other documents concerned.

REMY de COURCELLE, Daniel de: Governor of New France (1665-1672). Showed great ability and drew the respect of the French as well as the Indians. In 1669 he did not hesitate to condemn to death 3 soldiers of the garrison of Montreal who had assassinated a Seneca chief. The Iroquois were very impressed by this «3 for 1» and war was avoided. He checked the attacks of the Iroquois against Indian allies (the Algonquins and the Ottawians) of the French. Asked himself to return to France, leaving the colony in peace and prestige of France enchanced.

SAGAMITE: ground corn, seasoned with dried fish, meat, oil or all other condiments.

SAINT-FRANCIS, Lake: widening of the Saint Lawrence River.

SAINT-FRANCIS-XAVIER-DES-PRÉS: name of the Mission when it was located at LaPrairie.

SAINT IGNATIUS: Founder of the Society of Jesus.

SAINTE MARIE: chapel of Tionnontoguen, built by the Mohawks.

SAINTE-MARIE de GANENTAA: see Ganentaa.

SAINT-PIERRE: (Saint Peter) chapel of Caughnawaga.

SAINT-SACRAMENT, Lake: (Blessed Sacrament), see Andiatarocte.

SAINT-VALLIER: see La Croix de Chevrières.

SANGLE FRONTALE (frontal strad) : Leather band held by the forehead and which went down the shoulders, allowing to carry a basket or any other kind of load on the back.

SAULT SAINT-LOUIS: site on the Saint Lawrence, close to the Rapids of Lachine. Land granted to the Jesuits and the Indians by the intendant Duchesneau in 1675, conceded in 1680 by Louis XIV; today, city of Saint Catherine. See also Mission of the Sault.

SATEHON: wife of the Grand Mohawk.

SCHENECTADY: small Dutch town, close to Fort Albany.

SENECAS: one of the Five Iroquois Cantons, the one located further west.

SKANDEGONRAKSEN, Martin: close relative to the Grand Mohawk, lay apostle who might have had apparitions of the Blessed Virgin. Died as a predestined in 1675.

SKANUDHAROUA, Genevieve-Agnes, so-called "after all the saints": Augustinian Hospitaller, first Indian known to have entered religious life; born in 1642, died in 1657 at Quebec. Daughter of the Great Huron Chief, Pierre Ondakion, whose family was the first of this nation to embrace christianity.

SKARICHIONS, Marie: Huron woman of Lorette migrated to Saint Francis Xavier Mission, friend of Kateri.

SOSE: Joseph, in Iroquois.

SOUART, M. le Cure Gabriel: Sulpician (1610-1691), pastor of Ville Marie, one of the founders of the Holy Family Society. Practiced surgery at the Hotel Dieu of Montreal.

TEGIAGWENTA, Marie-Thérèse: Onondaga, widow, intimate friend of Kateri.

TEGANANKOA, Etienne: first martyr of the mission. See Ch. XXVI.

TEGONHATSIONGO, Anastasie: friend of the mother of Kateri in Caughnawaga; teacher of Kateri in Kahnawake.

TEKAKWITHA: the one who advances gropingly.

TERTIAN FEVER (fièvre tierce): recurs every 3 days, the last one included, the paroxysms take place every two days. In the double fever which recurs every second day, the caractaristic symptons reveal themselves daily.

TIONNONTOGUEN: the most important village of the Mohawks, town of the Wolf clan, Saint Mary's Chapel.

TIOTIAKE: (on-the-other-side-of-the-river) Iroquois name for Montreal.

TOGWIROUI, Joseph: See Grand Mohawk.

TONSAHOTEN, François-Xavier: Iroquoised Huron, husband of Catherine Gandeaktenha, founder of the Saint Francis Xavier Mission of La Prairie.

TURTLE: clan of the Mohawks, who lived in Caughnawaga.

TURTLE, River of the: tributary of the Saint-Lawrence, west of La Prairie.

TRACY: see Prouville.

THREE SISTERS: name given to corn, squash and beans.

TSIAWENTES, Marie: oyander and catechist at Caughnawaga, at the time of Frs. Pierron and Boniface; also called "the precious lady."

TSONNATOUAN, François: called «big log» by the French; his wife Marguerite; new exemplary Christian couple, they asked the advice of Marie-Thérèse and Kateri.

VILLE-MARIE: ancient name of Montreal.

VIRAGO: friend of Kateri.

VRAIS-FAISEURS-de-HACHES (Real-makers-of-the-Axes): name given by the French to the Hurons.

WARI: Mary, in Iroquois.

WAMPUM: (a necklace for exhortation) this necklace was conserved at the Saint Francis Xavier Mission at Kahnawake, where it was stolen. Necklace made of procelain beads; the symbols depicted on it carried a message; this one given by the Hurons begging their brothers of Kahnawake to stay firm in their faith.

WOLVES: clan of the village of Tionnontaguen in the country of the Mohawks; refers also to the Mahicans of any other non-identified Indians, especially in the Region of the Hudson River.

BIBLIOGRAPHY

MANUSCRIPTS

CHAUCHETIÈRE, Claude

- Lettre du P. Claude Chauchetière touchant la mission des Iroquois du Sault St-François-Xavier proche Montréal, 14 octobre 1682, Ms. Archives de la Compagnie de Jésus, Province de Paris, Vanves.

- La Vie de la B. Catherine Tégakoüita dite à présent La Sainte Sauvagesse, (1695), Archives ASJCF, Saint-Jérôme, No 343.

- Notes autobiographiques du Père Claude Chauchetière (1695), Archives ASJCF, Saint-Jérôme, No 390.

- Catherine Tegagouita. Recueil de ce qui s'est passé depuis le décès de Catherine, Archives ASJCF, Saint-Jérôme, N 350.

CHOLENEC, Pierre

- Extraict d'une lettre du père Chonelec (Cholenec) contenant le Recit de la Ste vie Et pénitence Extraordinaires de quelques femmes sauvagesses, escrittes de St François Savier du Sault proche le montreal au mois de février 1680, dans Des missions iroquoises en l'année 1676. Cette lettre se trouve dans un cahier relié, contenant d'anciens livrets manuscrits, conservé aux Archives du Séminaire de Québec.

- La Vie de Catherine Tégakoüita. Première Vierge Iroquoise, Ms. Archives du Monastère de l'Hôtel-Dieu de Québec, (1696).

GUEN,

Ouvr. de Mr Guen, No 35. Règles et prières de la Ste-Famille.

REMY, Pierre

Certificat de Mr Remy, curé de la Chine, des miracles faits en sa paroisse par l'intercession de la B. Cath. Tegakwita, la Chine 1696, Archives ASJCF, Saint-Jérôme, No 46.

WORKS AND PUBLISHED ARTICLES

- AMHD-Q. LETTRES CIRCULAIRES ET NOTICES BIOGRAPHIQUES, 1641-1755, vol. I, Archives du monastère, Hôtel-Dieu de Québec, p. 8-11.

- Prise de possession de l'Isle au héron par les filles de la congrégation de Montréal, le 2 mars 1674. - Archives de Montréal, No: 1003.

- Lettres édifiantes et curieuses, écrites des missions étrangères, A. Lyon, 1819, t. IV.

- Histoire de la Congrégation Notre-Dame de Montréal, C.N.D., 1910, t. I, 265 p.; 1913, t. II, 372p.

- Beatificationis et Canonizationis, Servae Dei, Catharinae Tekakwitha, Virginis Indianae, Positio super virtutibus, Roma, Typis Pont. Universitatis Gregorianae, 1940, 412p.

- Sainte Geneviève et son temps, Tours, Maison Alfred Mame et fils, s.d. 304p.

- Dictionnaire biographique du Canada Québec, Les Presses de l'Université Laval, 1966, volume premier, 774p.

BÉCHARD, Henri, S.J.

- The Original Caughnawaga Indians, Montréal, International Publishers', 1976, 258 p.

- L'héroïque Indienne Kateri Tekakwitha, 2e édition, Montréal, Fides, 1980, 202p.

- Revue trimestrielle Kateri, C.P. 70, Kahnawaké, Qc, J0L 1B0

CAMPEAU, Lucien, S.J.

GANNENTAHA,

Première mission iroquoise (1653-1665), Cahiers d'histoire des Jésuites No 6, Montréal, Bellarmin, 1983, 95 p.

CHARLEVOIX, F.-X. De,

Histoire et description générale de la Nouvelle France, avec le journal historique d'un Voyage fait par ordre du Roi dans l'Amérique Septentrionnale, Paris, Giffart, 1744, tome I, 664p., tome II, 638p.

CHATEAUBRIAND, François René de

Oeuvres romanesques et voyages, Texte établi, présenté et annoté par Maurice Regard, Collection la Pléïade, Paris, Gallimard, 1969, Vol. I, 1420p.

CHAUCHETIERE, Claude,

Narration Annuelle de la Mission du Sault depuis La fondation jusques a 1 an 1686; dans TH vol. 63, p. 140-245.

CHAUMONOT, Pierre Joseph Marie,

La vie du R. P. Pierre Joseph Marie CHAUMONOT, de la Compagnie de Jésus, missionnaire de la Nouvelle France, écrite par lui-même par ordre de son Supérieur, l'an 1688. Nouvelle York, Isle Manate, A la Presse Cramoisy de Jean-Marie Shea, M. DCCC. LVIII.

DEVINE, E.J., S.J.

Historic Caughnawaga, Montreal, Messenger Press, 1922, 443p.

GIROUARD, Désiré,

Le vieux Lachine et le massacre du 5 aout 1689, Montréal, Gebhardt-Berthiaume, 1889, 74p.

GROULX, Lionel, ptre

Histoire du Canada français depuis la découverte, Montréal, L'Action nationale, 1950, 221 p.

GRASSMAN, Thomas, O.F.M. Conv.

The Mohawk Indians and Their Valley, Schenectady, J.S. Lischynsky. 1969, 724p.

HALE, Horatio

The Iroquois Book of Rites. Philadelphia, D.G. Brinton, 1883, 222p.

LOYOLA, Ignace de

Exercices Spirituels, Traduction du texte Autographe par Edouard Gueydan, s.j. en collaboration. Collection Christus, No 61. Paris, Desclée de Brouwer, 1986, 302p.

MARTIN, Félix, S.J.

Une Vierge iroquoise ou Vie de Catherine Tegakoüita, ronéo, 89p.

MORGAN, Lewis H.

League of the Ho-de-no saunee or Iroquois, New Haven, Human Relations Area Files, 1954, 2 volumes, 338 et 332p.

OURY, Dom Guy

Marie de l'Incarnation, Ursuline (1599-1672), Correspondance, Solesmes, Abbaye Saint-Pierre, 1971, 1075p.

ROCHEMONTAIX, Camille de

Les Jésuites et la Nouvelle-France au XVIIe Siècel, Paris, Letouzey et Ané, éditeurs, 1895, 3 tomes.

ROY, Pierre-Georges,

Ordonnances, Commissions, etc, etc, des gouverneurs et intendants de la Nouvelle-France, 1639-1706, Archives Province de Québec, vol. II, Beauceville, L'"Éclaireur" Ltée, 1924.

SAINT-VALLIER, Mgr Jean-Baptiste de

Estat présent de l'Église et de la colonie française dans la Nouvelle-France, Québec, Augustin Coté & Cie, 1856, 102 p.

TRIGGER, Bruce G., editor

Handbook of North American Indians, Smithsonian Institute, Washington, 1978, Vol. 15, Northeast, 924p.

THWAITES, Reuben Gold, editor

The Jesuit Relations and Allied Documents, New York, Pageant Book Company, 1959, 73 volumes.

WALWORTH, Ellen H.

The Life and Times of Kateri Tekakwitha. The Lily of the Mohawks, Albany, N.Y., J.B. Lyons Company, 1926, 314p.